The science of safety

Other books by this author:

The Science of Speed
Today's high-tech world of Formula 1

Ferrari
Formula 1 racing team

Jordan
Formula 1 racing team

Stewart
Formula 1 racing team

Front endpaper: Solitude in Germany was a circuit made for the brave; fittingly, Innes Ireland won there for Lotus in 1961. (LAT)

Rear endpaper: Benetton driver Alexander Wurz got off to a flying start during the Canadian GP in 1998. The Austrian vaulted over Jean Alesi's Sauber and Heinz-Harald Frentzen's Williams, before getting involved with Jarno Trulli's Prost as he came in to land on the opposite side of the road. Once again, the inherent strength of modern F1 cars saved the drivers from injury. (Sutton)

The science of safety

The battle against unacceptable risk in motor racing

David Tremayne Foreword by Professor Sid Watkins

DEDICATION
This book is dedicated to those who fought to make motor racing safer; to those who paid its ultimate price; and to their loved ones left behind, who go on paying.

First published in October 2000

British Library cataloguing-in-publication data:
A catalogue record for this book is available from the British Library.

Published by Haynes Publishing,
Sparkford, Nr Yeovil, Somerset BA22 7JJ

Tel: 01963 442030 Fax: 01963 440001
Int. tel: +44 1963 442030 Fax: +44 1963 440001
E-mail: sales@haynes-manuals.co.uk
Web site: www.haynes.co.uk

ISBN 1 85960 664 4

Library of Congress catalog card number 00-134250

Haynes North America Inc.
861 Lawrence Drive, Newbury Park,

Contents

Introduction

We've all heard the joke: What's the first thing that goes through a fly's mind when it hits the windscreen of a car travelling at 100mph? Answer: It's backside.

A crude way of expressing it, granted, but essentially that summarises the inherent problem in all high-speed impacts. Different things slow down at different rates.

There is a three-stage effect when the objects in the decelerative mix are a racing car, its driver, and parts of the surrounding scenery. It goes like this:

Speeding car hits object;

Driver in no longer speeding car hits parts of car;

Driver's internal organs hit inside of driver's now slowing skeleton.

Not to put too fine a point on it, this is what tends to kill racing drivers these days. In the past it was usually the inadvertent flight from a crashing car, or later the conflagration that occurred when the relatively flimsy spaceframe or aluminium monocoque of the typical 'fifties or 'sixties car suffered high-speed impacts and folded up around the driver, trapping him in its twisted metal embrace.

There was a time, long before the modern age of political correctness, when the fact that a few racing drivers got killed every season appeared to excite little or no comment from sporting bodies and circuit organisers, beyond the usual show of public remorse. Some might argue that today the pendulum has swung too far in the opposite direction, when some observers indulge in hysterics because a driver has suffered broken legs.

After Olivier Panis's unpleasant accident in Montreal in 1997, World Champion-elect Jacques Villeneuve came in for stinging criticism from many quarters. 'What's all the fuss about?' he wanted to know. 'It's sad that Olivier has been hurt, sure, but it's only broken legs. That happens to ordinary people every day on ski slopes all over the world.'

Villeneuve wasn't being insensitive, merely speaking his mind. He has a habit of doing that. But Formula One had moved into an era in which safety had become an obsession, to the point that no injury was deemed acceptable. People were still understandably horrified by the sight of a broken racing car and an injured driver, a natural enough reaction among caring humans; but perspectives had changed. It was easy to forget that, horrible though such accidents might be, there was a time when the same incident would probably have resulted in the driver's obituary. In the over-protective modern era a small minority of fans still want to see a gladiatorial battle, but the majority want to see the laws of physics challenged without the risk of blood and guts and broken bones. In among them, the purists appreciate that to the men in the cockpits the late Peter Revson's adage still holds good: everything is sweetened by risk. It's just that the risk has to be better calculated today than it had been in the past.

The line of common sense lies somewhere between the two opposite swings of the pendulum, between fatal consequences from an accident, and the removal of all risk. Many things that man chooses to do are dangerous. For many sportsmen that is the whole point. The downhill skier gets an extra rush of adrenalin because he knows what he is doing courts danger and the risk of injury. Likewise the bullfighter and the mountaineer who work with millimetric precision, knowing that an error of even the tiniest magnitude may be their last. And so it was with the racing driver from the advent of the motor car right through until the 'sixties, when a series of events conspired to set in motion a catalogue of change that gradually forced a hitherto largely unconcerned sport to start putting its house in order.

The next time that you are communing with nature, take a good look at a tree. Any tree will do, but one with a six-inch (15cm) diameter trunk or greater is a good start. Give it a shake and see how much you can actually bend it. Note how solid it feels. Then imagine that you are driving your road car into that tree, at 100mph. Consider how much harder that tree has suddenly become. How unforgiving. How utterly unyielding.

It seems incomprehensible today that motor races – especially at Grand Prix level – used to be run where relatively fragile cars regularly passed by all manner of trees at speeds in excess of 150mph. And hardly anyone ever really saw anything wrong with that!

For the purposes of this book, safety in motorsport can be divided into four eras. First there were the pioneering days of Louis Renault, Charles Jarrott, and Selwyn Francis Edge, when the Red Flag Act had been repealed and the horseless carriage was given full rein. From those raw and destructive days motor racing developed its own character and its own heroes. Many crashed to their deaths, but by and large the ultimate heroes – the Tazio Nuvolaris, the Juan Manuel Fangios, and the Stirling Mosses – crashed yet survived to fight another day. It was as if some magic talisman kept them from terminal harm, while the others, in the parlance of the 'fifties test pilots of Edwards Air Force Base in California's Mojave Desert, didn't quite have The Right Stuff. It was as comfortable a way as any of shrugging away fears for one's own mortality, even if it was frequently illusory.

But then Jim Clark died at Hockenheim on 7 April 1968, and the sport went into shock, for Jimmy was arguably the greatest there has ever been. No comment better summarised his rivals' feelings than that of Chris Amon. 'If it could happen to Jimmy,' the bewildered New Zealander asked, 'what chance did the rest of us have?' Jackie Stewart said that Clark's death was to motor racing what the atomic bomb had been to the world.

Drivers were left frightened, naked, and vulnerable, for Clark was the measure by which they were judged, and the yardstick by which they judged themselves. The King of motorsport had gone, and with his departure each had to find his own private way of coming to terms with the loss – and the risks they faced.

Clark's death thus brought the first era to an end. Stewart had already begun to devote much energy to the safety campaign that would revolutionise the sport, and with his friend and fellow countryman's passing he redoubled his efforts.

During the immediate post-Clark period, motor racing moved gradually out of the Dark Ages, though the 'seventies remained a dangerous era nonetheless. But at the start of the 'eighties, with the advent of carbon fibre composite monocoque chassis, safety standards took another quantum leap forward, into what may retrospectively be called the pre-Senna era. Up until Clark's death, 25 of his fellow Grand Prix competitors had perished in international races or while testing. From then until 1980, and the end of the second era, that number dropped slightly to 21. From 1981 up until 1994 and the end of the third era, the number mercifully dropped lower still, to six.

And then came the terrible events of Imola, that godless weekend in 1994 when Rubens Barrichello was lucky to escape almost unharmed from a dramatic accident on the Friday, Roland Ratzenberger was killed on the Saturday, and Ayrton Senna died on the Sunday.

When the great Brazilian succumbed, the sport went into the same shock it had experienced with Jim Clark, but there were some crucial differences. In Clark's era motorsport had yet to fall under the spell of the great god television; it had much less of a global following and was recognised as a life-taker, even if nobody had ever expected one as gifted as the Scot to become a victim. But Senna, equally gifted in his era and every bit the yardstick to his fellows that Clark had been, operated in a period when F1 was being beamed into homes all over the globe, and was beginning to think that it had the thorny problem of safety licked. So many brilliant designers had devoted so much thought to making cars and circuits safer, that there was universal amazement when the harsh realisation dawned that loopholes still existed. For years nobody had been killed in a F1 car (even though there had been deaths in lower formulae), and now, in one awful weekend, two drivers had succumbed, one of the them the best of his time.

And Senna had been killed 'live' on television, in front of millions of viewers world-wide. They had seen it all. Right there, on the box, in their living rooms.

It is an evolution in public mores which has led to so much change in what can be called the post-Senna or present era; for today many people find it unacceptable that sportsmen should risk death while indulging in their chosen pastime.

The politics and psychology of such an esoteric argument are fascinating and complex, but need not detain us here, in a book which seeks instead to identify the changes that have occurred in motor racing safety, and the reasons why they have been made. Regardless of the semantics of the situation, action had to be taken. Looking at things with the benefit of more than six years of hindsight, much of the change that occurred in the immediate aftermath of Imola was of the knee-jerk variety, and necessarily so, for nobody had an absolute answer to any of the myriad questions that were asked. What was important was that action was at least seen to be taken.

Since Imola, the best brains in the sport have been devoted to eradicating whatever complacency may (with a degree of justification) have begun to creep back in during the pre-Senna era. With the benefit of cool, unhurried rational thinking, allied to intensive research and total commitment to the goal, much good has been done. Without question the sport is safer now than at any time in its frequently bloody and turbulent history.

It has metamorphosed from the early era, when trench warfare mentality ensured that there was always a supply of enthusiastic young men ready to take the places of the fallen. It has surpassed the days when it was deemed better for a driver to be thrown clear as a car went berserk, and outlived the days when the machinery crumpled around the driver like a fiery, fatal cocoon. And it has created structures strong enough to give every driver excellent odds of surviving the most fearsome impacts that would undoubtedly have been fatal in years gone by.

But this is not enough. It goes back to that old joke about the fly. Today the biomechanics of accidents are as crucial as the design of any F1 monocoque. As leading designer John Barnard remarked immediately after Imola: 'We know that we can build structures that are strong enough to withstand the toughest impacts an F1 car is likely to experience. But we have to be careful that, in making the car so strong, we do not arrive at an accident scene to find it all but intact, but the driver marmalised in the cockpit.'

If the pre-Senna era focused on making cars strong enough, the legacy of his death has been to investigate even more intently all means of ensuring that the very strength of the cars acts in a driver's favour without simultaneously compromising his chances of survival.

Will this research prove to be the last piece in a highly complex jigsaw? It would be far too naïve and dangerous to respond affirmatively, for safety in motorsport is a statistical science. It needs time for the new patterns and spikes to become apparent in the wake of change, and it will perforce remain an ongoing investigation whose solutions must change continually to cater for frequent changes in technology. The purpose of this book is to highlight what has been achieved so far, and to examine what lies ahead.

If there is one abiding lesson to be learned from not just the Clark and Senna tragedies, but from all of those incidents in which a young man has paid with his life for pursuing a sport that he loves, it is that no man should ever be turned into a pariah merely because he speaks out in the name of safety and common sense. All parties should have a voice.

Historically, governing administrations have been loathe to listen too much to the men who drive the cars – partly because they see them as only transient players in a long-term game, and perceive themselves as the target of any insurance claim in the event of a disaster such as the one which occurred at Le Mans in 1955. But now the sport's governing body, the FIA (*Federation Internationale d'Automobile*), is itself in the vanguard of the safety crusade. It believes that it is no longer acceptable that drivers risk being killed. The drivers are only too keen to remain with the living, but they operate to a different agenda. They do not all want to be wrapped in cotton wool or to see the visceral appeal of their sport emasculated, and most accept that everything is sweetened by risk. But that risk must be finely calculated and controlled, so that they can take their chances and make their mistakes without suffering fatal consequences because of either the lack of foresight of others or their own ignorance.

The science of safety is not an exact one. It is experimental, with all that this implies. Today's knowledge is the result of yesterday's experience. But now there is a huge data bank that extremely able and organised people are sifting through in the endless search for improvement.

How well all of the disparate groups inter-react – in particular the FIA and the drivers – may well hold the key to the future safety of motorsport at all levels.

David Tremayne
Harrow and Stapleton
September 2000

Acknowledgements

The writer who is better versed in books about people walks a challenging tightrope when he tries to unravel some of F1's technical mysteries. As was the case with *The Science of Speed*, he must be aware of the old adage that 'a little bit of knowledge is a dangerous thing'. But thankfully the sea changes that have flooded through F1 in the first 50 years of the FIA Formula One World Championship owed nothing to nature and everything to the courage, determination, and sheer persistence of some very fine fellows.

F1 has always attracted an unusual blend of human beings, from the second-rate grafters out for whatever they can get, to opportunists, professionally miserable millionaires, and those who have turned their backs on dying racing drivers as if they were nothing more than a blown light bulb. But their oleaginous presence is offset by others who carry the spirit of competition and sportsmanship like shields. Men who have paid very heavy dues in the pursuit of their profession, and who have worked tirelessly and selflessly – no matter how unpopular it might have made them – to bring about the changes that have banished the dark days, when F1 could expect to lose at least three of its protagonists with every passing season. If I wore a hat I'd take it off to these guys, while saluting the progress they have achieved and will go on achieving. It's been my personal good fortune to know them and to benefit from their advice, knowledge, and recollections in the preparation of this book.

Speaking of which, my thanks and appreciation go to: Gary Anderson; Jean-Marie Balestre; John Barnard; Gerhard Berger; Ross Brawn; Tony Brooks; David Coulthard; Ron Dennis; Frank Dernie; Bernie Ecclestone; Vicki Flack (Jardine PR); Mike Gasgoyne; Mika Hakkinen; Patrick Head; Innes Ireland; Eddie Irvine; Alan Jenkins; Lisa Kanani (Jardine PR); Karl Kling; Ed McDonough; Roberto Mieres; Max Mosley; Sir Stirling Moss; Adrian Newey; Jackie Oliver; the late Harvey Postlethwaite; Louis Stanley; Jackie Stewart; John Surtees; Trevor Taylor; Jos Verstappen; Jacques Villeneuve; Professor Sid Watkins; Charlie Whiting; and Peter Wright.

Foreword

by Professor Sid Watkins

the FIA's chief medical delegate

In the six years since the tragic events of the 1994 San Marino Grand Prix at Imola that changed the face and philosophy of Formula One motor racing, the search for safety has been intense. Under the immediate scrutiny of governments, and even the Vatican, the changes were unavoidable and have largely been received favourably by a world which itself had already changed.

Attitudes to safety measures and even proper medical support were once dismissive, and the proponents of such were treated with contempt or even aggression. In fact, at a national motorsport medical committee in 1970 – the only year in which motorsport has crowned a posthumous World Champion, and in which three top line drivers died – the chairman stated that 'racing drivers deserve no more medical facilities or response than an ordinary road car driver might expect'.

These attitudes, fortunately, started to change in the 'seventies and by the time my involvement in Formula One began in 1978 much progress had already been made. The early advances in safety were due to the efforts of many people but

(Sutton)

prominent amongst them were Jackie Stewart and Louis Stanley. Even in these comparatively recent times, however, their efforts were decried and even at times obstructed and vilified.

Subsequently Niki Lauda, Jody Scheckter, Mario Andretti and James Hunt became vocal in their concerns and also pressed hard for change. A major step forward occurred in 1978 when Bernie Ecclestone – worried by a spate of accidents in which clearly the management had been inadequate, if not negligent – decided to establish a worldwide standard of medical facilities and response for Formula One. Significant changes then occurred but were resisted at more than one circuit on the grounds of expense or, at times, with a sneering disregard for injury or even death. With the accession of Jean-Marie Balestre and his political weight as President of the FISA, the speed of change accelerated. The engineers, designers and circuit owners made massive contributions in car, circuit and barrier protection design.

From 1982 to 1994 a period of relative calm ensued, but concerns about speeds and protection arose in the early 'nineties, and as Ayrton Senna was preparing to launch a new safety initiative he was killed before he could get it off the ground. Since then Max Mosley, who succeeded Balestre as President of the FIA, has led the crusade.

This sensitive, scientific and heavily researched book deals in depth with the story of the search for safety from the earliest days of motor racing and recounts the progress with detailed interviews with many motor racing personalities. It is a work of the history of the subject – I learned much from it.

The best of friends: Ayrton Senna and Sid Watkins had a profound respect for one another's abilities and personalities, something which made the events of the 1994 San Marino GP at Imola all the harder for the FIA chief medical delegate to bear. (Sutton)

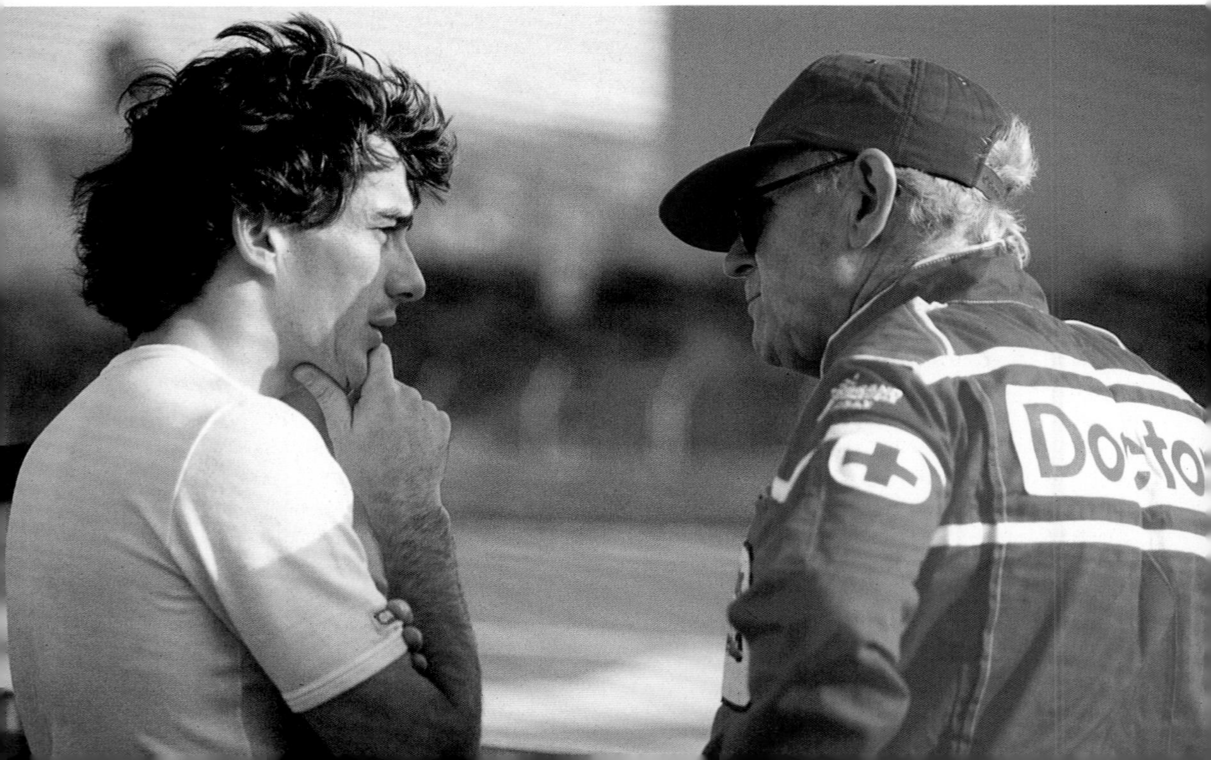

Chapter 1

Gay cavaliers

My philosophy was that I would rather lose a race driving fast enough to win, than win a race driving slow enough to lose. I was a racer, not a driver.

Sir Stirling Moss

In April 1996 Mercedes-Benz used the Grand Prix of Europe at the new Nürburgring as a useful opportunity to allow journalists to experience laps of the old Nürburgring, in road cars driven by luminaries such as Bernd Schneider and Jan Magnussen. But there was a treat of a different kind in store, too, for the three-pointed star also brought along 'fifties Grand Prix racer Karl Kling, who had a store of anecdotes to share. In company with the media men, he watched a film of the 1955 German GP round the grand old Nordschliefe circuit.

'I have to say that it is interesting to see it,' he said, 'because I have never watched it before. I'm pleasantly surprised to see a number of things!' What he added next demonstrated a different perspective, which wiped away the rose-coloured tints. 'On my first tank-full of fuel the tank split at a welded seam,' he revealed. 'I had fuel spraying on my back, and I knew I would have to pit for more. I was driving round there like a madman anyway, because I was certain at the time that the rear axle was giving trouble. The car wasn't running quietly any more.

'It turned out that the steel sheet supporting the top link in the rear suspension had broken. One of the things I did was test for Mercedes, and in those days we were testing things during races. We had used a bit less steel in that area on my car, and the top link broke as a result. It just wasn't strong enough. Normally we would pit after 500km [300 miles] for one tank of fuel and one set of tyres, but when I stopped there were frantic signs. I was attacking Fangio at the time; the Nürburgring was my home track and I was faster than him because of my lower fuel load. Maybe I could have won. Certainly I had to attack him to make time for my stop, and after the repair the car was not perfect.'

It was all said so matter-of-factly, as if everyone drove cars round the most dangerous and demanding circuit in the world with breaking suspension, and fuel slopping down their necks. Truth was, most of them did from time to time.

Racing has changed diametrically since Kling's days, just as it had since

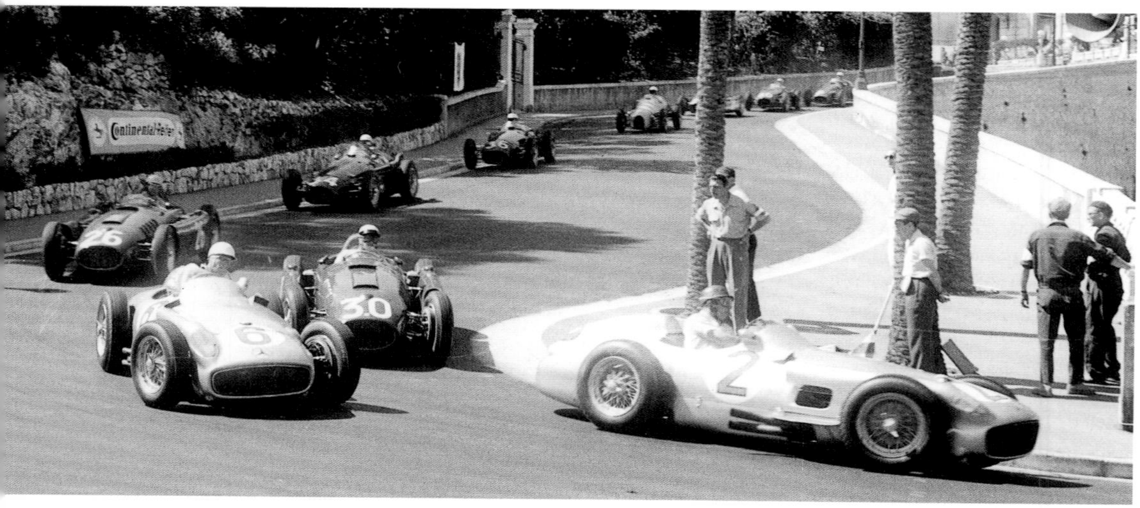

The way it was: at Monaco in 1955 Juan Manuel Fangio leads Stirling Moss, Eugenio Castellotti and Alberto Ascari, none of them giving a second thought to the open pavements and exposed trees. (LAT)

the days of Paris–Madrid when he was in his heyday. 'We had no assistance for the brakes and steering in those days, and needed 60km [40 miles] to run in the clutch and 80 [50] before the brakes came in. There was a lot of strain on the man and on his machine. But there isn't any less now; in fact, the g-force is much more now. It's unbelievable! You can see it in individual drivers, some can take it and some can't. You can't say that we had it tougher.

'I've always been a sporty character. I always lived healthily, as far as eating and drinking were concerned. I didn't smoke or drink alcohol. Drink is the worst thing for motor racing. We had two types of drivers, those who drank and those who didn't. One time when we were testing at the Nürburgring, engineering chief Rudolf Uhlenhaut made a deliberate test. After a day's running we drank in the bar in the evening. Next day those who'd been drinking couldn't get near their previous day's times. Then I tried it myself, and I couldn't beat my times. The next night nobody drank, and the next day we all went quicker!'

McLaren Mercedes-Benz driver David Coulthard was among those who watched the old black and white film that afternoon. It would be unfair to single out the Scot, for his views are similar to those of many current racing drivers, but what he said that day was an enlightening illustration of the gulfs that develop between different eras.

Coulthard had once tested a Maserati 250F for *Autosport*, but now he shook his head in disbelief and repeated over and again: 'They must have been absolutely mad. Just look, no belts, no proper helmets, and all that at the old Nürburgring of all places.'

'There was no way we ever thought of safety in our day,' Kling smiled, with the good cheer that is the legacy – luxury? – of a man who survived. 'If you had an accident the engine came back at you. I had my share of bad crashes, but as you can see, I survived quite well actually!'

Coulthard is a child of the modern era of Formula One, the period which began with the deaths of Roland Ratzenberger and Ayrton Senna at the 1994 San Marino GP. This race summarised the sea change that had taken place since the 'fifties concerning the acceptability of a human being risking his life. The freedom to do with one's life whatever one wishes to, regardless of risk, is one of the greatest personal liberties, but in the over-caring 'nineties it was one that was fast being eroded by the nanny state. Thankfully, however, we are long past the unfortunate days when several drivers were killed during a season, and at the time of the 1994 event at Imola it had been 12 years since F1 had last seen a fatality at a race, and eight since there had been one in testing.

Back in 1968 Jim Clark's death had been no less shattering, and had thrown the sport into turmoil. But now, as a similarly revered figurehead perished, there was a significant difference: in the politically correct 'nineties Senna's death had occurred 'live' in full view of the television cameras, which beamed it to billions of fans across the globe. FIA president Max Mosley was not indulging his penchant for hyperbole when he declared that motor racing was under the microscope in many European countries, such was the profound sense not just of shock but of disgust and outrage. The cold fact that this would not have been the case had only Ratzenberger died is neither here nor there, for in the immediate aftermath of the Senna tragedy there was an orgy of self-righteous indignation. Something or someone had to be held accountable, even if it was only the sport which both men had loved so much.

Mosley had already prepared an emergency plan (wing modifications, shortened diffusers, etc) when, at the very next race – the high profile Monaco GP – Austrian driver Karl Wendlinger slumped into a coma after an accident in practice. These events, and the FIA's reaction to them, were to have a very far-reaching influence on the entire format of future F1 racing.

But before we move on to examine the latest advances in motor racing safety, we need to go a long way back, not just to understand why and how the changes have been made, but also to appreciate how much resistance there once was to what is taken for granted today.

Death was an occupational hazard for men who wished to call themselves racing drivers, right from the early days of motorsport, when the brutal Paris–Madrid road race of 1903 had to be halted to bring an end to its bloody carnage. Death was simply the other side of the racers' coin, the one that all of them hoped they would not flip in their game of chance. It was what happened to the other guy, and few consciously allowed themselves to think about it. They barely considered what today we call 'safety'. Motor racing was dangerous, but you shoved that to the back of your mind and participated with an oft-misplaced blind faith that none of the bul-

At Le Mans the same year – scene of the sport's worst disaster when a Mercedes ploughed into the crowd killing more than 80 people – there was no wall to safeguard those in the pits, nor adequate run-off area to protect spectators packed into the tribunes. (LAT)

lets would have your name on them. It was as simple as that.

All too often, however, the bullets did carry names. Looking back, it is perhaps surprising that motor racing actually survived the Paris–Madrid fiasco in 1903. The horseless carriage was still a relatively unproven entity then, even if Leon Serpollet had proved its potential with his 120.79kph (75.06mph) land speed record. But the sheer scale of carnage along the public roads of this epic contest might well have swept the sport away on a tide of public indignation. More than 300,000 spectators watched the start of this much-trumpeted event, but before long Marcel Renault had died as a result of injuries received when a mistake sent him off the road at Poitiers. Lorraine Barrow's mechanic was reported killed when the driver ran over a dog, while Barrow himself was badly hurt. An English driver named Stead was also injured after crashing. Porter was crushed when he overturned his Wolseley, and his passenger, Nixon, was killed. Tourand and his mechanic were also seriously injured, as were a number of spectators. Confusion reigned in these days of primitive communication, and the paucity of coherent reports did not do racing any favours. Where there was doubt about the welfare of those who crashed, reports erred on the gory side. Headlines such as 'Jehu the Juggernaut', 'Motor Massacre', and 'The Petrol Death' did immeasurable harm to racing's image.

The race was stopped at Bordeaux, and the disgraced cars towed to the local station for dispatch by train to Paris.

Genuine road racing survived that bloody episode, and would remain popular even after the Le Mans disaster of 1955, when the veteran Frenchman Pierre Levegh became the first unwitting victim of a series of circumstances as evening settled on the famous circuit in France's La Sarthe region, where Grand Prix aces Mike Hawthorn, in his Jaguar D Type, and Juan Manuel Fangio in his Mercedes-Benz 300SLR, had been engaged in a furious battle for the lead. This struggle involved not only their personal honour and that of Jaguar and Mercedes-Benz, but, in this post-war period, also embraced national honour. World War Two might have ended a decade earlier, but this was France and feelings died hard.

As Hawthorn and Fangio swept through the fast section of road known as White House, and on towards the pits, Hawthorn overtook fellow Briton Lance Macklin, who was driving an Austin-Healey that was no match for his powerful streamliner. But having done so, Hawthorn then braked sharply in order to make it into the pits to refuel with minimal delay. Perhaps because of the power of the Jaguar's still relatively innovative disc brakes, perhaps because Hawthorn's move was so unexpected given the speed at which he had just overtaken the Healey, perhaps for any one of a number of other reasons, Macklin was taken by surprise. After all, he could have had no appreciation of the intensity of the battle for the lead, nor of Hawthorn's almost pathological hatred of German cars. Whatever the reason, it was to trigger the greatest carnage the sport has ever witnessed.

Macklin was obliged to swerve the Healey to the left to avoid running into the back of the Jaguar, and this put him squarely in the path of Levegh in the sister Mercedes to Fangio's. At that very moment the great Argentinian champion himself was also preparing to lap the two slower cars. The trouble was, all four cars were travelling at differing speeds. Hawthorn was now slowing into the pits; Macklin was unsettled as he pulled out to clear him; Levegh was closing fast on the Healey; and Fangio was closing faster still on the French veteran's Mercedes. Levegh was left with nowhere to go and no time in which to shed his speed advantage over Macklin. He ran into and over the Healey's sloping tail, spinning it into the pit road. The Mercedes, meanwhile, was launched into the unprotected grandstand to the left of the track, where hundreds were watching the race. As it scythed through the spectators and exploded as it broke up, killing Levegh instantly, it left a terrible trail of destruction in its wake.

The official death toll of Le Mans 1955 was 81, but it was likely more, perhaps double that figure, with hundreds more grievously injured. It was the worst toll in motorsport's roll of honour, but this time it was not just the combatants cut down by the bullets, but those who had paid to come and watch – those who had every right to believe that they would be safe from whatever happened on the racetrack.

Shortly before dusk Grand Prix racer Roberto Mieres' Maserati was forced into the pits by an electrical problem. As a result, the Argentinian was an unwilling witness as the drama unfolded. 'The dynamo was not charging properly,' he recalls, 'and as we would soon be needing our lights I stopped at the boxes [pits]. I was there, speaking with Perdisa, my wife, and Maserati's test driver Bertocchi, when it happened.

'Macklin [he pronounced it 'Mack-lean'] touched Levegh and then made a tête a queue [a spin] as Levegh in the Mercedes started to fly. Bang! It was terrible. When the car hit the concrete, it was like a grenade. A thousand pieces, whoosh, into the people. And I was there, standing in front of the boxes. I saw it all right before me. It was a terrible, terrible thing: I saw legs, arms, other things. Black smoke. I said to the team, "I'm very sorry, I cannot drive any more". They pleaded with me to continue, but how could I? I remember later, with the coming night, that the sun was blood red as it began to sink. I went to Paris to get away from it all. It was a terrible thing to see.'

Somehow motorsport survived that catastrophe too. While the venerable British magazine *Motor Sport* did what it believed to be its bit by acting as if nothing had happened, the national newspapers saw the tragedy in a totally different light and went into overdrive.

It was the same two years later, when Italy's glorious Mille Miglia cross-country road race ended with the deaths of driver Fon de Portago, his co-driver Ed Nelson, and the 11 spectators that their errant Ferrari cut down at Giudozzolo di

Monaco again, in 1958, with poles and straw bales intended to keep cars from the trees and lamp-posts. (LAT)

Mantova when it suffered a tyre failure at around 280kph (170mph).

Terrible as all this was – 1955 alone also saw the great Alberto Ascari killed at Monza, and Indianapolis legend Bill Vukovich and foul-mouthed sprint car racer Mike Nazaruk crash to their deaths – the world largely and, to modern eyes, unaccountably remained sanguine. There had been the usual outcry in Italy, where the Vatican had its say on Enzo Ferrari's role in the Mille Miglia tragedy and the Government banned the contest, but the world was still only one decade past the infinitely greater carnage of World War Two. While life was not cheap, death was nevertheless greeted stoically. Attitudes were different back then.

The 'fifties was a decade in which many bright young men lived for the moment, cramming their existences with all the pleasures of life as if some sixth sense was warning them how little time they had been allotted. Dashing blades such as quintessential Englishmen Hawthorn and Peter Collins, Italians Eugenio Castellotti and Luigi Musso, and good-time Franco-American Harry Schell, all paid the highest price. The Englishman Tony Brooks stood out among this colourful crowd. He was only 23 years old when, as a relative novice, he had gone out to race at Syracuse in Italy in the year of the Le Mans disaster, feverishly swotting for his dentistry exams when he was not challenging the might of Maserati with his Connaught. Yet he came back a man after scoring one of the greatest upsets in history. A quiet young fellow of unusually phlegmatic character, he was the prototype of the breed of racer who would step into the arena in future decades: the calm professional who stood apart from his hell-for-leather rivals. Yet Brooks was no softie, as victories at Spa-Francorchamps, Nürburgring, and Monza – the three fastest and most demanding tracks on the calendar – testified in 1958.

'I think all of us on the Vanwall driving strength did feel different from the others,' he admits. 'Stirling Moss was a real pro, and my other team-mate, Stuart Lewis-Evans, was also a quiet guy. I cer-

At Oporto the same season it was the same story as championship contenders Moss and Hawthorn blast past the straw bales. (LAT)

tainly felt different, because I thought that motor racing was too serious to fool about. I felt that you had to be totally fit and totally focused on what you were doing.

'Stirling was a totally committed professional, which I entirely respected. I think that behind the wheel I was just as committed and professional. You were putting your life on the line anyway, and not to be professional behind the wheel was just loading the dice against you.'

Ahead of his time in other ways, too, Brooks also demonstrated an unusual and unfashionable penchant for understanding the technicalities of his car. 'I put it down to my dentistry,' he laughs. 'There you have to be able to analyse and clear your thoughts to progress in a logical way, so I just applied my general degree training to get my car as good as I could, and to be as good as I could as a driver.'

A Musso or a Castellotti would drive over his head in the quest to coerce a better performance from his car. But if Brooks couldn't squeeze anything more from it without overstretching his own technique, he accepted the fact and could live with it. He was not troubled by machismo. 'I think that I was very fortunate. I was blessed with natural ability, and I found that driving to the limit of it was good enough to win races.'

Brooks was the most cerebral driver of his age, and was unusually aware of the risks of his profession. A year after Syracuse he found out the hard way what happened when you pushed a bad car too far. That season's BRM P25 was an unforgiving monster. His had broken its throttle cable during the British GP, but he remained anxious to impress the crowd who had come along to applaud him as the hero of Syracuse. After a pit stop to have repairs effected he found the throttle still sticking, but he kept pressing on, taking Abbey Curve flat out. 'I must have been a bit thick, really,' he recalls in his self-deprecating manner.

Luigi Musso was one of the young lions who overstepped the line once too often, at Reims in 1958. (David Tremayne Archive)

'You had to corner that car geometrically, you couldn't drift it. A bit more oil and rubber had gone down there and I needed a quick lift. But the throttle stuck, so I finished a little on the grass. In any decent car you'd have eased back on to the circuit, but it just went completely out of control, hit a bank, tossed me out, and then did the only decent thing and set itself on fire.'

In his heart he knew he should not have taken the risk. Another reminder of his own mortality lay in store at Le Mans in 1957, when he overturned his Aston Martin at the Tertre Rouge corner. He'd been looking down into the cockpit trying to figure out why the car was stuck in fourth gear. The Aston mounted a sandbank before flopping over on him, trapping him in the cockpit. These were the days when fire was the racing driver's greatest fear.

'It was three o'clock in the morning, and I was too far round the corner for anybody else to see that there was a car and driver lying in the road. I was thinking, "What's best, being run over or being cremated?" I was very lucky. Umberto Maglioli came round in his Porsche, hit the tail of my car, and knocked it off me. So I got up and ran to the side of the road. I was pretty carved up, but the adrenalin was running high at the time.'

The two close shaves gave Brooks pause for thought. 'Either time it could have been curtains through stupidity – not what I would call driving errors of judgement. I'd been very lucky, and I thought that in future I would not try to drive at competitive speeds in a sub-standard car. I made this solemn promise to myself.'

In 1959 Brooks led the Ferrari team and touched the hem of the World Championship after glorious victories at the fast tracks, Reims and Avus. But after a start-line brush in the final race, where he could have clinched the title, his discretion won over his valour and he made a precautionary pit stop. It cost him any chance of the crown.

'It wasn't a massive impact,' he recalled nearly four decades later. 'But if you stress things in the direction they aren't supposed to be stressed, a relatively small bump can do a lot of damage. I had one and a half minutes to decide what to do, and believe me those must have been the most difficult minutes of my life. If I stopped, the World Championship would be gone. On the other hand, if I didn't I would have betrayed the solemn promise that I'd made to myself …'

He once made a throwaway comment that one had a responsibility to take *reasonable* care of one's life. To him, that meant being sensible and not overstepping the mark. 'If I had approached a 150 mile an hour corner and said, "I want to win this race. I'm not comfortable but I'm going to go for it although it may be beyond my capabilities," in my book that would be taking unreasonable care of my life. But I rationalised that I was being reasonable going up to the limit of my natural ability, and not screwing myself up to do something I really didn't feel confident I could do. Without being dramatic about it, I had got away with my life twice, and therefore I made that promise to myself that I would not drive a sub-standard car quickly again, and if I did, would I deserve anything else but to be pushing up the daisies?'

Brooks was never intimidated by the greatest circuits – Spa or the Nürburgring – and thrived on them with his beautiful, precise style. 'I just did what came naturally, really,' he says diffidently. 'All sorts of drivers, great ones, said they hated Spa and Nürburgring, and I just don't understand that. That suggests to me that they must have been pushing their limits a bit far. It didn't matter to me whether it was an aerodrome circuit or Spa, I would drive in exactly the same manner, with the idea of going as fast as I could. But all that was available to me was the road. The last thing that would occur to me would be that I would leave this road. So one is almost led to the conclusion that some of these guys were pushing too hard.

'I never pressured myself and said, "Well, I don't feel comfortable but I'm going to go through this corner flat, come what may". If it were possible to go through it flat then I would, but I wouldn't screw up my courage and say, "I'm going to do it this time".'

Jim Clark hated Spa after the death of Archie Scott-Brown there in 1958 and Chris Bristow in 1960. Stirling Moss had enough accidents there, that were no fault of his own, to develop a distrust of the place. Jackie Stewart was always mindful of his shunt there in 1966. None of them ever let that be reflected in their driving there – indeed, Clark won four times in a row from 1962 – but they were ... wary. Many of Brooks's rivals lacked his self-control, and many paid a high price for this deficiency.

Stirling Moss ran in 66 Grands Prix and won 16 of them. He started from pole position 16 times, and from the front row of the grid 37 times. He set fastest lap on 20 occasions. Between 1955 and 1958 he was second in the World Championship, and between 1959 and 1961, third. Together with Fangio, he was the yardstick of his era. Yet he had a different philosophy to Brooks's.

'Racing is what mattered,' he said, not long before his knighthood in 1999. 'My philosophy was that I would rather lose a race driving fast enough to win, than win a race driving slow enough to lose. I was a racer, not a driver. And I think that was not an intelligent thing to be; one should be a driver and a racer as well, but I enjoyed racing. I enjoyed dicing with other guys. To me that's what it was about.'

Pushing a car into a corner and looking in his mirror and seeing another driver behind, and then seeing that same driver three or four feet further back when he looked again as he exited the corner: that was what turned Moss on. And he was very good at it. Fantastically good. 'That's when I felt six feet tall,' he chuckles. 'You know, beat that! It's a very lonely place, leading a race on your own, not dicing. No two ways about it. But even when you're on your own, you're still dicing. You come out of a corner and look down and maybe you'll see 6,700 revs. And the next lap you try that little bit harder, just to try and see a little bit more. You're dicing with yourself. And you are your own toughest critic.'

Yet though Moss could justly lay claim to having been the greatest F1 driver in history, he admits that he did not spin a racing car for the first four years

The Avus staged only one German GP, in 1959; note the steepness of the fearsome banking, and the big drop at the bottom of the curve. Tony Brooks leads Moss and Masten Gregory. (LAT)

Stirling Moss's Lotus 21 offered scant protection from severe impact. When he crashed at Goodwood in April 1962 the spaceframe chassis folded up around him, and he had to be cut free of the wreckage. (Phipps/Sutton)

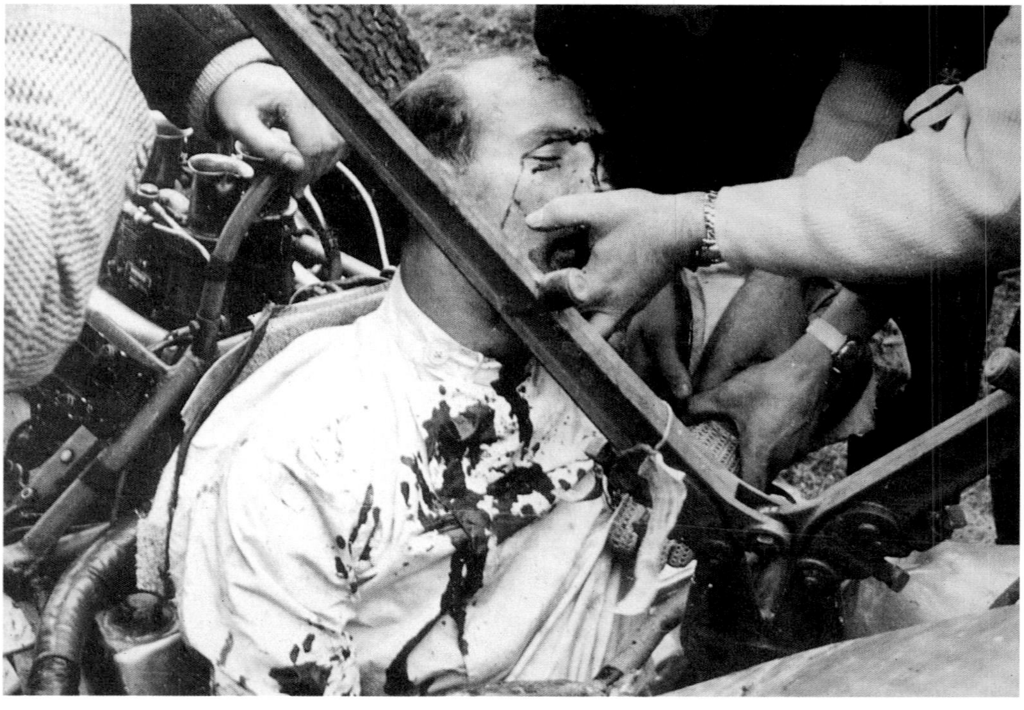

of his career. 'That's because I wasn't courageous,' he confides. 'You see, danger was always on my shoulder. The problem motor racing has today is that the way safety has changed has bred a contempt of danger. And I never had that contempt. I was always really quite frightened of hurting myself. Of dying. And I would always drive sufficiently within my capabilities because I just didn't want to spin. I was afraid that if I did I might hit the kerb and turn over, and be seriously hurt. I didn't actually spin until quite a long time after I'd started.

'When I did finally spin, it didn't change my outlook too much because I could see the reason I'd done it and it was my own fault. I came round this corner and there was dust, so I had a reason for doing it. But I didn't like it. The thing that would really worry me, mentally – because motor racing is very much a mental thing – is if something happened and I didn't know why. I mean, if I went off because a wheel fell off, I'd know why. I'd be pretty upset, naturally, but you have to remember that in those days the cars weren't built like they are now. But providing I knew what had happened, I wasn't mentally upset about it as far as my confidence was concerned.'

He admits that his attitude changed when he lost the title to Hawthorn. 'I really believed that year that I ought to be the champion, but I didn't win. And it was against Mike Hawthorn, and I thought, well, Mike drinks, and he runs around, and he does everything that I would like to do, and still I've been punished for not doing it. What the hell, I'm going to go out and enjoy myself.'

Moss never knew why his UDT Laystall Lotus-Climax crashed so heavily at St Mary's corner, during the Easter Glover Trophy race at Goodwood in 1962. The impact, and the comatose days that followed, erased the memory banks, leaving him with no inkling why his pale green racer speared off the track, careened over the grass and then crashed so heavily into the bank.

'I really don't have any idea,' he insists. 'All I can do is surmise. I was coming up to pass Graham Hill and I think that if a marshal had put a flag out, which he might have done, Graham may have acknowledged him with a wave to say, "Okay". And I may have seen that as a sign to say come past. In any case, Graham had an unusual line there, and if I had seen him over to the right there and seen that happen, I might have thought, "He knows I'm not competing with him, so I'll go past".' Moss was running well back after pit stops to have the Lotus's Colotti gearbox adjusted. 'Thinking that nobody would go by him there, Graham could have pulled over and I might have thought, "Crikey, I'd better get over," and pulled over and gone off. That's the only construction I can make. Graham wasn't the sort of guy who'd push you off. But like I said, it's all just surmise.'

In many cases back then surmise was not necessary. The great Raymond Sommer had suffered a steering arm failure at Cadours in 1950. The unfortunate Alan Stacey had lost control at Spa ten years later after a bird flew into his face. Eugenio Castellotti, Luigi Musso, Peter Collins, Stuart Lewis-Evans, Archie Scott-Brown, Jean Behra, Chris Bristow, Harry Schell, and Wolfgang von Trips – all of them had simply taken one step too many over the line.

Stirling Moss did not succumb to his accident. He survived, and appeared to have left his sport on his own terms. Somehow that seemed to make things all right by the curious mores of the time. There was no outcry against the unprotected earth bank that shattered his Lotus and left him battered and trapped inside. No distress at the way in which the chassis had folded up around him. No call for greater safety measures. But what lay ahead, at Hockenheim on 7 April 1968, would change all that.

Chapter 2

The physics of an accident

I just went a bit too late into the corner. The data says I was doing 179mph on the grass and I went in at about 6g. I suppose I was quite fortunate.

Mark Blundell

Though we need not concern ourselves overmuch with the reasons for accidents, those involving driver error are generally recognised to break down into five main groups: errors of judgement, possibly through lack of experience or complacency; poor technique; refusal to obey certain conventions, possibly through overconfidence; carelessness, again possibly through overconfidence; and negligence, where overconfidence may yet again be a contributory factor.

What we are more concerned with is what happens once an accident is in progress, regardless of the reason for it. The convention is to define acceleration and deceleration (which is really only acceleration in reverse) in multiples of the force of gravity, or 'g'. This is 9.81m (about 32ft) per second per second. A deceleration force is calculated as g being equal to the square of the speed at impact, divided by the distance available for deceleration. These two factors – the energy that must be dissipated, and the rate of deceleration – are the two most critical factors in any impact.

The level of energy defines the amount by which a car or safety structure must deform or break in order for that energy to be dissipated without injury to the driver. This in turn can influence, via the level of jeopardy to which the car's structure is subjected, the likelihood that its components will intrude into the survival cell and inflict injury to the driver.

The deceleration determines the subsequent parts of the crash equation: the driver's impact speed with parts of the car; and the impact speed of his internal organs with his own body structure. This is a very complex area of investigation in any accident, but in all research the overriding factors influencing a driver's chances of escape from serious harm, disregarding the actual structural integrity of the car itself, are the distance over which the car can decelerate before striking anything; and the progressive deformation of whatever it finally hits.

Thus all current thinking on racing car safety is structured around a desire to minimise the speed of impact while maximising the distance over which an errant car can be decelerated. Once the impact has begun, it then focuses on maximising the dissipation of energy in the object that the car finally strikes, rather than in the car itself; and in the extreme case where the car itself is also required to dissipate energy, it must deform in such a way as to offer its driver maximum protection within a survival cell which will not suffer any breaches of structural integrity.

In accidents where a car strikes an unyielding object with minimal deceleration, injury is more likely to result than in situations where the car runs for a long time before striking something deformable a glancing blow. Martin Donnelly's accident in Jerez in September 1990 (see Chapter 9) illustrated the desirability of gradual rather than immediate deceleration once control has been lost.

Many things pose an injury risk to the driver. There are the objects outside the car, with which it collides: Armco barrier, catchfencing, concrete wall, water butt, tyre wall, other vehicles, etc. Then there is the risk of injury from coming into contact with the car itself, since when a racing car hits something the driver's body will try to continue at the speed the car was travelling prior to the impact. One of the purposes of seat belts, of course, is to restrain the driver in order to prevent this, though some degree of 'give' in the belts remains desirable. The American driver Cliff Hansen, who undertook a season of F3 racing in Britain in 1981, delighted in relating the tale of a Formula Atlantic accident he suffered in which, though he was securely strapped in, his head actually struck the dashboard on impact because of the stretch in his seat belts. Alex Zanardi, too, struck his Lotus's dashboard when he crashed very heavily in the infamous Eau Rouge bend at Spa-Francorchamps during practice for the 1993 Belgian GP.

While such extremes may not be desirable, the driver must nonetheless have some movement in such instances if he is

Running is excellent cardiovascular activity, as World Champion Mika Hakkinen demonstrates. (Sutton)

Alexander Wurz's exercise rate is being monitored as he works out in Benetton's Human Performance Centre. (Batchelor/Sutton)

Even back in his Formula Ford days, aged 18, Williams' 2000 sensation Jenson Button worked out at F1 pitch. (Sutton)

to avoid his innards coming to a very sudden stop against the inside of his skeleton. It goes back to that old joke mentioned in the introduction.

The greater the distance over which an impact to a driver may be spread, the more significant will be the effect on his ability to withstand it. Two incidents illustrate this, both at the Fontana Speedway in California, which caters for ChampCars. In 1997, double champion Zanardi endured 88g after his Reynard-Honda collided with the concrete outer wall at close to 322kph (200mph). Two years later Canadian racer Greg Moore was killed when his Reynard-Mercedes struck a concrete inner wall cockpit first at similar speed.

No human being has the power to alter the pure physics of impact between a driver's internal organs and his skeleton. That's just the way humans are built, so everything else has to start from that inflexible point and take it as a given. Deformability of the structure and any objects with which it impacts are thus critical to a driver's chances of survival.

'Every accident is unique, in the tiny details,' says the FIA's technical consultant Peter Wright, formerly the technical director of Team Lotus. 'Basically the cars are very safe and the circuits are very safe, if you get all the details right. If you get one or two of the tiny details wrong, little things like seat belt tension not being quite tight enough, or the detail which lets something catch the driver's helmet and rotate his head, something like that, you can hurt the bloke. If you get all the details right, the cars and drivers can withstand a phenomenal amount.

'One of the worst accidents I looked at was a head-on in CART ChampCar racing, because of the g angle. And we said, "How come the guy wasn't hurt?" You look at the impact, and you know it's going to be serious. The answer was that he was a very experienced guy who saw it was coming, so he put his head on his chest, tucked his hands into the belts, and there was no problem. He had no g-related injuries, because he did exactly the right thing. Drivers are learning now, with all this head padding, to put their head back into it before they hit.'

But in America's rival series, the Indy Racing League (IRL), some crashes in the late 'nineties were paralysing the drivers. Wright's assessment is chilling to hear. 'What happens is this. Dr Terry Trammell, CART's well-known medical representative, has worked out that the driver's head goes back into the crash padding. That's great. But then the body tries to ride up with it; but if the head is fixed to the head pad by friction, the neck becomes bent by the compression, and then you chip the vertebrae. And those chips don't have to go very wrong to damage the spinal cord. So there is a lot of work to do there. Like I said, it is the tiny details of things that happen in milliseconds.

'Our function at the FIA is one of co-ordination more than anything else, and what we are doing is pulling in more and more experts, and tying in with people doing similar work in the States. In many ways they are ahead of us, for two reasons. One is that it is the big car companies doing the work; and two is that they have these horrific accidents on ovals. We don't have them, so our crash pulses look totally different from the Americans'. If we see a solid 40g, you start worrying. You can get peaks that are much higher than that. I know Alex saw that 88g peak at the Fontana oval. But I have seen peaks where a driver has gone over a kerb and the step in the undertray has seen 80g, and the driver hasn't even noticed it because it's very short. So the g level is not that important. It's the change in velocity in a given time that matters. Whereas in America, where they get these solid crash pulses of 120–130g, it's a completely different thing.

'Of course, they don't have barriers on ovals, and I've just been reading that it is building up that the drivers want something done about it. God knows what. It's hard to see what, because there is this very good safety function where if a car hits a concrete wall it tends to slide along it and not bounce back. But if you do have a component perpendicular to the wall, you need distance. The ones that hurt them are the 64 to 96kph [40 to 60mph] components, which doesn't sound very much. You are desperately looking for distance to decelerate the car in, and if you are going to do something about it you are talking about putting something in front of the concrete wall. That limits the track width, and you can imagine the cost ... And also, when you hit a tyre wall and crumple it, then what do you do next? Stop the race? Run under yellows while they repair it? It's not easy.'

Fitness guru Josef Leberer (centre) shares a joke with Johnny Herbert in the latter's Sauber Petronas days. (Sutton)

The infield is perhaps the bigger problem as far as the drivers are concerned, after Moore's fatal accident at Fontana. Richie Hearn had had an almost identical accident and got away with it only a few laps earlier.

'The difference between those two is that when it happened, Hearn banged on the brakes. The hotshots tend not to take their foot off the accelerator but try to spin it,' Wright points out. 'What happened was that Moore's car hooked up with full power on, and he accelerated. And then he went on to a different trajectory, hit the strip of gravel and the car appeared to take off and the aerodynamics rolled it over. Nobody would have predicted that.'

As we shall see later, racing drivers are an extraordinary breed of men. Their spirit and tenacity is typified by Mark Blundell's reaction to the accident that befell him at Suzuka during practice for the Japanese GP in 1995. He had lost control in the very fast 130R corner, spun, and then hit the barrier opposite almost head-on at an estimated 250kph (155mph). He was advised not to participate in the final qualifying session.

'I was sore and stiff, as you'd expect to be after a crash like that,' he admitted the following day. 'I just went a bit too late into the corner. The data says I was doing 288kph [179mph] on the grass and I went in at about 6 g. I suppose I was quite fortunate.'

Very often a driver will overstate his case to the point of whingeing when talking about minor things; but when the chips are really down and they venture into their own exclusive territory of speed and danger, which marks them out from their fellow men, the understatement is as dramatic as it is chilling. 'I think I was probably knocked out for a little bit, because I didn't move at first in the car,' Blundell added, matter-of-factly, as if discussing nothing more irritating than a missed golf shot. 'I was certainly winded and my vision was slightly blurred. I didn't feel 100 per cent fit. But I can assure you that walking away from qualifying was a harder thing than going out there and doing it.

'Obviously the body tries to recover, but despite a good night's sleep I'm still quite drained. And my neck is in a bit of a poor way. Considering that, I think I'm in quite good shape. This is a tough circuit physically, and mentally too with all the concentration. I don't know if it's the right thing to do, but I will start the race.'

He not only started, but finished. He went the distance to seventh place when a lesser racer would have given up. A normal human being would have taken a fortnight off work after a car crash at even 80kph (50mph), but Blundell just wanted to get straight back to pushing the outer edge of his McLaren's performance envelope.

Where all of the key factors exert their influences in the desired manner, a driver will walk away from an accident, and this is what viewers see more often than not on their television screens. The fact that this is so often the case is a tribute to the massive steps that safety engineering in motorsport has taken in the past 50 years.

At one stage at Monaco in 1993 it seemed as if a thumb injury would prevent Ayrton Senna from competing; after Leberer's ministrations he would go on to win his record sixth victory. (Sutton)

Chapter 3

Self-preservation – the first line of defence

If you or I had had the same accidents, forget it. The neck would be just nothing. General fitness is so important. The cardio-vascular system is so important, and having the right amount of muscles. The power and the energy has to be there and you have to train it all the time.

Josef Leberer

If you had to choose the least flappable F1 team pairing of all time, it might be a close-run thing between Jack Brabham and Jochen Rindt at Brabham in 1968, and Gilles Villeneuve and Didier Pironi at Ferrari in 1981. All four were pretty cool customers.

In 1967 Rindt was testing an Eagle Offenhauser at Indianapolis when he lost control and collided at high speed with the concrete outer wall. It was a hefty impact that badly damaged the car, and there was a brief fire. But Jochen calmly rode out the ensuing wild slide before stepping off just before the hulk came to rest. He was totally calm as the rescue team arrived, lit a cigarette nonchalantly, and had to help the driver to do likewise as he was carted away for the mandatory medical check-up. His heart and pulse rates barely registered the incident. Likewise, when Black Jack Brabham walloped the back end of John Surtees's BRM at Monaco in 1969, when Big John's car slowed suddenly, the ensuing ride over the top of the BRM scarcely affected Brabham's demeanour, even though his car had a wheel torn off.

Stories abound of the calm manner in which Villeneuve extricated himself from countless scrapes during his years at Ferrari, with his heartbeat and pulse never betraying the slightest inkling of how close he might have come to disaster. My colleagues Alan Henry and Nigel Roebuck tell a tale of Didier Pironi at Hockenheim in 1979, being berated by Hans Stuck following an incident in the BMW ProCar race. Pironi had apparently pulled a move that displeased Stuck, who was losing no time in relating the news to the Frenchman. Pironi had a reputation for glacial calm and, sure enough, merely gazed with complete lack of concern at Stuck even though the Austrian's red face was only millimetres from his own. He neither flinched nor blinked nervously during the aggressive harangue. Had his eyes not been open, he might have been completely oblivious to the verbal assault.

Villeneuve and Pironi were able to tell

A fiercely private man Nino Farina, the first World Champion, looks uncharacteristically cheerful as he models the well-dressed 'fifties racer's garb of linen coveralls and cloth helmet. (David Tremayne Archive)

us much about the effects of speed on a racing driver, for in 1981 they allowed themselves to be wired up to various monitors during testing at Ferrari's Fiorano circuit, and during the French GP at Dijon. Pironi was also wired for the Monaco GP.

One of the tests measured pulse rate per minute against the average speed for a lap, and interestingly revealed that while Pironi's pulse rate reached almost 200 beats per minute at maximum speed, Villeneuve's was usually no higher than a remarkable 175. It is worth mentioning that anything over 200 can be dangerous for ordinary mortals. At Monaco during practice Pironi again peaked at 198, though interestingly his highest point of stress, which raised his pulse rate to 212, came as he was leaving the circuit!

On one occasion in a press conference at Estoril, Nigel Mansell momentarily grabbed everyone's attention by discussing the 35g forces to which he had been subjected during his pole-winning lap, for the highest-g corner on the Portuguese track was believed to be around 3.5 or 4. It soon transpired that the Englishman was unwittingly adding up the g from each corner ...

Nevertheless, forces up to 4g are regular in F1, and under their influence the driver's weight changes dramatically. Since his torso is firmly strapped into the car, it follows that his head will be affected most, and that the greatest strain will be on his neck muscles. If a driver's helmeted head weighs about 6.5kg (14.3lb) when he is static, it thus follows that in a 4g corner his neck and shoulder muscles are required to support 26kg (57.3lb).

As an indication of the performance of the carbon disc brakes used on modern F1 cars, rates of deceleration can be even more impressive. During the San Marino GP at Imola in 1997, Heinz-Harald Frentzen recorded an amazing 5.99g deceleration on two occasions in his winning slick-tyred Williams-

Renault. In other words, his body momentarily multiplied its normal weight by a factor of almost six! And deceleration figures approaching 5g were then the norm.

Small wonder that today's drivers are highly trained athletes who combat such forces via rigorous exercise routines – though 1978 World Champion Mario Andretti insists that the only exercise which really works to strengthen neck muscles in order to drive an F1 car, is actually driving an F1 car. Double title-winner Mika Hakkinen agrees.

'And don't forget that testing is not the same as racing for 70 laps, either,' insists fitness guru Josef Leberer, an Austrian physiotherapist who worked for the legendary Willi Dungl for many years before setting up his own clinic in Salzburg. Leberer worked for McLaren from 1988 until 1993, when he switched to Williams together with Ayrton Senna. He subsequently returned to McLaren, and currently works with Red Bull Sauber Petronas. 'Racing brings a different pressure,' he continues. 'You have to try to build up the muscles. We use a lot of different exercises but even cross-country skiing is good because you use certain muscles. Then we use other equipment, to simulate sitting in a cockpit and putting some weights on the helmet just to make the right impulse on the muscles and the nerves.'

In keeping with his little-recognised reputation as one of F1's most far-thinking team owners, Ron Dennis at McLaren was one of the first to appreciate just how crucial physical fitness is to a driver's overall level of performance. He had good cause to be thankful for Leberer's ministrations, in the aftermath of Hakkinen's near-fatal accident in Adelaide in 1995. Like Martin Donnelly at Jerez in 1990, the Finn owed much of his survival to his innate fitness.

'If you or I had had the same accidents, forget it,' Leberer insists. 'The neck would be just nothing. General fitness is so important. The cardio-vascular system is so important, and having the right amount of muscles. The power and the energy has to be there and you have to train it all the time. If something doesn't work as it should, you can have major injuries in an accident and then you cannot come back.'

A peak of fitness can also help drivers for the future, by alleviating the stresses and strains of racing that might otherwise manifest themselves at a later date. More than one driver from the bone-shaking days of ground effect in the 'seventies and very early 'eighties now experiences a degree of spinal discomfort.

'Good training is very important,' Leberer continues. 'In my days at McLaren in 1996, for instance, David [Coulthard] would be across with me two or three times in the winter, at my place in Salzburg, to carry out my training programme. We did a lot. I favour cross-country skiing, at the right altitude, which is about 1,700m [5,577ft]. The higher you are the less oxygen there is, so you have to work harder. That gets your own oxygen flow going and stimulates the red blood corpuscles, so at the end David was able to perform better because his cardio-vascular system was at a peak.

'Cross-country skiing is hard work for your whole body and exercises a range of muscles. That's very important. And it's good on muscles and joints because it's not as hard on the joints as running or mountain biking. Overall you have to try and build up a good muscle system, without harming the ligaments or joints. Swimming is also a good exercise, fantastic – one of the very best. But you have to be careful to choose the right discipline. You need a variety of breast stroke and crawl, but backstroke is the best, because it trains the opposite muscle group to the one you use normally as a driver when you are sitting with your arms straight out in front of you.'

Leberer says that the fittest driver he

At Monaco in 1961, winner Stirling Moss shows off his cork Herbert Johnson helmet. (Phipps/Sutton)

ever worked with was probably Ayrton Senna, with whom he forged a very close working relationship in their McLaren years. Yet ironically, the Brazilian was perceived as relatively unfit at times during his rookie season with Toleman in 1984. In his second race for the team, in South Africa, he was almost overcome by heat exhaustion on his way to sixth place and his first World Championship point.

Many drivers deliberately train in high temperatures to get used to the effects of heat. Senna, for example, regularly ran in heat on the beach near his Brazilian hideaway at Angra dos Reis, working to a three-day cycle which saw a greater distance covered each day.

During the selection process for the driver of ThrustSSC, Richard Noble's British land speed record challenger – with which Andy Green went supersonic at a speed of 1227.968kph (763.035mph) in October 1997 – contenders were incarcerated in a room for 24 hours. During this time they were required to carry out a series of tasks, including some complex computer control. Later, when the temperature had been increased dramatically, they were required to fulfil the same tasks once more. The temperature rise had a dramatic negative effect on the efficiency of several candidates.

Besides Senna, Nelson Piquet and Brabham team-mate Riccardo Patrese suffered badly in high temperatures during the 1982 Brazilian GP. (Piquet collapsed on the victory rostrum, while Patrese spun helplessly several times.) Nigel Mansell collapsed from the effort of pushing his Lotus to the line during the US GP at Dallas in 1984. The ambient temperature there was so high that the race was started at 11 o'clock to avoid the worst of it. Race winner Keke Rosberg very shrewdly invested in a special 'cool cap', a silver skull cap which pumped water to his head to keep it cool throughout a gruelling race. It worked perfectly.

'Before long, though, Senna was very fit,' Leberer stresses. 'Since he started training really seriously, all of the new drivers saw that there was no way to be competitive without being fit. I think there is not much difference now between any of the drivers, especially the young ones.

'In my early days Gerhard Berger, though you wouldn't believe it, got really strong and really fit. David improved a lot too, I must say, and reached really good physical condition. Mika, too. It was unbelievable, how he came back after his accident. That really was more than you could expect. I said to him at his first race back, in Melbourne in 1996, "You've already won the first race, just by being here, so just be grateful. You are the winner just for being here".'

Leberer stayed in Australia for two and a half weeks with Hakkinen after the accident in Adelaide at the end of 1995 which nearly killed him. 'I wanted to see how bad it was in the beginning. He was gradually working up, up, up. We had to do a lot of physical therapy to work on that, because then you can combine everything. We concentrated on breathing properly, getting the energy out, then he opened up and I could change things. But it was always step by step.'

Give somebody a goal, or goad them, and you can often get more out of them than you might by gentle persuasion. 'It's very hard at the beginning and it hurts a guy, but if they're strong enough they think about it and see that maybe you are right. Even if they don't tell you, at least they do it. The most important thing is that I'm not a guy who always tells a driver what he wants to hear. These guys always seem to be surrounded by people who tell them what they want to hear, and that doesn't help.

'It was very special with Ayrton. We didn't have to talk a lot. Six years with McLaren, then I went with him to Williams. At the end we were very close; where he went to drive, I went. There was something very special. It was very difficult to talk about it, because some people don't understand, but everything we did together just worked.

'At the beginning, I remember when we were at Bali, when he had just won the World Championship for the first time by winning in Japan. He had a problem with his knee. And we did something, acupuncture, massage or whatever, with energy, combining your own energy to try and bring it in. Make no mistake, I'm not full of energy. I take it from mental training, from the earth or from the sun. You have to get the energy because we are constantly giving or losing it. With Ayrton it was fantastic. Everything I did it just worked.'

It helped, undoubtedly, that Senna was intelligent and open-minded enough to draw the maximum from any programme. 'He saw it, all right. In Mexico that year that he had the crash, 1992, we were working all Friday night. He was sleeping already in the day and he said that he was going home, that he couldn't race anyway. And I said, "Let's try it. Let's try it." But even I thought there was no way. The doctor said he couldn't race and it was so painful he could hardly walk. He'd really been shaken up. But we kept working there and I put all these packages on, trying to stimulate the lymphatic system in his body. After one and a half hours he fell asleep. I went back to my room to fill myself up with energy, and I said to myself, "We have to do it".

'We worked nearly all night. At one o'clock he slept a bit, and at five I came back. We worked for six or seven hours. But then he began to think, "This guy is working so long, he must believe in it. Maybe there is a chance." I had the feeling that he opened himself up.

'He slept for four or five hours and in the morning I came back and started work on the leg, a different kind of therapy. And he said, "What's going on? I have the feeling I slept 24 hours. It's unbelievable." He didn't talk a lot, but he said, "To me, it's like a miracle". This is where you get something back, you know? I mean, this was Senna and he said that to me! Wow!'

Senna, who thought he had broken both legs and described the pain as, 'like nothing I had ever felt before', went on to qualify sixth and ran third in the race until his transmission failed.

At Monaco in 1993 Senna was again in trouble, tearing the ligaments in his right thumb after a hefty head-on collision with the barriers at Ste Devote during practice. Again, intensive physiotherapy was the only answer. Leberer glows at the memory.

'He couldn't move that thumb. Everything was blue, with internal bleeding. You know how painful that can be. And in a car with all that vibration – it was impossible. We worked all night, with muscle herbs on the thumb, a special bandage. Thank God it was Monaco with practice on the Thursday, so that we had a day off on Friday. I said to him, "We can do it, I tell you". And he said, "Okay, I leave it to you".

'It was tricky, because he had to be able to move the thumb, so we couldn't use an injection or a cast, but we tried a lot. At the end I made him a special tape bandage, quite a complicated thing, to allow movement but also to give support to the damaged ligaments. He said, "It's fantastic! It works, it works!" And then he went out and won the race.' It was to be the Brazilian's sixth and final victory in the Principality. 'On the victory rostrum he held up his hand to me and showed it to me like this.' Leberer gave a thumbs-up gesture. 'This was fantastic. Nobody else knew what he meant. This was just for me, and I just kept it for myself.'

He makes a simple point about training racing drivers to peak physical fitness. 'The main thing for the driver is that you have to be flexible, you have to find the right way for yourself and for them. They have to believe in you completely, to trust you, and then you can be successful. It's not always easy, but it can be so rewarding. Whatever the time, you have to support the driver, give him the feeling that there is always someone there to help him. I think with Ron Dennis and Marlboro at McLaren we were the first team truly to understand this.'

It was after a back-packing break that took her through Nepal and Venezuela and thence to Adelaide, where the final Grand Prix of 1995 was being staged, that Sonia Irvine accepted brother Eddie's invitation to work with him when he went to Ferrari for 1996. A trained physiotherapist who had taken time off from her own London practice, she found that her own daily physical fitness routine was a priceless asset as she kept pace with his unusual lifestyle. She would normally drive him to and from the circuits, but would also go into the gym to workout while he was doing his own programme.

'The thing I liked most was probably the fact that I could be there, and feel that I could be a positive influence on Edmund,' she explains. 'There were a lot of things that he hadn't adapted to in the past, and if I could keep going on at him in subtle ways, I figured I could only improve things for him.'

Irvine has a notably long neck and back, both of which created problems in the early days, driving for the Jordan team at a time when cars tended to have cramped cockpits. That situation improved thanks to changes in the regulations for 1995, but Sonia was also able to help Eddie avoid other situations that might otherwise have aggravated his unusual stature.

A racing driver's physical well-being must also be complemented by the right diet, not just to nurture the system and keep it at its peak, but also to avoid embarrassing and potentially dangerous reversals once the race has begun. This was an aspect of every racer's regime that increased in importance during the 'nineties. 'Eddie knows what he should eat,' Sonia explains. 'After he's come out of the car he'll go into his pastas. I plug on at him to eat more vegetables, and he knows he should be eating rice – any form of carbohydrates – rice, bread, pasta. He doesn't really have to be weight conscious, and although he says he doesn't, he does do a lot of training, so that burns it all off.'

Leberer agrees. 'Wherever you are racing, the food has to be fresh, of course, and naturally grown, with plenty of vitamins, proteins, and carbohydrates. And then it's important how much a driver eats, and when. You certainly don't feed them heavy food before a race. You also have to work out a driver's metabolic system, and what sort of food is important for him, and how much. For example, with Nigel Mansell at McLaren in 1995, it was different. We had to cut him back a lot! At the beginning I was quite strict with him, and had to say, "Look, this is not necessary, you know".

'In one test he lost about four kilos. That was a lot. He was quite happy, and he and his wife Rosanne said they wanted to continue the diet. The problem in the beginning was that Nigel ate double what I gave him. I knew him from his days at Williams and he chose good food; he liked pasta quite a lot, but he also liked pudding. It makes quite a difference if you have three scoops of ice cream and not just one, for example. He knew what was good for him, but it was just the amount. We cut it down. He always made a joke of it, putting it on the side of his plate. And it worked. But then he got frustrated that the car didn't go, and he started eating again. When he missed the first two races of 1995 and then came back at Imola, he was the same weight as when he started the season.

'Mika and David were already quite healthy when I worked with them at McLaren in 1996, so I could give them high quality food and the amount didn't matter. They were no problem at all. I gave them muesli, fruits, cereals, tea, pasta, soups, vegetables, salads. Sometimes it was fruit tea, herbal tea, but why should they change everything? David liked his English tea so we made it weak. And they drank lots of water. It's fantastic for cleansing the system. Senna nearly always had flat mineral water. For David, sparkling Highland Spring mineral water was perfect. We checked what was in it, and it was perfect.'

To combat dehydration, especially at the hotter races, drivers also tend to use onboard drinks bottles. After one celebrated incident when racer Philippe Streiff threw up his energy drink in his helmet at a race in Rio in 1987, most drivers prefer ordinary water or a flat glucose mix. 'I just put water in,' Leberer says. 'My opinion is that the drivers should have got everything they need in their system before the race. They are strong enough, and the energy store should be full if they have had a good training programme and we have emptied them enough in the four or five days before a race. It was very easy with Mika

By 1968 Jackie Stewart was in the vanguard of safety wear, insisting on triple-layer flameproof Nomex overalls. (Phipps/Sutton)

and David because they ate my food. They are quite clever as well. Food and drink was particularly important for Mika, and I was very happy for him. It was good for his recovery programme.'

Dehydration can be debilitating for athletes working in extreme temperatures, especially the cockpit of a racing car. A driver who sweats a lot can lose as much as two litres per hour, which means he may lose up to 4kg (8.8lb) of body weight during a full-distance two-hour Grand Prix.

There was an amusing incident after the French GP at Paul Ricard in 1990, which serves to illustrate the different reaction rates of drivers to the effects of dehydration. Mansell was uneasy all season with Alain Prost as his team-mate at Ferrari, and his mood was ugly in the immediate aftermath of a botched first start which had seen Mauricio Gugelmin catapult his Leyton House over a group of other cars in the first corner, before landing on top of Mansell's car. Before the restart Mansell, in clearly agitated state, angrily denounced the Brazilian's error to anyone who would listen in the Ferrari garage. Prost then streaked home an easy winner, while the unsettled Mansell retired with engine failure in the spare car, ironically enough after running behind Gugelmin's team-mate Ivan Capelli in the other Leyton House.

Afterwards, the three of them were whisked off for F1's first-ever 'drugs test'. Capelli was able to oblige with the mandatory urine sample, but Mansell – a very physical driver who always sweated profusely during the course of a race – required many litres of liquid intake before he could follow suit. What made matters worse was that Prost, having won so insouciantly that he stepped from his car looking as if he was preparing for the start rather than the victory celebrations, was able to oblige the medical attendants immediately. Mansell was definitely not amused. Needless to say, all three tested negative.

Under Professor Sid Watkins, the FISA's Medical Commission issued guidelines for diet and fluid management as far back as 1982, when it recommended that drivers take a litre of liquid aboard before the race, two litres during it, and another two afterwards to maintain their correct levels. Interestingly, Watkins was also scathing in his scepticism over the value of 'high energy' concoctions brewed up for drivers by their personal fitness gurus.

* * *

If the manner in which drivers train themselves, and manage their diet and fluid intake, has changed dramatically since the halcyon days at Le Mans when private entrant Rob Walker so famously stopped for a glass of champagne before changing into evening dress, the means by which they choose to protect themselves have also improved significantly over the years.

Once the dust masks, greatcoats, and gauntlets of the very early 1900s had given way to linen caps and coveralls in the 'twenties, motor racing seemed to exist in some sort of time capsule. Though drivers often crashed and in particular sustained burns, little or nothing was done for decades.

One of the few exceptions was motorsport's first knight errant, Sir Henry O'Neal de Hane Segrave. Besides being the first Briton in a British car to win a Grand Prix, when he and mechanic Paul Dutoit took their Sunbeam to victory at Tours in the 1923 French GP, Segrave broke the land speed record three times and the water speed record once. He was the first man ever to travel at 321kph (200mph) on land, and 160kph (100mph) on water. A deep thinker, he shrugged off the amusement of his fellow competitors by regularly wearing a cork crash helmet at a time when soft linen 'head covers' offering no protection whatsoever were fashionable.

It was not until the 'fifties that these

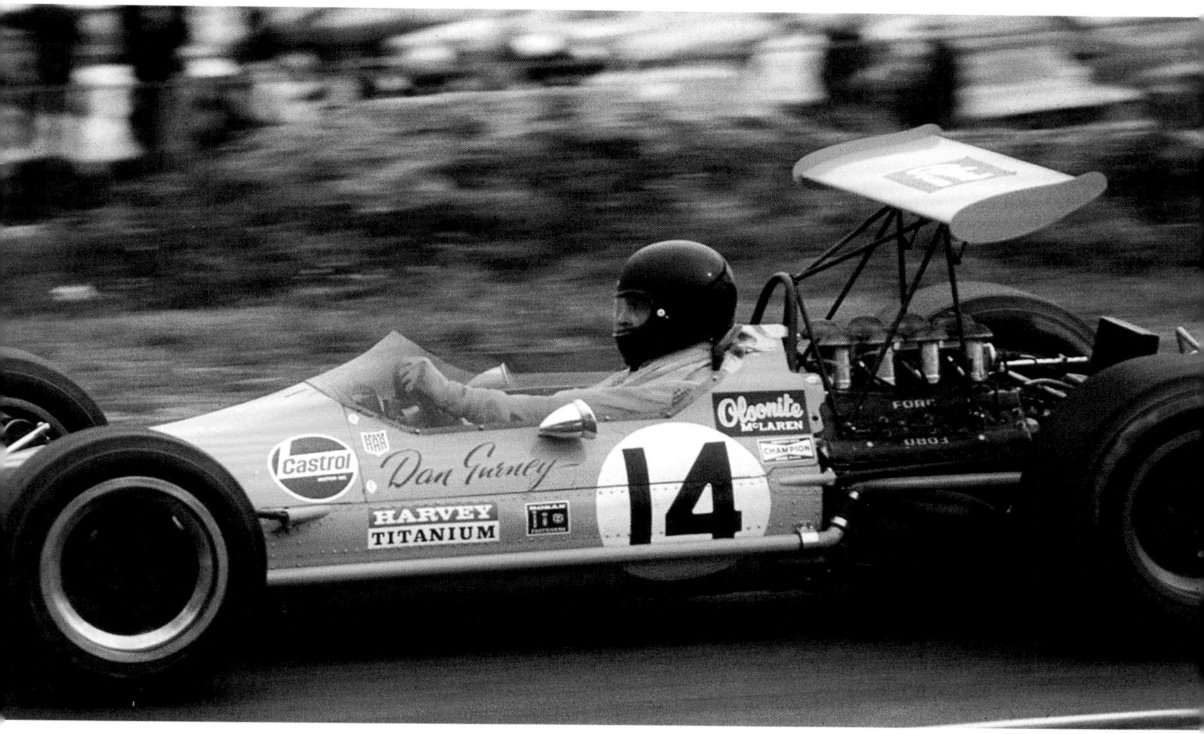

Later that season Californian Dan Gurney became the first man to race with one of Bell's dramatic new full-face Star helmets. (Phipps/Sutton)

old linen 'helmets' finally began to give way to the trusty Herbert Johnson pudding basin cork helmets, which were similar to Segrave's. These afforded a sensible measure of protection, at least to the top of a driver's head. The sides remained unprotected below the level of the ears, but it was a start. These British products endured into the 'sixties, when they were finally supplanted by the more advanced glass-fibre designs of Buco and the American newcomer, Bell. These covered the temples and the sides of the head too, right down to the nape of the neck, and by the mid-'sixties were frequently complemented by bandannas worn to cover the driver's exposed mouth. On the best helmets the straps ended in a cup that went over the driver's chin to effect the strongest possible means of attaching the helmet securely. At some circuits, notably Enna, drivers also took to taping over their goggle glasses and nose to protect themselves from the myriad stones that other cars' wheels threw up.

Californian driver Dan Gurney was the first on the international scene to experiment, in 1968, with a brand new type of helmet produced by Bell, the famous Bell Star. This resembled an opaque fishbowl which fully covered the driver's head, with only a postal slot through which he had forward vision. Jackie Stewart was also up to speed with Bell's and Buco's wares. Though they looked strange back then, they represented the future, and today the only open-faced helmets tend to be seen in touring or rally cars. In single-seaters, full-face helmets are de rigeur.

Besides the greater protection afforded the driver from the airflow around the cockpit, full-face helmets also enhanced the level of head protection in serious accidents or fire. And as manufacturing techniques have improved, and different materials have been used, they have become ever lighter yet stronger. Today, the top-of-the-range offerings from manufacturers such as Arai, Shoei, Bell, Bieffe, and Simpson incorporate composite construction for maximum strength and security. They also employ shotgun-proof Lexan visors. The need for the latter was unfortunately highlighted at the notoriously stony Clermont-Ferrand track in France during the 1972 French GP. In one of those unpleasant ironies of life, BRM driver Helmut Marko was having the best race of his burgeoning F1 career, chasing World Champion-elect Emerson Fittipaldi's Lotus for sixth place. Then one of the Brazilian's fat rear tyres spat up a stone which penetrated Marko's visor and struck him in the left eye. He suffered optical damage that left him blind in that eye, and ended his driving career.

When Ayrton Senna was killed at Imola 22 years later, much was made of how a suspension component on his Williams-Renault penetrated his Bell helmet's visor and inflicted fatal wounds. In the author's book *Echoes of Imola*, Bernie Ecclestone was adamant that this is what killed the great Brazilian.

Professor Watkins, however, expressed a different view. 'I have no evidence that anything penetrated his helmet,' he said. 'I saw the helmet only briefly at the scene – certainly it was cracked or fractured linearly, but I believe that the visor was intact. My best guess is that the right front wheel struck his helmet, and no helmet would have prevented the head injury that he suffered from the blunt impact and energy release.'

Looking back to the 'fifties, or even the 'sixties, it is staggering to minds trained to think along contemporary lines how little attention drivers used to pay to their own protection. Look at photographs of Fangio in action, even as late as 1957 when he won his last title, and there is the Argentinian with only his linen helmet, racing in shirtsleeves. Not for him the pale blue Dunlop coveralls that were just becoming popular. Fast forward to Spa in 1961, when men such as Phil Hill had followed Stirling Moss's lead with neat one-piece coveralls, and there are Belgian rivals Willy Mairesse and Olivier Gendebien quite happily driving their Ferraris in their shirtsleeves. Fortunately for him, Mairesse had some form of coveralls the following year when his Ferrari met a fiery demise after colliding with Trevor Taylor's Lotus.

The 'fifties and 'sixties were undoubtedly the most dangerous years for F1, and more often than not fire was the great bogey. Then out of Jackie Stewart's safety crusade of the late 'sixties came the first fire-resistant overalls, produced in Dupont's Nomex flameproof material.

In conjunction with similarly treated underwear, triple-layer Nomex driving suits finally provided racing drivers with the means of withstanding fire for long enough for rescuers to extract them from burning cars. Perhaps more than any other safety development of the era, they were instrumental in saving lives. Today the FIA lays down stringent rules on material specifications, and the offerings from manufacturers such as Sparco, OMP, Stand21, Momo Corse, and Advanced Wear & Safety are even more advanced. While offering the latest fire-resistant materials, they also incorporate sophisticated nuances such as 'floating' sleeves, strategically located elasticated gussets, and soft collars, which afford all the protection that has come to be taken for granted over the years, while ensuring that the driver has complete freedom of movement and comfort while racing.

Meanwhile, in France, tests continue on an advanced and as yet unnamed chain mail material that offers quite remarkable protection from fire. It is being developed primarily for aerospace applications at this stage, but the likelihood of a development appearing in F1 in the long term cannot be discounted.

At the same time as overalls developed, fireproof balaclavas, gloves, and driving boots completed a driver's armoury against fire. By the 'seventies there was not a professional racing driver who did not take his own protection with absolute seriousness. By the 'eighties, such developments, in conjunction with significant technical progress on the cars, had finally made fire the least of a driver's concerns rather than the foremost.

Now the FIA is conducting fresh research into helmet standards, and Professor Watkins is very excited about a new means of removing a driver's helmet after an accident. 'We saw a gentleman from America a few years ago with this balloon which takes the helmet off. It is a folded, collapsed plastic bladder with a long tube that hangs down the side of the helmet. We would use a simple CO^2 gun to inflate the bladder, and as that inflates it lifts the helmet gently off the driver's head.' It was originally called Dehat, but now it's known as Hats-Off and is being used in America's ChampCars series.

'It's awfully difficult to take a helmet off,' Watkins stresses. 'The driver may have a neck injury, so we have one person supporting the driver's neck, and a second person has to spread the helmet and take it off. These boys wear their helmets so tight, which is correct because the tighter they are the better, but that makes them hard to take off. One of the things that often happens in an accident is that the helmet moves on the head, and you can get into trouble from that point of view. So this device is a tremendous help.'

The research into Hats-Off is being carried out in association with Snell and Arai, and the helmet manufacturers have recently been very co-operative, after some initial caution. They, too, take safety issues very seriously.

Hats-Off may appear in F1 at the beginning of 2001. 'We don't like to waste any time,' Watkins says. 'And we have a small group to make the decisions, so it's very flexible.'

Michael Schumacher models the latest wear: flameproof overalls and boots, and fullface helmet. (Sutton)

Chapter 4

Impetus – and resistance

When I came to I was gasping for air, and it felt like I'd punctured a lung, so I rolled over on my stomach, crawled to a hedge, and pulled myself up with the branches. I thought to myself, 'Wow, if this is Formula One ...'

Bob Bondurant

Formula One in the 'fifties and 'sixties was a far cry from the organised, cohesive affair that we take for granted today. Back then individual organisers ran their own races, in their own way, and the teams and drivers had far less influence. Some organisers levied petty penalties on those who dared to criticise their way of doing things. Even the mighty RAC in Britain took the astonishing view that if drivers didn't care for trees alongside the Brands Hatch circuit, they were quite at liberty to remove them themselves.

It seems curious today that it apparently did not to occur to officialdom that the old practices were dangerous, much less that the responsibility for protecting the drivers – and spectators – should rest with governing groups, and not with the competitors.

In the sport's very early days there was nothing to separate an errant driver and his riding mechanic from a grisly collision with a solid object, unless it was the soft, yielding body of a spectator who happened to have chosen the wrong place to stand. Study the early footage of the sport's Edwardian days, and it is hard to believe that the world could have changed so quickly. In a few short years it had embraced the motor car and all it represented, and switched its philosophy from the ludicrous demand that a man with a red flag must precede any horseless carriage to the equally foolhardy, and reckless, acceptance of unchecked speed.

Since the days of Paris–Madrid style road races, in which several spectators died, motorsport had moved gently on to its own purpose-built venues, such as Brooklands, by 1907. Later still there would be other private venues which did not have to rely on the closure of public roads. Monza opened in 1922. The great Nürburgring was built during Germany's depression of the 'twenties. Gradually such tracks would all but replace the old road courses, while the increasingly popular street circuits of the 'seventies and 'eighties would take their cue from Monaco, which first hosted a Grand Prix in 1929.

After Hubert Locke-King opened his

vast concrete saucer in Weybridge in 1907, Brooklands soon established itself as a fearsomely quick, if bumpy, track. By the time it closed in 1939, its lap speed was so far ahead of Indianapolis's that in a modern-day comparison Brooklands would see averages of almost 450kph (280mph) compared to Indy's 378kph (235mph). Yet in places there was not even a fence at the top of the treacherous banking to restrain errant drivers. When Clive Dunfee lost control of his Bentley in the 1932 BRDC 500-mile race, and dropped a wheel over the edge while riding the banking too high on Member's Hill in an overtaking manoeuvre, it ploughed through fir saplings before striking a larger tree. Dunfee was thrown out and the Bentley crashed through the trees and fell to the entrance road below.

The same mentality that permitted such follies persisted well into the 'sixties. In retrospect it seems that there must have been some secret agenda to resist the imposition of common sense; but in reality that was simply the way things were in those days. Nobody knew any better, despite the frequent tragic reminders.

One of the catalysts for change came in the late 'fifties and 'sixties, when Stirling Moss emerged as the sport's first real professional racing driver. By the standards of the 'nineties, drivers' remuneration was indeed meagre in those infinitely more dangerous days, but Moss was the first to consciously market himself as a commodity. As a result, circuit owners had to pay higher start money to favourites such as Moss, and the more he became known the more he could command and the more he could call the shots.

The situation was exacerbated in the mid-'sixties by the rise of another financially astute racer of similar stature: John Young 'Jackie' Stewart, whose arrival with BRM in 1965 sent a clear signal round the world that Jimmy Clark was not the only raider to cross the border from Scotland. But it would take many years for the reality finally to dawn that it was no longer acceptable for drivers to face unnecessary risks simply because organisers and governing authorities could not be bothered to make changes. Partly this new philosophy was simply long-stifled common sense coming to the fore via different social attitudes; partly it was a backlash arising from relaxation of the rules on advertising and sponsorship which

Bleak and stony scrubland await those who stray off the hot road at Casablanca, during the Moroccan GP of 1958. (LAT)

would come in the cathartic 1968 season. After all, people pumping money into Grand Prix racing could see the downside to their logos adorning the front pages of local newspapers as a driver burned to death. Stewart took it upon himself to make such views crystal clear to one and all, and his popularity undoubtedly suffered for it.

Looking back, everything seems so simple, almost naïve, but hindsight plays unfair tricks, both on the viewer and the viewed. Today it seems incredible that drivers ever raced at more than 240kph (150mph) past trees which grew right on the very edge of a track. But these were the days when the public held dear to the image of the racing driver as a steely hero who brushed aside such risks without a backward glance; and when gate-conscious organisers did little to disabuse them of it. It was a comfortable enough opinion to hold, especially if you weren't the one who had to find out the hard way how it felt to hit something solid at two and a half miles a minute. But the drivers knew, and gradually all but the most fatalistic of them came to realise that the situation had to change.

Many tracks came and went in the years preceding Jim Clark's death. Those used in the 'fifties, such as Switzerland's hazardous Bremgarten, which had taken the life of the legendary Achille Varzi and ended the career of the equally lustrous Rudolph Caracciola, were no different to what they had been in preceding decades. Others, such as the 25.8km (16-mile) Pescara in Italy and 6.3km (3.9-mile) Pedralbes in Spain, were a throwback to the age of dusty heroes.

Monte Carlo, Nürburgring, Zandvoort, Monza, and Spa were all great tracks in their own individual ways. Each imposed different challenges, and would prove resilient and resistant to the changes that would sweep away the other venues of the time. While the Monaco, German, Dutch, Italian, and Belgian races thus stayed put, the French and British GPs were itinerant.

Reims in France's champagne region hosted the former seven times in the 'fifties and three times in the 'sixties, before enjoying its last hurrah in 1966 when Jack Brabham became the first man ever to win a GP in a car bearing his own name. Reims was flat and very quick, essentially comprising a triangle of fast local roads bordering champagne fields. And it was here, during the 1958 race, that Italy's young lion, Luigi Musso, crossed the line once too often and paid dearly for it.

Rouen, which held the race five times between 1952 and 1968, was also very

Jack Brabham dukes it out with Dan Gurney at Spa in 1961, where the first signs of Armco barrier are in evidence as they breast Raidillon. (LAT)

quick, but of very different make-up. Its terrifying flat-out downhill curves past the pits were the stuff of legend, where the abnormally brave David Purley would admit in later years to adapting his old paratrooper training and screaming in his helmet to summon the adrenalin to help him keep his right foot nailed to the floor. In the 1968 French GP Rouen claimed the life of veteran racer Jo Schlesser, who was taking part in only his second Grand Prix at the wheel of an experimental Honda that team leader John Surtees had declared unfit to race (see Chapter 15).

Clermont-Ferrand, an interloper in 1965, 1969, 1970, and 1972, was another much-loved venue, a sweeping ribbon of roller coaster road that was France's switchback answer to the Nürburgring.

When it held the French GP in 1967, the permanent Bugatti Circuit that was located within the main perimeter of the famous Le Mans road network was generally regarded as a sick joke. It was feeble, dull, and completely devoid of challenge in comparison with Reims, Rouen, or Clermont-Ferrand. But little did anyone who raced there realise that it was the forerunner of the sterile modern circuit.

Britain had its trusty airfield at Silverstone, where the World Championship had been born in 1950, but initially alternated it with the interesting Aintree venue alongside the famous Liverpudlian horse racing course. After 1961 and 1962, however, Aintree was dropped, and from 1964 Brands Hatch staged the race biennially. Where Silverstone was fast and wide, with challenging, sweeping corners, Brands was equally popular on account of its undulations, several demanding corners, and its natural amphitheatre layout.

In 1960 America finally found itself a proper round of the World Championship, in the final year in which its legendary Indianapolis 500 needed to be included as a qualifying round as a sop to the desire to make the championship seem truly international. At the end of the season the charismatic Riverside track in California's fragrant Orange County hosted the first US GP. A year later picturesque Watkins Glen, near New York State's Finger Lakes, took over the honour.

In 1960 F1 also went back to Portugal, but the race round the hazard-laden streets of Oporto was a one-off not emulated for another 24 seasons. Mexico also got in on the act with its autodrome in Mexico City, which matched a couple of long straights to a hairpin, some tricky esses, and a wonderful banked 180° right-hander called Peraltada at the end of the lap. The Canadian venues which appeared in the late 'sixties – Mosport Park and Mont Tremblant St Jovite – were equally well accepted as drivers' tracks. So too was Kyalami, which quickly replaced East London as the home of the South African GP.

The Spanish GP was also revived. In 1968 the new Jarama track near Madrid finally staged a Grand Prix, after running a non-championship event the previous year. But it only did so after some cliffhanging moments arising out of the safety considerations dealt with at length in the following chapter.

Prior to that, safety considerations tended to receive as little attention on the circuits as they did on the cars. Car designers everywhere did as much as they considered right, but in all truthfulness safety was rarely the uppermost factor in their minds. These were times when priorities were very different. Nobody saw any peril in photographers standing right on the edge of the track, even at a driver's clipping point; nor in them crossing the track during the course of a race, even though Dale von Trebra was once famously missed by millimetres by Jim Hall's speeding CanAm Chaparral when the jumbo-sized American stumbled and fell. Photographers, journalists, hangers-on, and mechanics all habitually stood on the track either side of the grid as the races began.

With the four by three by four grids which were used at some venues the first few moments of a race were even more hectic than they seem with today's two by two staggered grids. Raymond 'Toto' Roche, who was the official starter of the French GP when it was staged at Reims, and sometimes at the other national venues, did his best to make matters worse. In his mind, Roche seemed to feel that he was a matador among a field of rampant bulls, and had to prove his masculinity by showing complete disdain for them. He would deliberately make the most of his moment in the limelight. His plentiful bulk augmented by his renowned predilection for whipped cream, he sneered away death while carrying out his duties and would turn his back on the field before unpredictably bringing down the *Tricolore* to start the race. More than one driver held the secret ambition to despatch the rotund Frenchman, but somehow he always got away with his antics.

Nor was it just the starts that could be fraught with danger. Only good fortune avoided a tragic end to the 1962 French GP at Rouen, when the local gendarmes mistakenly believed that the race finished when winner Dan Gurney crossed the line in his Porsche. Linking arms in a typically arrogant show of force, they unwisely united across the pit lane entrance after the silver car had flashed by, forgetting that other drivers had yet to complete their own race. John Surtees, for instance, was heading for fifth place in his Lola-Climax but was in trouble. Since he had sufficient margin over Carol de Beaufort's Porsche he decided to head for the pit road with the

Racing was hard in the 'sixties, as Trevor Taylor and Willy Mairesse demonstrated with their celebrated collision at Spa in 1962. The Yorkshireman's Lotus 24 was totalled, while the Belgian's Ferrari was burned out. Both had miraculous escapes. (Phipps/Sutton)

intention of crossing the line there rather than having to embark on a slowing down lap that the Lola was unlikely to complete. Surtees knew nothing of the blockage ahead until he suddenly encountered the linked and unyielding arms of the law and was forced to take immediate avoiding action which placed him squarely in the path of fast-finishing Frenchman Maurice Trintignant. He, in turn, was forced to swerve left. At what he later estimated to be 193kph (120mph), delayed Lotus number two Trevor Taylor struck the back of Trintignant's Rob Walker Lotus.

Both cars were seriously damaged, and potential carnage was avoided only by good fortune. 'That were one of the daftest things anyone did to me in my years in F1,' blunt-spoken Yorkshireman Taylor recalled in later years. 'I've no idea what the silly buggers thought they were up to, but they were bloody lucky there wasn't a massive accident.'

Even after the Le Mans disaster of 1955, pit lanes remained open to cars passing at their maximum speed. The idea of a protective wall lay well into the future, and was indeed resisted strongly even by such normally erudite circuit designers as Zandvoort's John Hugenholz. 'Zandvoort was a generally good design let down by its execution, and you couldn't believe the huge resistance we got from circuit owners,' Stewart recalls. 'It was just incomprehensible. At places such as Spa, Reims, and Rouen it was just bloody dangerous to have cars going by the pits at 257kph [160mph] while mechanics were working there. It was even worse in practice, when you had journalists and hangers-on walking up and down too. Just imagine what could have happened if a driver had lost control ...'

At the beginning of the decade straw bales were still the popular means of keeping cars from departing from the grey stuff. At Monaco bales were all that protected the drivers from the lamp posts and horribly solid mooring posts along the harbour, which themselves were the only things likely to prevent errant cars from launching into the water. During the 1955 race former champion Alberto Ascari became the first man to risk drowning in a Grand Prix when he crashed his Lancia into the Mediterranean. Ten years later the colourful Australian Paul 'Hawkeye' Hawkins likewise managed to avoid all of the iron mooring posts to throw his DW Racing Enterprises Lotus 33 into the drink. Typically, the wry Hawkeye

The cockpit of Giancarlo Baghetti's ATS, tried here by team-mate Phil Hill at Spa in 1963, afforded him about as much protection as spectators at La Source enjoyed. (LAT)

reckoned the resultant soaking was preferable to hitting anything solid.

It was straw bales that triggered Lorenzo Bandini's tragic demise at Monaco two years later. Ferrari's team leader was challenging eventual victor Denny Hulme, but crashed in the closing stages. As rescue efforts proved inept (see Chapter 15), he suffered burns which would prove fatal.

Elsewhere, the means for restraining errant cars would have been laughable had they not been so dangerous, and the risks they posed so severe. At the Nürburgring feeble wooden trestles attempted to perform the same function, and were no better than the other sections of the track where, early in the decade, there was nothing apart from grass banks and, beyond them, the unforgiving trees. Silverstone, today in the vanguard of the world's safest tracks, relied on the sort of low concrete wall that typified photographs shot from the inside of Copse, while a makeshift scaffold tubing fence was at one time the only thing to stop cars which left the road on the exit.

Perhaps the one aspect that was better then than in the environmentally conscientious 'nineties was that the trees were deemed expendable once circuit owners had been persuaded that having them so close to the edge of the track was not a good idea. 'Leaving them unprotected made absolutely no sense,' Stewart argued. 'There was just no point in adding needlessly to the danger.' Either they had to be cut down, or protected by a layer of barrier. The distinctively corrugated steel Armco barrier would eventually prove the most popular (see Chapter 6).

At Monza in 1964 American Bob Bondurant had an accident while testing which encapsulated the risks that drivers faced back then. An opportunity to try the hitherto hopeless ATS F1 car came while Bondurant was at Monza testing the Ford GT40 for John Wyer's team. At that time Bondurant was still climbing the racing ladder and he jumped at the chance when it was offered by legendary mechanic Alf Francis, who had revamped the ATS into something rather more respectable.

'The car felt pretty reasonable in the few laps I did that day,' Bondurant recalls. 'I think they'd redesigned the rear suspension, among other things, and I went out and just got used to driving it. That night we got talking about the Curva Grande and how guys like Clark were taking it flat out. We went back the next morning and I'm thinking, "Well, maybe it *is* flat". I figured the ATS didn't have that strong a motor, so I wouldn't be going *that* fast, and after a few laps I got through it flat out. And on the way to the Lesmos I'd picked up 500rpm. Quite a difference. By the end of an hour, I'd done it several times, and then I got the IN signal. I thought, "Well, who knows when I'll be back here? I'm going to do it one more time."

'As I went through Curva Grande a halfshaft broke. I was doing 241kph (150mph), and the axle broke at the left rear. I went through the hedge backwards, and remember thinking, "Bondurant, you just wrote yourself off ..." I went down a ravine, and got thrown out of the car. I was wearing one of those bubble shield visors we had at the time and it got shredded, but it saved my face. I landed on my back, of all things on a pile of leaves! Just lucked out, I guess. When I came to I was gasping for air, and it felt like I'd punctured a lung, so I rolled over on my stomach, crawled to a hedge, and pulled myself up with the branches. I thought to myself, "Wow, if this is Formula One ...".'

Bondurant was lucky on many counts, but if there had been a barrier in the Curva Grande, he might have had a much easier walk away from a damaged car.

By 1967 Stewart's safety campaign was well under way, triggered by the accident he suffered in the Belgian GP the previous year (see Chapter 5). There was barrier at the top of Spa's famous Eau Rouge corner by that year's Belgian GP, though it was not enough and there were still many unprotected areas lined by buildings close to the edge of the track as it swooped and twisted through the Ardennes. Burnenville in particular, which was flat-out in top gear, was rippled and bumpy yet provided no means of containing cars which escaped their drivers' control. It was the same along the Masta Straight with its infamous kink.

The pit wall at Mosport was also separated from the track by a strip of barrier, and there was plenty now at Monza, albeit still only single tier apart from the exit to the Parabolica. Barrier was now also positioned at the bottom of that bank, in an attempt to discourage any repeat launchings. 'Ironically though,' Stewart noted at the time, 'it was only on the left-hand side. There was none on the right!'

There was more and more barrier in Mexico the following year, including the hairpin and the esses, and by then it had become familiar though certainly not widespread elsewhere. Brands Hatch was still largely an Armco-free zone that year, and Stewart's impassioned pleas for greater safety on his home track fell on shamelessly deaf ears.

It was a time when tradition ruled and the resistance to change was massive. The fundamental attitudes were wrong, for there was a general complacency based on habit. This was the way things had always been done, so why change? And there was another unspoken but underlying attitude that smacked of chilling pragmatism: there would always be a another crop of drivers coming through, so why invest so much just to appease the current bunch?

This was a difficult period, when entrenched views gave rise to acrimony in the face of Stewart's persistence, and had the Scot been of weaker character his crusade would simply have faded away. But there were lights on the horizon. 'Alex Blignault out in South Africa was a very switched-on man who took a progressive view,' Stewart recalls warmly. 'He continually made numerous modifications when he was persuaded that they were sensible, and we were always careful not to make unnecessary demands. The Mexicans, too, always had an enlightened attitude. We didn't like the half tyres that they liked to use in the esses, but they listened to our requests to have their barriers angled so that a driver couldn't hit them head-on, and they were always enthusiastic and open-minded.'

During the mid-'sixties an important development occurred when the *Commission Sportif Internationale* (the CSI, which was the forerunner of the FIA) took over responsibility from the national authorities for circuit safety inspections. This was a major step forward, since it led at last towards homogeneity of safety standards. As a result, the Grand Prix Drivers' Association (GPDA) was able to work in co-operation with the CSI to hammer out a universal specification for Armco barriers. It was a slow process, but it was significant progress.

Bob Bondurant was another lucky man, after his shunt while testing for ATS at Monza in 1964. (LAT)

Sadly, it was not enough to save Jim Clark. The Hockenheim Formula Two race in April 1968 was typical of the slip-streaming epics that this undiluted track produced in those days, and was held in dreary weather. Clark was unusually far down the field, well out of contention, as his Gold Leaf Lotus was running poorly. Other drivers reported hearing it misfiring as he struggled along in eighth place in the first of two scheduled heats.

Despite the Lotus 48's shortcomings, Clark accelerated hard on to the straight that took cars far out into the pine forest. These were the days when there were no chicanes to interrupt the full throttle blast out to the Ost Kurve. Nor was there anything to prevent a car going into the trees. Eye witnesses reported the Scot struggling as his car twitched first right, then left, close to its likely maximum speed of 257kph (160mph). Then it plunged off to the left, smashing into trees which struck it broadside at cockpit level before breaking in half just behind the cockpit bulk-

head. Clark, for all his greatness, had no chance whatsoever. Despite reports to the contrary many years later, it seems certain that he died immediately of unsurvivable head injuries.

Investigation later suggested strongly that he had been the victim of a slow puncture in a rear tyre, which then led the tyre to decompress suddenly. When this caused it to lose the internal pressure upon which it relied to keep its beads firmly secured to the wheel rim, the tyre popped into the wheel well, destabilising the Lotus to the point where not even a Clark could bring it back under control. When you look forward to the 1999 German GP, where Mika Hakkinen's McLaren suffered a similarly explosive rear tyre failure approaching the stadium at around 305kph (190mph), you appreciate the progress that has been made in the name of safety. Hakkinen spun violently, but walked away. For Clark there was no escape. Had the road at that point been lined with Armco barrier, he would likely have got away with bruising after a hefty impact. Perhaps he might even just have glanced the rail. Instead, the sport's great champion was brought down by a nine-inch (23cm) diameter tree – little more than a sapling, really.

Motor racing, and the world, were stunned. Jim Clark had always been thought of as invincible, such was the magnitude of his talent. Other drivers perished, but not men of Clark's unique calibre. It was simply unthinkable. Clark, dead.

There were to be none of the knee-jerk reactions that would come in the aftermath of Ayrton Senna's death 26 years later, for these were different times. But Jimmy Clark's death soaked with gasoline the fuse which had already been burning within Jackie Stewart.

Nobody could have known, but it was only the beginning of a horrible catalogue of tragedy that would force motor racing to take a long, critical look at itself.

Chapter 5

The road to Stavelot

The first thing I asked Ken when I pulled into the pits after taking the flag was, 'Who died?'

Jackie Stewart

'Helen and I once counted the friends we had lost in racing,' Jackie Stewart admits. 'We stopped when we got beyond 50. It was just a terrible time, with so many people losing their lives. It just didn't make sense to me.'

His sons Paul and Mark were still small at that time, Paul a rising eight, Mark five. Once, Paul had come back from school in Switzerland and shaken his mother rigid when, with all the innocence of youth, he had asked Helen Stewart when his Daddy was going to die. Jochen Rindt and Jo Bonnier had died, and Natasha Rindt and Joakim and Jonas Bonnier all went to the same school. Somebody had told Paul that if you were a racing driver, you got killed.

'When I think back,' Jackie says, 'it's remarkable how well Helen coped. I think she did a great job and handled it in a really mature way. She managed to isolate herself. I think back to the number of hotel rooms she had to go into, to pack the things for a wife whose husband had been killed. Drivers today just don't understand that side of the sport.'

Stewart invested a lot more in motor racing than he ever received in return. Without his unflinching safety crusade in the 'sixties, the sport would never have progressed beyond the senseless risk-taking days before Armco barriers protected drivers from trees. There is no question that many drivers survived who otherwise would not have on circuits where Stewart's plea for tree-paring or barrier-erection had dramatically increased the margin for error. 'I'm proud to have been part of that progress,' he says today. But he was there in the darkest times. He saw it from the depths, and peered many times into the blackest pit that can sometimes be motor racing. Throughout, he coped with the style and courage of a champion.

Death was then a constant companion of the men who pushed the outer limits of the speed envelope. It was, with cruel irony, a fact of life. Racing drivers went fast, and sometimes Death reached out for them. It went with the badge. There was not a single driver who went to the starting line believing that it could happen to him. Like the test pilots of yore, each always held the utter conviction that it was something that would happen to the other guy. 'If you had thought in any other way,' New Zealand star Chris Amon recalled, 'then you would never have raced in the first place.' But happen it did, to far too many young men.

Stewart freely confesses that he thought precisely the same way, and that in his early years in racing he gave nothing more than a passing thought to safety. This was the time when race organisers and the CSI turned a conveniently blind eye and refused to do anything to lengthen the odds of surviving a serious accident. If each appeared to take a cavalier attitude to safety, it has to be said that nobody else was doing anything different.

Then came the 1966 Belgian Grand Prix, in which the up-and-coming Stewart was involved in an accident which could have led to a grisly death, trapped in a burning racing car.

Sudden rainstorms are typical in the Hautes Fagnes region. That day in 1966, one fell on the far side of the circuit, at Burnenville, only moments after the 16-car field had left a dry starting grid. Jo Bonnier, Mike Spence, Jo Siffert, and Guy Ligier all went aquaplaning off the track there, Bonnier's car ending up dangling over a sizeable drop. Then, after Jochen Rindt had got away with a series of wild rotations there, Stewart spun on the super-fast Masta Straight when he encountered a river of water running across the road just at the point where it kinked between two houses. His BRM went off the road at high speed and demolished an outbuilding before sliding into a ditch. There he remained, trapped by the damage inflicted on the

In 1967 Stewart drove the hefty BRM H16, seen here at Zandvoort. Before the season was out, it became the first F1 car to be fitted with a full safety harness. (David Tremayne Archive)

1968 British GP winner Jo Siffert flashes past the sort of trees that Stewart was told he could cut down himself if he didn't like the geography of Brands Hatch. (Phipps/Sutton)

cigar-tube monocoque chassis, and the steering wheel, which was bolted to the steering column. His overalls were soaked in fuel which had leaked out of the ruptured tanks, and he had an uncomfortably long time to consider his plight as team-mates Hill and Bondurant, who had also spun, sought the necessary tools to release him. Eventually they managed to borrow spanners from a spectator.

This accident on the road to Stavelot had a profound effect on the young Scot, who had turned 27 the previous day. 'It was a terrifying situation. There I was, trapped and conscious in the car, and all the time able to smell all the fuel around me. One spark was all it needed.'

There was a note of dark humour when Hill and Bondurant got Stewart out of the car and transferred him to the cellar of a nearby farmhouse while they awaited the ambulance. 'They began stripping off my overalls, because the fuel was really starting to irritate my skin, and suddenly a pair of nuns appeared at the door. They were horrified by the sight of this semi-naked man lying on the floor. It was a while before they could be persuaded to do anything …'

But there was nothing remotely funny about the closeness of Stewart's brush with death. 'It completely focused my mind,' he revealed later. 'Sitting in that fuel bath, waiting for the thing to catch fire, gave me a very long time in which to consider things. Afterwards I became very angry when I thought of how close I had come to being just another statistic of motor racing.'

The first manifestation of his new role as the sport's leading safety campaigner was banal. When he returned to the cockpit at Brands Hatch for the British GP a month later, he insisted on having a spanner taped to the steering wheel. The days of quickly detachable wheels still lay some way in the future. Little by little, however, Stewart began to take far greater care of himself as he took over the mantle hitherto entrusted to the taciturn Bonnier. By 1967 his BRM H16 was the first F1 car to be fitted with seat belts. He was in the vanguard of the development of superior racewear, too, selecting the best fireproof overalls. He and Dan Gurney were the first F1 drivers to wear the innovative full-face helmets when they appeared at the end of 1968. But drivers' and cars' equipment were only the start of Stewart's newfound safety crusade.

There were two circuits which he came to loathe from the safety point of view: Spa Francorchamps, and the Nürburgring. Both offered fantastic challenges to racing drivers, yet each was a minefield of traps awaiting the careless or the unlucky. Despite his 1966 misfortune Stewart's driving performance never suffered at either venue. The opposite happened. Ever the complete professional, he always shone at both.

In the 1967 Belgian GP he drove what was without doubt one of his finest races in the recalcitrant BRM H16. It was seriously overweight, but at Spa the multicylinder powerplant could really open up. Stewart got the big green car flying. He was leading the race until Dan Gurney overcame an initial delay and put the Eagle Weslake into an impregnable lead. But an honourable second place that day was as good as a victory, particularly since the Scot had pushed the monster along with one hand, holding it in gear at more than 257kph (160mph) with the other.

A year later at Nürburgring he was peerless as he scored the greatest win of his career. This was the race that was run

Though he was all too aware of the dangers of the track, Stewart never gave a poor performance at the old Nürburgring. Here in 1968 he won the German GP by four minutes, despite appalling conditions. (Phipps/Sutton)

in terrible rain and fog. Once Ken Tyrrell persuaded his man to start, Stewart streaked home a brilliant four minutes ahead of Graham Hill. It was the largest margin of victory since Stirling Moss had beaten Mike Hawthorn by 5m 12.8s at Oporto ten years earlier. To win at the 'Ring was truly the mark of greatness, but he had no misgivings about admitting how much he detested the place. 'I never did a lap of the Nürburgring that I didn't have to do,' he says. 'I defy anyone to say they really liked it, if they went properly quick there. You'd do your warming up on the South loop, then when you went out on to the big lap you'd nail it. But I never did a lap more than I had to.'

The victory was cathartic for F1, for 1968 was a terrible season. Jim Clark had died at Hockenheim on 7 April. On 8 May Clark's former Lotus team-mate Mike Spence succumbed at Indianapolis. On 8 June Lodovico Scarfiotti was killed at the Rossfeld hill climb, and on 7 July came Jo Schlesser's fatal accident in the French GP at Rouen. The racing world was stunned. The macabre coincidence of dates left drivers nervous and full of foreboding as they gathered at the Nürburgring, the greatest circuit of them all. To make matters worse, the Eifel mountains were shrouded in mist and fog, and it was four weeks to the day since the last tragedy. Whose turn would it be this time? Many drivers went to the grid convinced that one of their number was not going to make it. 'The first thing I asked Ken when I pulled into the pits after taking the flag,' Stewart admits, 'was, "Who died?" It was such a blessed relief when he said, "Nobody!"'

There were some die-hards who called Stewart a 'milk and water' driver because of his safety crusade, and certainly the man himself was never bird-mouthed when something needed saying. And there were plenty of things which fell into that category in that dangerous era. But even his detractors had to admit that whatever his personal views about a circuit, he never once drew back from giving his utmost commitment once he climbed into the cockpit.

He raced in what was arguably the most dangerous period of Grand Prix motorsport. During a career that stretched over 99 GPs between 1965 and 1973, 17 Grand Prix drivers were killed in either F1 races or test sessions, an average of two per year. At Spa in 1968

Fullface helmet, Nomex overalls and safety harness: Stewart prepares for his final season in 1973 in a Tyrrell that had also benefited from his tireless safety campaigning. (Phipps/Sutton)

only a stop for fuel lost him the race. Next time the F1 cars went there, in 1970, the milk and water man was in pole position. There was a name for what he did: professionalism. The more successful and famous he became and the more people there were who would listen to his voice, the more he was prepared to use it until common sense prevailed. If it meant the demise of the old Spa, so be it. And if others chose to criticise him for it, so be that, too. Stewart was prepared to put his reputation where his mouth was, on and off the track. It was a tough campaign, but he stuck to his guns. One man could not bring about a complete revolution, but without the safety crusade fought by John Young Stewart in the 'sixties there are survivors of hair-raising accidents around today who would otherwise most certainly not have made old bones.

The situation at Brands Hatch in 1968 typified the sort of intransigent officialdom that Stewart had to overcome. It was hard to believe that the great Clark had been dead but three months. The British GP didn't take place in some far-flung part of the globe where organisers new to the sport might have just about been forgiven for lacking such knowledge, or for under-estimating or misunderstanding the dangers of motor racing. It happened in England – at Brands Hatch, one of the self-styled hearts of British motorsport, where Clark had scored so many brilliant triumphs. The attitude of the organisers of the British GP, the RAC, was shameful, as they behaved with abominable insensitivity.

'We had been in correspondence with the organisers early in the year,' Stewart recalled, 'but their response could only be described as childish. We thought that a wooded area was potentially dangerous, and asked for a fence to be erected. It wasn't just something we were thinking of for ourselves, but for any driver in any race on what was a very busy circuit. Everyone racing at Brands Hatch would benefit.

'The RAC told us they didn't think that this was necessary, because they were only "small" trees. Any larger ones could be protected by straw bales. Well, we'd seen what straw bales did for poor Bandini at Monaco ... When we pressed the RAC harder we were told that if we wanted a fence, then we could have one if we paid for it! And they didn't even own the circuit, so it wasn't as if they had to pay for it themselves!' At other times he was advised that if he wanted to have trees removed, the drivers could do it themselves!

Looking back from the 'nineties, with the perspective of Ayrton Senna's death at Imola in 1994, it scarcely seemed credible that Clark's death should have excited so little in the way of change. Stunned though the motor racing world undoubtedly was, Stewart's often tended to be a lone voice crying out for things to be made better. By contrast, in the immediate aftermath of Senna's death, everything seemed to change. Perhaps that itself is a definition of progress.

At the end of 1973, the year in which he won his third and last title, Stewart's Tyrrell team-mate François Cevert was killed during practice at Watkins Glen for what was to have been the Scot's 100th GP. As it was, the Frenchman's violent and horrible death brought two careers to an end, for the Tyrrell team withdrew as a mark of respect and Stewart did not take part in the subsequent race, and he had already long since decided to retire from racing. Typically, he had made it as easy as possible on Helen.

'I had made the decision in April that year. Helen never knew. I only told Ken, and Walter Hayes and John Waddell at Ford – we had lunch in London – but I didn't want anyone else to know. I didn't want Helen thinking of ten green bottles ... I didn't tell her until the afternoon that François died. Even François didn't know.'

Chapter 6

The Armco revolution

The peak of my helmet was sticking up and I could not move my head. It was wedged between the Armco ...

Jackie Stewart

It says much for the thinking of the time that, in the immediate aftermath of Jim Clark's death, the focus of safety lobbying centred more on changing the circuits than it did on changing the cars.

Contrary to the belief of his critics, Armco barrier was in use long before Jackie Stewart's crusade reached maximum revs. Barrier that had sprouted initially as protection for the pit area at Monza in 1962 also spread soon to the pit straight and other areas, and the Italian track was one of the pioneers of improved safety. Its attitude had its roots in the tragedy which killed Wolfgang von Trips and 14 spectators in the 1961 Italian GP, when the German Count had been vying for the World Championship with his Ferrari team-mate Phil Hill.

The accident occurred in the braking area for the Parabolica, the fast turn that takes cars through 180° at the end of the super-fast back straight, and on back past the pits. At the typically hit-and-

Single-tier Armco stands ready to restrain the errant as Jack Brabham climbs Massenet at Monte Carlo in 1964. (Phipps/Sutton)

miss start of the race, Jim Clark had thrust his underpowered Lotus up among the more powerful Ferraris, and was slipstreaming them like mad. Trips, meanwhile, had made a poor start and was cutting back through the field. Having passed Clark on top speed, he then assumed that he had dealt with the tenacious Scot and failed to see him pulling alongside again under braking at the end of the straight. When Trips, who was in a tight bunch of cars, pulled over to his left he found Clark already there, and the Ferrari and the Lotus collided. 'Trips's car was launched up the sloped bank there and just hydraulicked a load of spectators,' recalled Hill, who won the title as a result of this tragedy.

By 1964 Armco barrier was employed at Monaco, where a single tier of the grey steel lined the pit straight. There was more at Ste Devote and down the hill to Mirabeau, though they were relatively short lengths.

The greatest benefit of Armco barrier lay in the manner in which, if installed correctly, it would deform progressively. Where a tree would be totally unyielding and would exert its point of impact over a dangerously narrow area, with Armco there was more chance of spreading the load across a wider area. This, allied to its deformability, further helped to dissipate the car's energy. But installing it was a costly and laborious business, and many circuit owners refused to do so on principle. The underlying attitude was that they weren't going to all that expense simply because a Scottish racing driver said they had to. To an extent, it was possible to sympathise with their view.

'Everyone thinks that we were hell-bent on having wall-to-wall Armco barrier,' Stewart says, 'but that wasn't the case. What we were asking was for them to install it in strategic places where it would do most good.

Monza 1963. Dan Gurney, Jimmy Clark and Graham Hill flash past the Parabolica where, in 1961, Wolfgang von Trips perished. Single-tier Armco and safety fencing help to protect the spectators, after 14 had died when the German count's Ferrari tangled with Clark's Lotus. (LAT)

'The problem was that there were no standards, and there was usually nothing between the racetrack and spectators, or the earth banks that were historically used at places such as Goodwood or Silverstone or Clermont Ferrand. They were launching pads, because they were never straight-edged. So what happened then was that they put railway sleepers in. Silverstone was one of the first to do that. The Woodcote sleepers were really there to hold up the wall, because otherwise weather eroded it, which chamfered the bank down so that it became a launching pad.'

One of the jokes of the era was: How do you get to Jackie Stewart's house? Answer: You just follow the Armco barrier. Looking back, Stewart chuckles. 'Yes, that's because then we were really putting Armco in everywhere. In my shunt at Spa there was barbed wire fencing between the track and the cows – and it was there to keep the cows off the track!

'So the Armco thing happened because there wasn't much alternative. We went to Barcelona and ringed the whole place. Monaco, we ringed the whole place. There was no other option. And to begin with, where there was Armco in some places before we really got going, it was on the outside of a straight, but not near the pits. Single height. And we all know that that doesn't work. Then in addition to that I remember going through layers of Armco at Jarama. I had a tyre deflate in the Formula Two Matra and I went through between two layers. The peak of my helmet was sticking up and I could not move my head. It was wedged between the Armco ...'

Where Stewart had been a passionate campaigner for Armco long before Jim Clark's passing, now he redoubled his efforts. It was deeply ironic that the very day of his fellow Scot's death, the very moment that Jackie learned of it, he was making a safety inspection of Jarama, being unable to race at that time himself because of an injury to his scaphoid sus-

Just visible as Pedro Rodriguez boils into the lead of the 1968 Spanish GP at Jarama is the Armco which caused so much heartache for the Spanish organisers. (Phipps/Sutton)

tained in his earlier accident there.

Nothing better epitomised the irritation that could breed between drivers and circuit owners than the situation that arose during this inspection. In keeping with a regulation of the time, the organisers had staged a make-weight non-championship race the previous year, which Jim Clark had won for Lotus. Then had come the F2 race in which Stewart had been injured. Now, on 7 April, he made an alarming discovery as he inspected the Armco barrier which had been installed along the pit straight. To his dismay he realised that the not insignificant work that had been carried out by the willing organisers was almost completely useless because the mounting posts had simply been driven into sand, and had no extra means of support. The CSI informed the Spaniards that their race could not go ahead unless the problem was rectified. The problem was typical of the era in which even the willing were having to learn as they went along.

The Spaniards were understandably disgruntled, because they felt they had done everything that had been required of them, by drivers and CSI alike, and now they were being told that what they had done at great cost was not good enough. It was a situation that called for every ounce of Stewart's tact to explain to them precisely why their efforts had fallen short of what was needed; but there was no way that the problem could have been ignored. As future events were to show, badly installed Armco could be as much a terror as no Armco at all, with the possibility that a car could be launched into the air as the rail bent back under impact.

'That situation at Jarama was hugely difficult for our cause,' Stewart admits. 'The job had been done, they were try-

Later in that race the Mexican had cause to be thankful for the catchfencing, which arrested his BRM after he slid off the road on oil. (Phipps/Sutton)

ing to do right thing. But here was Jackie Stewart saying it needed doing properly. That was a problem, and that's why I didn't win any popularity polls.' But he was right to insist.

The GPDA eventually helped to hammer out a standard specification for barriers, but history is nevertheless littered with incidents in which poorly installed Armco proved appallingly dangerous. Besides Stewart, it was only by the grace of God that fellow GP drivers Clay Regazzoni and John Love lived to tell their tales of intimate acquaintance with it. When the Swiss driver hit the barriers in his F3 Tecno at the Monaco chicane exit in 1968, the two tier barrier split in such an extraordinary way that the Tecno ran under the upper rail, right up to the rollover hoop. 'I threw myself down into the cockpit and just managed to duck under in time,' Regga told photographer Bernard Cahier. Love, like Stewart, found his Surtees spearing between the tiers at Kyalami and coming to rest with the car buried in the steel and his helmet crammed up against it. He was able to walk away.

At Monza in 1968 the barrier supports had not been properly treated and had sheared on impact when Chris Amon's Ferrari slid off on its own hydraulic fluid. As the barrier bent back, the car was launched into the trees. Thanks partly to his seat belt, Amon survived.

Two years later Giovanni Salvati, an ebullient Italian/Brazilian Formula Two racer, was beheaded after crashing into barrier in a race at Taruma in Brazil.

In 1973 the dashing Frenchman François Cevert had died in the fast kink at Watkins Glen when he lost control of his Tyrrell and was virtually cut in half as the car landed upside down on the barrier on the opposite side of the road and its structure was torn into jagged edges.

Early in 1974 popular American Peter Revson died during a test session at Kyalami when the front suspension of his Shadow DN3 broke and threw him into a barrier. The bottom rail was torn from its post, while the upper inflicted fatal head and chest injuries as the black car was pitched over.

Unfortunately, the catchfencing visible in this shot taken at Zandvoort two years later did not help Piers Courage, who lost his life after crashing his de Tomaso. (Phipps/Sutton)

Months later, at Jarama, the Italian racer Arturo Merzario was fortunate to escape – as indeed were a number of photographers and spectators – when the front wings of his Williams-entered Iso Marlboro collapsed. With no frontal downforce, Art speared across the track and into the barriers, before his car climbed atop the steel and slid precariously along it until finally coming to rest.

Helmuth Koinigg died at the Glen at the end of that year when a left rear tyre lost air at the end of the main straight and his Surtees slewed off at 45° through

When Brian Redman's Cooper-BRM broke its front suspension at Spa's Les Combes during the 1968 Belgian GP, he crashed off the road into a parked Vauxhall Cresta. Despite a serious arm injury, he was hauled unceremoniously from the wreckage by untrained helpers. (Phipps/Sutton)

three layers of catchfencing before running head-first into a barrier. The bottom rail had not been secured properly and as it tore off its mounting post it allowed the car to slide beneath the upper rail. The unfortunate Austrian was beheaded as the Surtees buried itself up to its gearbox.

Armco was also at the centre of one of F1's greatest scandals, during the Spanish GP at Montjuich Park in 1975. Had the paddock for the race not been located within a derelict sports stadium in the picturesque park, the race would never have taken place. When the teams arrived, they were appalled at the standard of construction of the barriers around this demanding circuit – so much so that Jacky Ickx was the only man to drive in both of the first two practice sessions, with Vittorio Brambilla joining him in the first and Bob Evans and Roelof Wunderink in the second. The rest of the teams and drivers boycotted the sessions.

They had a point. When Jean-Pierre Beltoise had made his initial inspection in accordance with CSI rules, much of the work had not been completed to turn the public roads into a race course. When the drivers finally got a look at the supposedly finished article, they became extremely agitated. Most of the Armco was old, lengths did not match and, worst of all, thousands of nuts and bolts had visibly only been tightened by hand.

After the 1969 race, when Jochen Rindt and Graham Hill had crashed heavily into Armco barriers at Montjuich after wing failures on their Lotus 49Bs, the circuit had earned accolades as the epitome of Armco-lined safety. Now the organisers had done a terrible job. The GPDA spoke of boycotting the event, remembering only too vividly the recent accidents which had taken Roger Williamson, Cevert, Revson, and Koinigg from their number. In particular, they knew that after the Cevert accident they should have taken more of a stand at Watkins Glen, and that their apathy had contributed to Koinigg's death.

GPDA president Graham Hill convened a press conference, backed by an irate Niki Lauda, Jody Scheckter, and Emerson Fittipaldi. He said the matter was one between the organisers and the CSI. But he also said that the drivers and teams would take up the matter themselves in the absence of any sign of leadership from the representatives of the governing body.

Work was supposed to take place overnight, but on Saturday morning the drivers reported little but cosmetic evidence of it. As a noon deadline for action approached, several team representatives, among them Ken Tyrrell and John Surtees, took things – including their own spanners – into their own hands, and set to work. It was a ludicrous situation that reflected no credit on either the organisers or the CSI. The drivers were under enormous pressure, especially from a public used to bullfighting, who couldn't see what all the safety fuss was about. But by Sunday they would, and they would react accordingly.

There was so much talk of the teams withdrawing that the officials panicked and let it be known that they would have the police impound all of the cars and transporters if the race did not go ahead. Such was the enlightenment of F1 at that time. The GPDA and the teams were forced to concede that they were over a barrel, for all the organisers had the whip hand. All they had to do was lock the two pairs of stadium gates, and F1 would be a prisoner.

Eventually, in this spirit of camaraderie, practice went ahead. The race itself was initially marred by accidents. The Ferraris of Lauda and Regazzoni, Hunt's Hesketh, and Andretti's Parnelli all crashed. Then came tragedy on the 26th lap.

Rolf Stommelen's Embassy Hill was

The hapless Austrian Helmuth Koinigg made quite an impression in his two races for Surtees in 1974, but perished when his TS16 slid at high speed through three layers of catchfencing and the steel barriers at Watkins Glen. (David Tremayne Archive)

one of the first cars to use carbon fibre; its rear wing support was made of this aerospace material, but had been drilled once already to prevent a crack elongating further. On the 26th lap the strut failed, pitching the hapless German into and over a guardrail. The car was thrown back across the road, where it slid along the upper rail before plunging into a marshal's post. Four bystanders were killed including a Spanish fireman and an American photographer, while Stommelen suffered broken legs.

The crowd, which had been immune to such dangers only 24 hours before, now literally bayed for blood as the fuel from Stommelen's car flooded down the gutters. Chaos reigned on one of the blackest days in the sport's history. Fittingly, the debacle was stopped and the win awarded to Jochen Mass, who was almost moved to physical violence against officials who stood around smiling happily.

F1 writer Nigel Roebuck was at the time working on Embassy's behalf. 'In between his spells at *Autosport*, Quentin Spurring and I ran the Embassy Racing Club for punters. After the accident the Guardia Civil was just lashing out at anyone and everyone. There was complete bedlam. The gutters were awash with fuel from Rolf's car, and all it needed was for somebody to drop a fag end … Luckily there was no fire, but the crowd was in such a mood that Quentin ran the gauntlet getting back to the paddock. At the accident scene he was quickly advised to get rid of his Embassy jacket.

'It was just unforgettable, seeing Rolf still slumped in the wreckage of the car at the top of the hill, conscious and staring straight ahead, and clearly in huge pain from broken legs. Under the monocoque there was a body and the place was strewn with wreckage. It really was a scene from Hell. There was a total absence of control.'

'It's hard to believe how many times the Armco barriers weren't assembled correctly,' Stewart concedes unhappily. 'I actually went round Barcelona myself, checking for loose bolts.'

* * *

Armco was not the only method of restraint to supersede straw bales. Another means was tried by John Hugenholtz, the innovative yet sometimes curiously blinkered designer of Zandvoort and Suzuka. At Zandvoort in 1960 Dan Gurney had left the track and a wheel torn from his BRM had killed a small boy. By 1962 Hugenholtz had come up with a potentially strong alternative to steel barriers – strategically sited chainlink fencing. In all the fuss about Armco, however, it would go almost unnoticed for a while.

John Surtees had reason to be grateful for it that year, however, when his Lola-Climax left the road but was arrested by the fencing before it could hit anything hard. 'I was a big advocate of catchfencing and worked closely on it with Hugenholz,' Surtees says today. 'What happened was that the Lola broke a steering arm as I was coming over the rise and into the corner leading on to the main straight. There were two things I recall: one is that the fencing slowed me down, the other is that I ended up in the

Top left: This is why the drivers and teams were so disgusted at Montjuich Park when they arrived for the Spanish GP in 1975 … (Phipps/Sutton)

Top right: Team mechanics took to tightening the loose Armco nuts and bolts themselves, in a desperate effort to ease an ugly situation. (Phipps/Sutton)

Right: Backed by Niki Lauda and Emerson Fittipaldi, spokesman Graham Hill outlines the drivers' concerns. (Phipps/Sutton)

Far right: Fittipaldi himself relayed the drivers' views to the increasingly intransigent organisers. (Phipps/Sutton)

Team Tyrrell

TEXACO

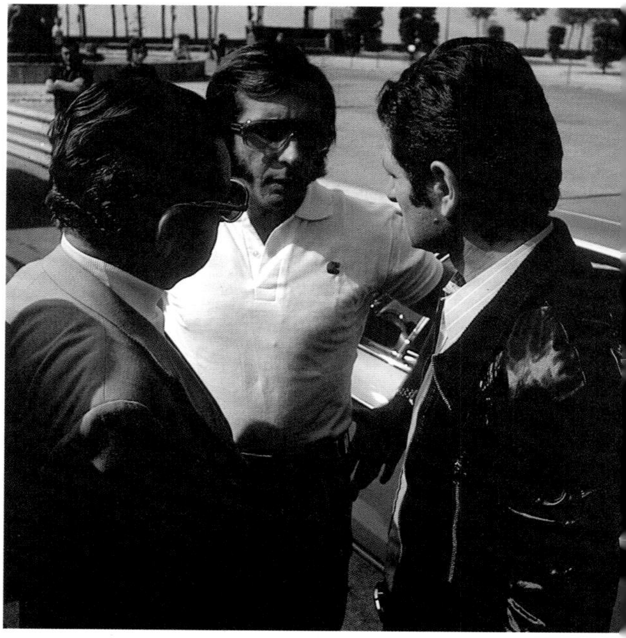

bicycle park. I landed there, but the fencing undoubtedly slowed me down. Without it, it would have been an enormous accident because I had no steering.'

Stewart was another fan. 'I always liked it,' he admits. 'It was one of the best safety devices I had the misfortune to experience. In those days the cars had no deformable structure. The driver was effectively the deformable structure. There was an aluminium tub. My F1 BRM had a full tub, but it was still alloy. So at the time the only other deformable structure was chainlink fencing, which was Hugenholtz's concept and a very good idea.'

It did not go unnoticed by any of the drivers, however, when Jack Brabham crashed team-mate Rolf Stommelen's Brabham BT33 and got trapped in the fencing during testing at Zandvoort prior to the Dutch GP in 1970. The Australian triple champion was not prone to accidents of his own making, and went off when a tyre failed as he passed the pits. The turquoise car turned over and Brabham found himself trapped, trussed up like a chicken, until help arrived. Mercifully, the car did not catch fire.

'That posed a big question,' Stewart admits, 'but on the other hand what it had probably achieved in saving other lives had been fast forgotten. It really only got into full swing in other places in the late 'sixties and early 'seventies, but of course everyone who shunned it said the same thing about seat belts. People would get trapped in a fire and/or drown in a river. But it saved an awful lot more people than they could have saved had nobody been wearing seat belts. The same thing was really the case with catchfencing.'

To compound the problems, Lauda and Regazzoni collided in their Ferraris during the opening lap of what would be a tragic race. (Phipps/Sutton)

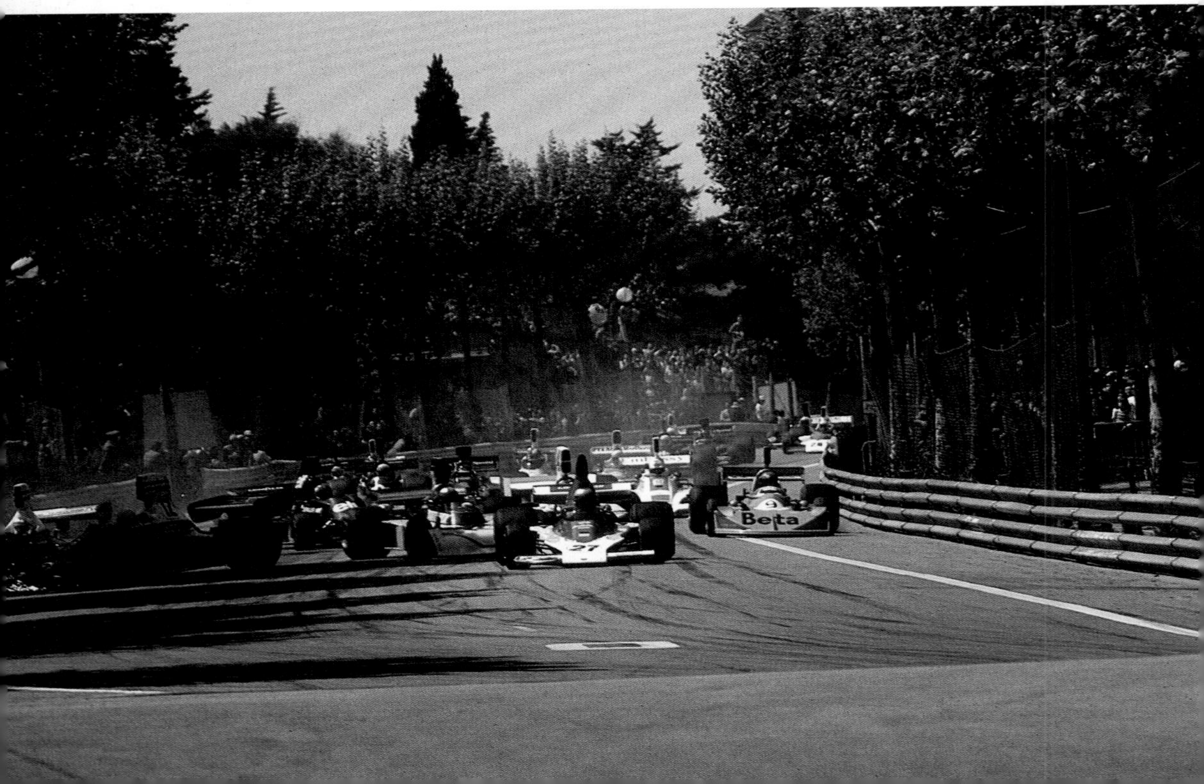

Stewart is still adamant that catchfencing saved his life in the fearful accident he had at Kyalami during practice for the South African GP in 1973. 'I had a brake failure. Had chainlink fencing not been there, I would have died. There is no question about that. I was doing 283kph [176mph], and I had only one master cylinder working and the car just was not going to stop. Even spinning did nothing to wipe off speed. I just tried to forget about it, until I opened my eyes and there was a white wall in front of me, which was the concrete. The fencing had slowed me down, otherwise that really would have been a big shunt.'

Catchfencing's height of popularity was in the 'seventies. But several incidents in the British GP at Silverstone in 1975, where Tony Brise's Griffin helmet was knocked off by one of the half-cut fence poles that were used to support the chainlink, were followed by tragedy at the Osterreichring which sealed its fate.

Mark Donohue crashed during unofficial practice on the morning of the Austrian GP. The irony is that he seemed unharmed as rescuers helped him from his Penske March 751, which had left the road at the Hella Licht chicane at the top of the hill after the pits – the corner that Jackie Stewart once described as one of the toughest in racing. It is likely that the left front tyre of the car burst, sending it off the road and through 50yd (45m) of catchfencing. As it smashed through the posts and wire, they rolled up under the car and effectively pitched it over the Armco when Donohue's momentum had used up all the space he had left. On its way it struck two marshals, who were badly injured. Worse still, Donohue struck some scaffold poles which formed an advertisement hoarding, and by the time the March came to a halt some of these were still bent around his form in the cockpit.

The former CanAm champion got out of his damaged car okay and was taken back to the pits, where he appeared to be perfectly calm and lucid. But then he suffered an epileptic fit, and was unconscious as he was flown by helicopter to a hospital in Graz. By the time he arrived there his pupils were 'fully blown', had dilated fully in indication of very high pressure in his head, and by the time he was operated on it was too late to save

Rolf Stommelen's Embassy Hill dangles from a crane, its damage all too apparent after its rear wing had broken and sent it vaulting atop one of the controversial barriers, killing four spectators and seriously injuring the driver. (Phipps/Sutton)

him. By Tuesday, the man who had spoken lucidly with Emerson Fittipaldi shortly after the accident, was dead.

It is likely that it was the scaffold poles that inflicted the blow to Donohue's head, but uncertainty remained that it could have been a catchfence pole. 'I think chainlink fencing was a very important stage in the progression of safety,' Stewart says. 'And that's all you can say. Good chainlink fencing ideally had its lower edge located beneath the level of the ground so that the cars couldn't dig underneath it. And certainly, with the nose on F1 cars in those days, several that went in straight-on *did* go under it. With a security fence you put it below the level of the ground so that people cannot burrow underneath it; but the problem if you did that with catchfencing was the maintenance of it after one accident. The servicing was one of the biggest problems with it.'

Another answer, much employed to the chagrin of the drivers and spectators alike, was the chicane. Once it was merely an essential part of every kid's Scalextric set, but chicanes proliferated in the 'seventies, emasculating circuit after circuit in the name of safety. Banging in a chicane was the sticking plaster of the era, often applied regardless of the severity of the injury.

One of the first tracks to suffer was Monza. In 1971 Peter Gethin won for BRM the fastest race in history, at an average speed of 242.62kph (150.76mph). By 1972 the parkland track had chicanes at the end of the pit straight, and another at the corner named after Alberto Ascari. In ensuing years there would be more. The average speed that first year plummeted, to a miserable 211.80kph (131.61mph). The slipstreaming epics became a thing of the past.

Following Cevert's accident in 1973 and Koinigg's in 1974, Watkins Glen went the chicane route for 1975 with a clumsy affair nicknamed after Jody Scheckter. It was sited in the old Esses, where Cevert had met his end, and where, ironically, it had been Scheckter who had been first upon the horrible scene. This chicane, though the product of good intentions, was universally detested. Where fourth or fifth gear had been the norm though the Esses, now the drivers found themselves fumbling through the catchfence and kerbing edifice in second or third.

Amazingly, for all the so-called safety thinking behind the chicane, drivers reported many instances at the Glen of Armco attachment bolts which featured no washers. 1975 was indeed a lamentable year for the safety crusade.

Though it is easy to look back with 'nineties eyes on a time when priorities were different, the post-Clark years saw some progress in the quest for greater safety. At the beginning of the 'seventies the CSI published its considerations on circuit design. Track verges had to be a minimum width of three metres. All guardrails had to be double tier. Organisers were required to locate spectators at least three metres behind any safety fencing. At long last a barrier was mandatory between the pit lane and race track. Straw bales were finally banned, and tracks were to be subjected to mandatory CSI inspections. At the same time, new regulations were introduced governing track width, surface, and gradient change.

As the era progressed, more changes or clarifications were implemented. In 1972 criteria for circuit safety were published, together with specifications for debris fencing. A year later regulations on catchfences, rescue equipment, and starting grid dimensions were similarly tightened up. By 1977 the CSI had defined specifications for another new method of restraint that would have its day in the 'eighties and 'nineties and on into the current era – the gravel arrester beds more popularly known today as gravel beds.

Chapter 7

The spectre of fire

It sounds a horrible thing to say, but for a long time
I could never forget a smell like roasting pork.

F1 driver, 1968

Curiously the cars themselves changed little in the immediate post-Clark era. In many ways it was to take massive upheavals in circuit design before what we see today as the shortcomings of the cars were truly highlighted.

The 'fifties had served to move the sport gently away from the post-war era, but the technology of the day largely repeated what had gone before – until Charles and John Cooper began putting the engine behind the driver and thus gave birth to a new generation of Grand Prix car.

In the early years, teams such as Alfa Romeo and Ferrari relied on simple ladder frame chassis, flat two-dimensional platforms on which their coachbuilders mounted the framework for the hand-beaten body panels. Cockpits were roomy, ejection therefrom easy. But this was the era when the philosophy was that it was better to be thrown from the car in an accident, than to be subjected to the almost inevitable fire that would result from a serious shunt.

The true spaceframe, perfected by Colin Chapman with the Vanwall in 1956, was a significant improvement. Its greater torsional stiffness led in turn to better roadholding and general handling, but in itself it was only a small step forward as far as safety was concerned. However, drivers still favoured the idea of ejection, even as the 'sixties saw the advent of rear-engined cars with more supine driving positions.

The 2.5-litre regulations had been in force since 1954, having replaced the 2-litre Formula Two rules of 1952 and 1953, which had themselves overtaken the series' original 1.5-litre supercharged regulations. But all through 1959 there were rumblings about reducing engine capacity to 1.5-litres, non-supercharged, to reduce speeds. The idea filled the emergent British constructors with dismay and anger in equal measure. They thrust their heads into the sand and refused to believe that it would happen, thereby giving Ferrari a head start when the formula did indeed come to fruition in 1961. That refusal to assimilate the writing on the wall may have delayed the next significant safety step.

This was Chapman's Lotus 25 in 1962,

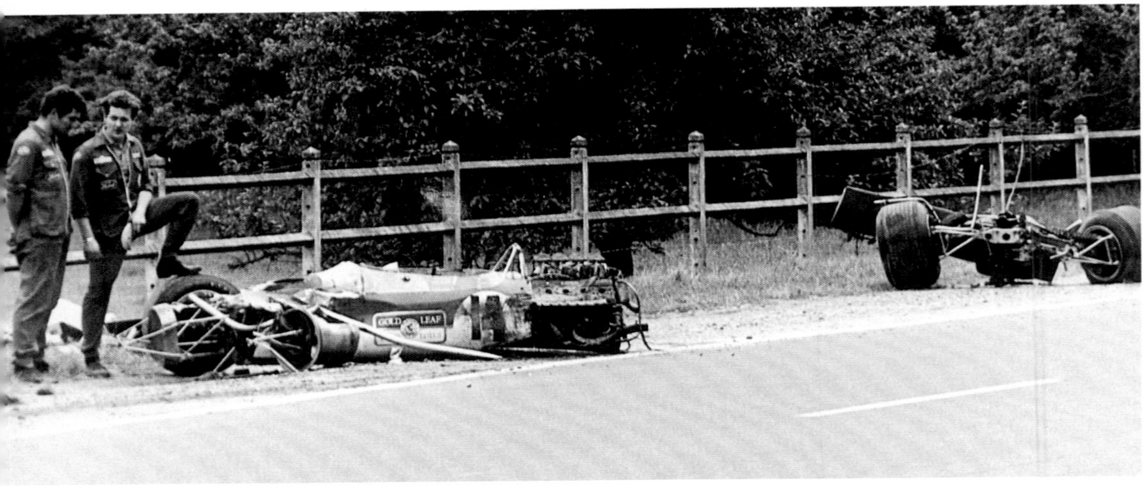

Jackie Oliver and his Lotus mechanics can't quite believe how he escaped after this hefty crash during practice for the 1968 French GP at Rouen. Wing failure, or the aerodynamic effect of running too close to another car, were blamed. (Phipps/Sutton)

which completely rewrote the performance parameters. Taking a note from the sports car racing Jaguar D-Type, the versatile designer came up with a slim single-seat bathtub monocoque chassis, which, while offering massively increased torsional stiffness and further enhanced handling, also went some way towards protecting the driver. The chassis had no round-section tubing to poke unpleasantly into his tender parts in an accident, but used bulkheads to tie together its aluminium skins. Instead of housing its fuel in vulnerable metal tanks it used rubber bags hidden within the monocoque walls. Before long everybody was toying with monocoques, though Brabham was the last to go that route, in 1970, by which time the regulations made them mandatory. In 1963

BRM went a step further, in both the rigidity and safety stakes, by producing a full cigar-tube monocoque which cocooned the driver better.

The 'sixties was a fertile period for Formula One technical development, for alongside such breakthroughs teams were also experimenting with wider tyres and four-wheel drive. Both held the promise of better roadholding, which itself might be deemed to have a beneficial impact on safety, though the flipside of that particular coin was the fact that cornering speeds were increasing dramatically so accident speeds could be expected to rise similarly.

To keep pace with the rapid development of the racing tyre, suspension systems were becoming increasingly more adjustable. It now became possible to adjust a car to suit a specific type of circuit, rather than making do with the basic design as had previously been the case. In its wake that versatility brought softer tyre compounds and wider contact patches and suddenly there was an explosion of lap speeds that would soon far outstrip the safety benefits of the monocoque.

In 1960 Chapman's spaceframe Lotus 18 had used Dunlop rear tyres that were no more than 152mm (6in) wide. When the 1.5-litre formula ended in 1965, his Lotus 33 used 229mm (9in) wide rear tyres. And more was to come, for 1966 saw F1 run to regulations permitting 3-litre normally aspirated engines, or 750cc supercharged. By 1968 Dan Gurney's Eagle Weslake had 406mm (16in) wide Goodyear rear tyres.

The 1.5-litre F1 had been relatively safe, but the 'Return to Power,' as the new formula was billed, would usher in a new and dangerous era. The magic power figure was 400bhp, with the possibility, it was thought, of as much as 500 after a few years' development. Honda's 1.5-litre V12 was the most powerful unit

One race later, at the British GP at Brands Hatch, every self-respecting F1 team was using the high overhead wings. (Phipps/Sutton)

After countless failures of the high wings, the CSI finally stepped in at Monaco in 1969. One day Graham Hill's Lotus 49B bore its elevated appendage, the next this upturned piece of aluminium. (Phipps/Sutton)

Before long, integrated wings were de rigueur. Jackie Oliver leads the Race of Champions for BRM in 1970, pursued by eventual winner Jackie Stewart and moral victor Jack Brabham. (Phipps/Sutton)

of the old formula, with 230bhp, so it is not difficult to see why the new regulations created so much excitement.

The BRM P83 and the Lotus 49 revived the 1954 Lancia D50's advanced thinking by using their engines as stressed chassis components from which suspension parts were hung, but one of the unseen innovations of the era came in 1966 from Robin Herd. He made the first use of composites, as Bruce McLaren followed Jack Brabham and Dan Gurney down the self-construction path. Herd's McLaren M2B used a monocoque made of Mallite balsa honeycomb aluminium, which gave great strength for lightness. But this was still an era when the focus was on performance, not safety, and the benefits of this construction method would take a while longer to sink in. There was greater focus on multi-valve technology and tyre development and then, suddenly, from 1968 onwards, the concept that would for evermore be F1's buzzword: downforce.

The idea of putting an upturned aerofoil, or wing, on a racing car was nothing new. Back in the 'twenties the rocket-propelled Opel RAK2 record car had mounted one either side of the cockpit. In 1955 Swiss engineer Michael May had placed an overhead wing amidships on his Porsche. But the first really successful application had come in the 'sixties, when the innovative Texan Jim Hall had gained terrific results with overhead wings on his remarkable CanAm racing Chaparral sports cars.

In F1 Chapman had begun moving towards the wedge-shaped body with his Lotus 49B, which appeared publicly at Monaco in 1968. It used small wings either side of the nose to reduce aerodynamic lift, and an upturned wedge tail. Then, at Spa-Francorchamps, both

Fire was still a major hazard in the 'seventies. At Kyalami in 1973 Mike Hailwood earned himself the George Medal after this dramatic rescue of Clay Regazzoni from his burning BRM. (Phipps/Sutton)

Mercedes-Benz's post-war W196 was a step forward, with its spaceframe chassis, but though it placed the engine at the opposite end, Cooper's late-decade contender did not differ too much from the German car's tubular concept. (Phipps/Sutton)

Ferrari and Brabham appeared with pukka aerofoils at the rear, mounted on stalks. Suddenly, everyone had down-force fever. Chapman caught the direction of the wind and soon the Lotuses had bigger and higher wings than anyone else, and more grip. Lap times began to fall further as the tyre companies got in on the act by creating softer compounds to generate even more grip. The age of aerodynamics had arrived, and in its wake came a serious threat to safety.

This finally became apparent during the Spanish GP at Barcelona's demanding Montjuich Park circuit in 1969. Broken wing struts were nothing new; Lotus had had failures in 1968, and one was suspected to have been the cause of a massive accident that befell Jackie Oliver in practice for the French GP at Rouen. Either that or some aerodynamic quirk from following another car very closely had caused a dramatic loss of control.

'Whatever it was,' Oliver recalls, 'it separated the engine from the monocoque and threw everything down the road at a fair old rate. I remember sort of coming to outside this big pair of gates. It was some old French chateau, but at the time I wasn't sure I hadn't arrived at the Pearly Gates!'

Brabham and Lotus had suffered further failures earlier in 1969, at the South African GP at Kyalami. Brabham, indeed, had persevered for a while in a foul-handling BT26A shorn of its wings after the rear one had collapsed and been cut off with hacksaws in the pits.

At Montjuich, however, enough became enough. Lotus team leader Jochen Rindt was already very nervous about wings, but they undoubtedly conferred a speed advantage on his 49B. He was leading the race when team-mate Graham Hill had a huge accident as his rear wing struts broke on the ninth lap. He was travelling close to 225kph (140mph) at the time, and hit the barriers on either side of the track before coming to a halt.

Hill studied the wreckage, seeking some indication of what had gone wrong, and was trying to get word to Chapman to check Rindt's car when the same thing happened to it at the same spot, on the 20th lap. Rindt's 49B slammed into Hill's wreck. Fortunately the Armco barriers on both sides of the road did what they were supposed to do, and though Rindt fractured his skull and broke his nose both drivers were fortunate to escape what could easily have been fatal accidents. But the writing was on the wall. The CSI had already ruled

Colin Chapman's revolutionary Lotus 25 of 1962 took safety a big step forward, as it introduced the aluminium monocoque with rubberised fuel tanks. (Phipps/Sutton)

that wings should act on the sprung mass, not the unsprung suspension uprights à la Lotus. But now, after one practice session at the next race, in Monaco, it acted overnight and outlawed the high wings altogether.

Despite Montjuich there was an outcry against the ruling, and eventually all parties were satisfied when the CSI relented and allowed wings so long as they were mounted low as part of the rear bodywork. It was a compromise, and it would not be the last time that the governing body and the teams would clash over the issue. Controlling the levels of downforce remains a bone of contention to this day.

By 1970 the concept of the monocoque F1 car had been refined. Spaceframes were banned, high wings were banned, and rubber bag fuel tanks were mandatory (some constructors had used ingenious means of storing fuel in other ways which the CSI came to disapprove of). But safety had only come so far.

Between 1963 and 1967 regulations were introduced either to mandate things such as dual braking circuits and seat belt anchorages, or to enhance the design of fire protection systems, fuel tanks, fillers and breathers. At the same time rollover hoops were required to be larger and stronger, though in truth, even though hoops protruding 5mm (0.02in) above the driver's head were required from 1968, it was 1969 before structures strong enough to support an upturned car began to appear.

From 1968 cars were required to have an electrical circuit breaker, reverse gear, and easy evacuation cockpits. An oil catch tank was also mandatory. There had been several accidents over the years where drivers went off on another's oil, and at Spa in 1967 British driver Mike Parkes had a nasty accident in which his Ferrari slid off the road at Blanchimont on the first lap, on oil spewed from Jackie Stewart's BRM. Parkes was thrown from his car and suffered serious leg injuries which ended his promising F1 career.

Safety belts had been a familiar feature in Indianapolis roadsters over the years, not so much to retain the drivers

The typical F1 car of the mid-'sixties was markedly less integrated than today's designs. Jochen Rindt's 1967 Cooper Maserati provides evidence of afterthought in the positioning of its ignition coils. (Phipps/Sutton)

Though it had been designed specifically around aerofoils, Chapman insisted on running his wedge-shaped Lotus 72 without them at Monza in 1970. This is the unfortunate Rindt shortly before his fatal accident. (Phipps/Sutton)

in an accident but to keep them in their bucking broncos in the first place, especially on the rougher tracks. Stewart was the first F1 driver to insist on belts, and they were fitted to his BRM for the German GP in 1967. 'I just didn't think that being thrown from the car was a sensible option,' he recalls, 'and in any case, being belted in gave me better control over the motor car.'

There were as many cases for as against belts at this time, when spaceframe and monocoque chassis alike could still crumple around drivers and trap them in a serious accident. After his adventure at Monza in 1964 (see Chapter 4), Bob Bondurant said, 'After I'd been thrown into a pile of leaves I picked myself up and wandered around a bit. I couldn't find the car, though. I thought, "Well I know I came down here in a car – where the hell is it?" Then, in the middle of the Curva Grande, I found the hole in the hedge – and then I found the car. At that time the bodywork was all one piece, and the front had come back, so the windscreen and the rollover bar were sheared off. If I'd been strapped in, I'd have been decapitated.'

Equally, Chris Amon probably would not have survived his unusual accident there in the 1968 Italian GP but for his seat belts. 'The car landed in the trees and I was upside down,' he remembers. 'They had to cut through the belts to get me out, but if I hadn't been wearing them I'd either have been thrown into the trees or would have had a long drop to the ground, which might not have done me any good …'

Fire was still the major fear. At the Nürburgring in 1966 John Taylor crashed his spaceframe Brabham and subsequently died a month later from the burns he received. A year later, as we have seen, Lorenzo Bandini died at Monaco, followed by Jo Schlesser at Rouen in 1968. 'It sounds a horrible thing to say,' one driver of the era admitted after the Honda tragedy, 'but for a long time I could never forget a smell like roasting pork.' Yet little seemed to be done to exorcise the spectre.

By 1969 cars had to be fitted with two onboard extinguisher systems. A year later came the bladder fuel tanks, but neither were sufficient to save Piers Courage at Zandvoort in 1970. The whole question of fire had already raised its head at Jarama that season, when Jackie Oliver's BRM broke a stub axle on the first lap, ran brakeless across a corner, and tee-boned Jacky Ickx's Ferrari. Both cars had full fuel tanks, which immediately ruptured, and burst into flames. Ickx ran from his car with his Nomex suit alight, but neither driver was seriously injured.

Not so Courage, who crashed on the 23rd lap of the Dutch GP at Zandvoort. The cause of the accident remains uncertain, though mechanical failure was a likely factor. The Englishman's de Tomaso slid wide at 241kph (150mph) on a right-hander before the Ost Tunnel, climbed up a bank and knocked down several poles, before striking another bank and rolling over in flames. Courage's helmet was torn off in the impact, and he was unconscious in the cockpit. The firefighting facilities were at best weak, and he had no chance of survival.

Later that year, which had already seen Bruce McLaren killed after the rear bodywork of his CanAm McLaren M8D flew off during a test at Goodwood, Rindt became the sport's only posthumous champion after crashing fatally during practice at Monza. Several factors contributed to the Austrian's death. One was Chapman's extraordinary insistence that he should run his Lotus 72 without the rear wings for which it had specifically been designed, in the search for greater speed with which to challenge the Ferraris. Another was the likely failure of one of the inboard front brake shafts, which pitched the car left into the Armco barriers at the approach to

After Jody Scheckter's McLaren spun at the end of the opening lap and hit the pit wall, the 1973 British GP had to be stopped amid a welter of damaged cars. (Phipps/Sutton)

Parabolica as he was decelerating from around 322kph (200mph). Yet another was the way in which the Lotus's wedge nose dug under the barrier close to a post, which arrested the front end of the car instantly and caused the back to slew round violently. Finally there was Rindt's detestation of crutch straps, and his habit of wearing only shoulder harnesses. His feet had already suffered badly in the initial impact, but now he literally submarined down inside the monocoque, whose front end had been torn off, and the seat belt buckle inflicted terrible injuries to his throat.

Chapman vehemently denied that a brake shaft had broken, and – as would happen in the Senna case – the car was impounded and a lengthy and inconclusive Italian investigation was conducted.

BRM and Surtees fared worst, the former losing two cars, the latter all three, but in common with the Scheckter McLaren the latest F1 cars proved the worth of their recently introduced deformable structures. (Phipps/Sutton)

But Rindt's team-mate, John Miles, had suffered a similar failure in practice for the previous race, in Austria, and privately was convinced the same thing had happened to Jochen's car.

In 1971 three more GP drivers died: Ignazio Giunti and Pedro Rodriguez in sports car accidents, Jo Siffert in a non-championship F1 race at Brands Hatch. All three accidents involved impacts and fire. Giunti and Rodriguez were incapacitated in the impacts, in Buenos Aires and Norisring respectively, but Siffert had only a broken leg and was asphyxiated. All three were reaching their peaks, and their loss, added to those in the previous season, prompted greater efforts to make the sport safer.

Safety foam became mandatory in fuel tanks from 1972, as the CSI introduced its FT3 specification. The use of magnesium in chassis components was limited, and there were other cosmetic changes, such as the requirement for a headrest for the driver to reduce whiplash, minimum cockpit dimensions, and a combined electrical cut-off with an external handle that marshals could activate. Cars were also required to carry red lights at the rear, for use in poor weather. More convincing were the changes for 1973, when deformable structures around the fuel tanks, which were usually in the sides of the cars, became mandatory.

These changes were quickly put to the test, when Clay Regazzoni's BRM and Mike Hailwood's Surtees collided during the South African GP. A serious fire immediately ensued, with Regazzoni still trapped in his car. In a performance that would subsequently earn him the George Medal for gallantry, Hailwood went back into the flames time and again until the Swiss driver was rescued. Once again, motor racing made the front page news. It did so again later that year with the multi-car shunt in the British GP, and then the Williamson tragedy at Zandvoort covered in Chapter 15.

Jody Scheckter was the man responsible for triggering the accident that put deformable structures to further test at the end of the first lap of the British GP at Silverstone. The young South African had made a strong start in his McLaren, but lost control and spun exiting the Woodcote corner, which at that time was very fast. He hit the pit wall nose-first, and behind him cars went all over the road trying to avoid him. Eight drivers were unsuccessful, and the race was stopped as the road became littered with debris which included the BRMs of Regazzoni and Jean-Pierre Beltoise, and all three Surtees cars. But despite the carnage, the new safety measures achieved their goal. Not a single car caught fire, and only one driver, Andrea de Adamich, had suffered injury. Scheckter reminded the Italian of that years later, when they met for the first time. 'The last time I saw you,' the 1979 World Champion said, 'I had just broken your ankle!'

But just as the sport was congratulating itself, came the Williamson tragedy. At the end of the season it was followed by François Cevert's death at Watkins Glen and, early in 1974, Peter Revson's at Kyalami. Cevert died after making a small error at very high speed; Revson was an innocent victim when a titanium suspension component broke and pitched his Shadow into an Armco barrier. Later that year Helmuth Koinigg died at the Glen, followed by Mark Donohue in Austria the year after. Then came Niki Lauda's horrendous accident at the old Nürburgring, when he crashed at Bergwerk and his Ferrari exploded into flames.

By a miracle Lauda not only survived, but would race again that very season. But his accident was a terrifying throwback to the sort of inferno that had killed the promising young Vanwall driver Stuart Lewis-Evans in Morocco back in 1958. It seemed that no matter what the best brains in the sport tried to do, the spectre of fire could not be beaten back.

Chapter 8

The man who walked through flames

When you are in there, surrounded by fire, you can't see and it is extremely claustrophobic. I must say, after 30 seconds I cheated and came out!

Louis Stanley

As the ripples began to spread through every corner of Formula One in the wake of Jackie Stewart's tireless safety crusade, one non-driver lent his stentorian voice to the campaign and stood head and shoulders above his fellows in the quest for greater safety.

In his heyday as a member of the Grand Prix circus, Louis T. Stanley cut an imposing figure with his tall and corpulent frame, and his swept-back silver hair. He had become a member of the Owen family – which owned BRM – when he married Jean Owen, sister of Sir Alfred, the industrial knight who had rescued the ailing team and whose businesses pumped in so much money to finance it over the years. Stanley's customary attire of blue blazer, light flannels, and old school tie stamped upon him an authority that could outmanoeuvre even the most intransigent gate man at any of the world's circuits. His firm but authoritative manner quelled many arguments before they had really got under way. He was wont to give vent to long-winded opinion on any number of subjects concerning the sport and the manner of its running. Accordingly, he was seen by many simply as a pompous fellow who liked the sound of his own voice. They called him 'Big Lou', 'Lord Louis', or 'Lord Trumpington' (the last in reference to his home near Cambridge), though few had the temerity to do so directly to his ruddy face. More than one of his drivers over the years tells the story of how he would never trouble to correct minions, particularly in America, who incorrectly addressed him as Sir Louis.

By the 'seventies Stanley was joint managing director of BRM, and, as one of the most outspoken and controversial figures in racing, continued to consider himself as the sport's self-appointed senior statesman. Jackie Stewart, who regarded him with great respect and affection, once remarked: 'Louis Stanley is an extraordinary man. He has many talents and some failings, not all of which are obvious to him. He writes a very amusing book, takes terrible pictures, and can be diplomatic or not depending on the circumstances.' But beyond the immediate impression he created, Louis Stanley was also ahead of his time. For he was a man of vision, albeit sometimes rose-tinted, who refused to accept that drivers had to be sacrificed in the name of the sport he loved.

Stewart's contribution to progress in safety rightly received due recognition, and the mantle that the Scot had taken over from Swiss driver Jo Bonnier would later pass without fanfare to Jean-Marie Balestre as he tackled the problem from the technical side during the 'eighties. But in truth Stanley, for all his bombast and his intransigent views on team management, may well have been the true father of the safety movement. There is little doubt that he influenced Bonnier and Stewart – both BRM drivers at some stage of their careers – to initiate their crusades in the first place. Like Balestre, it's easy to let a man's perceived public image, with all its associated dogma and pomposity, obscure just what he achieved behind the scenes.

Stanley succeeded *Autocar*'s sports editor, the late Peter Garnier, as honorary secretary of the GPDA. Later he became a trustee of the Jim Clark Foundation and the founder of the Jo Siffert Advisory Council. He was also the director general of the International Grand Prix Medical Service, created through his efforts in 1967 (see Chapter 16). This was a remarkable mobile hospital intended to travel to every European race and thereby guarantee the availability of a specific minimum level of care for any driver involved in an accident. However, this bold initiative ultimately failed through a mix of politics and vested interests. In the end it was sold off, but Stanley had made his point and had set the ball rolling.

In his later years he was, contrary to his image in the 'sixties and 'seventies, commendably modest about the role he had played as a prime mover of motor racing safety. 'Well, it would be nice to think I had played a part,' he says. 'With the GPDA I was always reluctant to hold press conferences, which may have been wrong. But these were private meetings, so we did not tell the press what had happened during them. We carried on the jobs we had to do without telling them. One or two of them got upset; to them, Bonnier was cowardly, Denny Hulme was yellow. That sort of remark was so silly. Of course, none of them said it to Denny's face, otherwise they would have had their own changed …

'But there were certain irritations which one ignored. The main thing was to try and make progress. I was put in charge of circuit safety and also had the authority to say no if a circuit didn't come up to scratch. That only happened twice, once with the AvD at Hockenheim, and the same at Le Mans.'

Stanley retained his outspoken views. Speaking of Senna's accident at Imola, he said: 'You were there in person, I saw it on the screen. The car comes to rest, the driver slumped. It was just on five minutes before medical help arrived. They said there was no question he was dead; they didn't know that. We did exercises with firefighting, and so with medicine; there must only be so many seconds before help arrives. There was no excuse for the delay.'

He agreed that the sport had not become complacent about safety at that time, but suggested that perhaps standards had slipped a little without anyone really appreciating it. 'Whatever you do in a racing car, it has to be potentially lethal. If you clout a pile of tyres, well … you're going to get more than a headache, aren't you?'

Professor Watkins disagrees utterly with that assessment. 'That view is ill-informed and simply isn't right,' he said. 'I was certainly at the accident scene within two minutes, and the first intervention car, carrying an Italian doctor, was already there when I arrived. The Italian doctor was cradling Ayrton's head.'

Eventually, BRM became an embarrassment in terms of performance and sank from the F1 grids. Stanley admits that it was difficult to walk away after more than 16 years, and that he missed racing badly at first. 'But after we closed Stanley BRM I had so many other interests, among them really streamlining our industrial works. You can't keep things going on sentiment. The bottom line has to be taken into account, and although they are unpopular people, accountants are the people in the end who talk sense.' In any case, he had come to detest the rampant commercialism of the sport and the way it had changed its face and character.

'You see, it has ceased to be a sport, as we knew it. In the old days – and not too far away – the drivers, team owners, everyone, stayed on after a race and enjoyed it. There was pleasure, instead of getting straight into a helicopter, or hiding in one of these motorhomes or having a press conference or whatever. That's not the same. Not many of today's drivers have charisma. And the fastest race some of them have is the race to the bank.'

His spat with Marlboro, whom he introduced to F1 in 1972 with BRM, was indicative of his manner when his dander was up. 'Speaking my mind has not always made me popular,' he concedes. 'But with Marlboro it was quite simple. We came to an agreement on terms, I went over to Geneva, and they tried to alter the contract. So I told them where to put it even though it was painful. I came back, they changed their mind and they came to the Dorchester and signed.

'Now, they had their job which was to sell cigarettes, and I wouldn't dream of telling them how to do that. And I don't expect a novice to tell a chief engineer what he should do with his engines or the drivers. I said, "You can obviously make suggestions and they will be considered, but I will not gatecrash your meetings on sales ..."' Today he bitterly regrets the deal.

At the official handing over ceremony at the Oulton Park Spring Cup meeting, Louis Stanley (facing camera) receives the keys to the International Grand Prix Medical Service. (LAT)

He and John Surtees, who endured a year of purgatory with BRM in 1969, were never going to the ballgame together. Surtees recalls: 'We'd have a meeting to discuss what we were going to do, shake hands on it, and go away believing everything had been mapped out. Then I would find everything would be overturned by a telephone call – usually at about 1:30 in the morning – from Louis Stanley. Something had made him change his mind …'

Not to be outdone, when Surtees quit to form his own team, Stanley was acidic. 'He came to see me and said he had two sponsors lined up, a cigarette firm and a rubber company. What did I think? I said, "I think it's pathetic," and he said, "Why?" I said, "Because your car's circulating with a fag at one end and a condom at the other. I don't call that progress."'

But then there was the other side of Louis Stanley. Fire in racing accidents is now little more than a ghost of the sport's dark past, partly thanks to his pioneering efforts in the early 'seventies when safety was still, to many, a dirty word.

In October 1971 Jo Siffert was killed during the Tribute to Jackie Stewart F1 race at Brands Hatch. It was intended as precisely that, a non-championship bit of fun, a chance for the British fans to greet their new champion. Instead, when Siffert's car suffered a suspected suspension failure on the 257kph (160mph) approach to Hawthorn's bend, it turned into a tragedy upon which Peter Gethin's victory in the sister car made not the slightest impact. Siffert's car struck the bank and overturned, pinning him beneath it. Though his only injury was a broken leg, the intensely popular Swiss driver succumbed to asphyxia in the flames. He was the only man ever to die in a BRM. 'Seppi should not have died,' said Stanley, using the Swiss racer's affectionate nickname. 'He died because of the ineffectiveness of Brands Hatch's firefighting. Those aren't my words, but from the coroner's report. All right, you

Accompanied by designer Tony Southgate, engine man Geoff Johnson and gearbox man Alec Stokes, Stanley admires the elegant lines of the 1971 BRM P160. (Phipps/Sutton)

couldn't bring him back, but their extinguishers didn't work, they were empty. It was terrible. A nightmare.'

Stanley was bereft, and took it upon himself to devise new means of combating fire, which at that time was still every driver's ultimate nightmare. He initiated a series of tests, where he insisted on being in the helicopter that was used in an experiment to fan away the flames in an attempt to find a new method of fighting fires. Stanley was criticised for many things, but the courage he showed in these tests was beyond that. He not only stood by his convictions, but insisted upon actually seeing them through, playing a key part – in conjunction with the dramatic improvements in car design that would follow in later decades – in ensuring that fire at motor races is now almost a thing of the past.

Stanley enlisted the help of the chief advisor at British Airways (then BOAC) and an expert representative from the Home Office for the tests. 'There were eight of us on the committee, and we devised these tests and gave the marshals so many seconds. The driver in a burning car doesn't die from burns, he dies from asphyxia. Along with former racer Dennis Poore, we devised a plan whereby no matter where a driver crashed a marshal with a proper extinguisher filled with proper extinguishant would be on the spot within five seconds. That was the maximum time allowable.'

The next thing was for them to source the right extinguishant, and here all sorts of clashing commercial interests arose. Stanley's oft-criticised traits came into their own. In the end it was the most suitable extinguishant that was chosen, not the most commercially viable.

'We developed a fresh backpack that

Still to be found on the racing scene from time to time, Louis and Jean Stanley visited the BRM-themed Coy's International Historic Festival in 1999. (Bearne/Sutton)

left both hands free, and then trained marshals to fight a fire in tests at Stansted. Then we tried the experiment with the helicopter and I went up with the pilot and told him that he had to drop to do the job effectively. When we were airborne I suddenly realised that the higher we went with my weight aboard, the quicker we'd drop! But it worked.'

Not content with that act of self-involvement, Stanley then decided that he personally needed to try out the fire-proof suits being introduced because of the need to get to the seat of a fire in order to put it out. 'I was told that I had 48 seconds, then my skin would start to prickle. It was childish really, because I knew I could walk through. But when you are in there, surrounded by fire, you can't see and it is extremely claustrophobic. I must say, after 30 seconds I cheated and came out!' But he had seen the horror for himself, at first hand.

Stanley recalled a time when Graham Hill visited him in his suite at London's Dorchester hotel for a GPDA meeting. 'We had all the drivers round one very hot summer day. Graham was trying a new driving suit to see what it felt like, and he kept it on to see how it was. He was like a lobster at the end!'

Louis Stanley may not have been everybody's cup of tea, but he was never afraid to stand up and be counted for his beliefs on matters concerning safety. 'He really did his best, and he got the medical unit going,' FIA president Max Mosley points out. 'People did not understand in those days how much could be done with the cars and the circuits, that came later. But he was altruistic. You can understand a driver being interested in safety, but Stanley was genuinely altruistic, and he achieved a lot.'

Veteran racing journalist Jabby Crombac also remembers Stanley fondly. 'He was a man whose pomposity was against him,' he says, 'but on the other hand he was the most kind-hearted person I've ever known. During his period as a regular in Formula One, if anyone was in trouble Louis and his wife Jean would be the first to come and help, sometimes at great expense to themselves.' In particular, Crombac remembers the tragedy of Jo Schlesser at Rouen in 1968. 'They helped Jo's widow Annie tremendously. Jean stayed up all night with her to stop her throwing herself from a window, when all of Annie's friends from Paris had left her.'

Jackie Stewart says of him: 'He was brutally frank, but I think that anyone of mature years who has lived through a period like that is allowed to be. I rather liked him.'

Say what you will about Big Lou, he stood his ground and refused to be bird-mouthed during one of motorsport's bloodiest eras. Time and again, like many of his contemporaries, he paid his dues. But the difference was that he did not simply don a sad but tolerant face in the wake of each tragedy. He did what he could to make things change.

Chapter 9

Consolidation and complacency

The teams were saying it was irrational, completely stupid, which I am fully prepared to agree that it was. But you had to do something. You had to be seen to be doing something.

Max Mosley

In retrospect it seems ironic that Jarama circuit should have been vilified at the time for its 'Mickey Mouse' character, for by today's watered down standards it seems pretty good. But back then, especially in comparison with the majestic Montjuich Park which would host the Spanish GP in 1969, it was deemed far too sterile by the drivers. And indeed it was.

But, like the Bugatti circuit at Le Mans, Jarama was a harbinger of the future. Though great circuits such as Montjuich Park (1969), Osterreichring (1970), Paul Ricard Le Castellet (1971), Parc Almirante Brown (1972), Interlagos (1973), Dijon-Prenois (1974) and Long Beach and Fuji (1976) would all bring bright new challenges in the post-Clark era, there was also a proliferation of Bugatti and Jarama-like venues.

Comfortably the worst of these was Nivelles, which replaced Spa for 1972 when the drivers refused to race on the super-quick Belgian track after the 1970 race. A barren, unimaginative facility, Nivelles was deeply unpopular with drivers, teams, and spectators alike, the last-named feeling that they were far too far away from the action because of the plethora of run-off areas. Nivelles lasted only two races (1972 and 1974) before the equally dull Zolder took over from 1975 after hosting its first Belgian GP in 1973. This in turn would give way to the shortened Spa-Francorchamps, which thankfully retained much of its former character. Anderstorp, which was built on swampland in Sweden, certainly lacked this, while Brazil's Jacarepagua track in Rio was no match for Interlagos's steely challenge.

Perhaps the most vilified circuit from the safety point of view was Canada's Mosport, which was finally deprived of the Grand Prix when Montreal took over in 1978. But Mosport was undoubtedly a paradox, for its climbs and swerves offered a serious challenge to the drivers. Things reached a climax there in the 1977 race, in which the unfortunate Ian Ashley suffered a massive accident in his rented Hesketh 308E.

The English F5000 racer was running

at around 273kph (170mph) in fifth gear when the car took off as it negotiated an infamous bump at the end of the main straight. In the past this had given luminaries such as Denny Hulme, Jackie Oliver and Brian Redman uncomfortable experience of the dubious joys of somersaulting CanAm sports cars, but this was the first time an open-wheeler had backflipped. The Hesketh was running a lot of rear wing, it is true, but the root cause was the hump itself. The car landed sideways, dug its nose into the soft earth, then vaulted the two-tier Armco barrier before demolishing the scaffolding of a television tower. The Hesketh was decimated, but Ashley could count himself extremely fortunate that when he was eventually released from the mangled remains he had only broken wrists and ankles. Drivers reported that it was an age before any help arrived. Jochen Mass said that he did two laps before he decided to stop and render assistance himself. It reminded them that the previous year an injured Chris Amon had been obliged to hobble to a road car after waiting for something as mundane yet essential as a pair of crutches to be delivered to the circuit.

Nor was the hump on the straight Mosport's only problem. Jackie Stewart had long been concerned that there were several sites at which, like Mont-Tremblant St Jovite, there was a risk of cars being launched up banks in a repeat of the von Trips accident at Monza. Back in 1968 Jacky Ickx had been launched up such a bank at St Jovite when his Ferrari's throttle stuck open, and only catchfencing had prevented the car going into a local river. That night the organisers had brought in a bulldozer and squared off the bank to avoid a repeat, though Ickx was out of things after breaking a leg.

At Mosport in 1977 the organisers were less amenable. The drivers, particularly Hans Stuck, complained that despite being passed following an inspection by the CSI's Basil Tye, the uprights to much of the Armco barrier lacked reinforcement, and there were places where it was still possible to hit the rail head-on. Compared with Silverstone or Brands Hatch, which by this time spent vast sums each year to keep their circuits up to speed with the cars that ran on them, Mosport was in desperate shape. 'And yet,' James Hunt said in a lament that summarised the paradox, 'it is such a beautiful circuit to drive on.'

This was a familiar attitude, particularly among those who wavered between Stewart's views and the traditional viewpoint. Some others, such as Ickx and the lion-hearted Pedro Rodriguez, were fatalists with little time for such sentiments, believing implacably that if the bullet had your name on it, nothing was going to save you.

As Formula One moved on the 'eighties became an era in which gravel beds and run-off areas multiplied, while catchfencing virtually died out and was outlawed altogether in 1985. Armco still proliferated, but tyre walls were also becoming de rigeur. Behind the scenes the CSI, now renamed the Federation Internationale du Sport Auto (FISA), under Jean Marie Balestre and the increasingly active Professor Sid Watkins, was getting its act together.

From 1980 it became mandatory for all F1 circuits to have a permanent medical centre. By 1981 tyre barriers were also mandatory, and at all but Monaco pit lanes had to be a minimum 10m (32.8ft) wide. By 1992 this was extended to 12m (39.4ft). Three years later it became acceptable, in certain agreed areas, for concrete walls to substitute for Armco.

In 1987 the FIA issued its criteria for temporary circuits, and in 1989 came a 1m (3.28ft) minimum height for trackside barriers and a 1.35m (4.4ft) minimum for pitwalls.

The tyre wall only did half a job at Zandvoort in 1982 when Rene Arnoux's Renault lost its left front wheel under braking for the Tarzan hairpin, but the car stayed clear of the crowd. The Frenchman walked away unharmed. (Phipps/Sutton)

The 1992 season brought mandatory chicanes on the entries to the pits.

All of these changes brought improvement, but there were still nasty accidents. In August 1980, for instance, that tough little French fighter Patrick Depailler died when his Alfa Romeo crashed at Hockenheim's Ost Kurve during testing for the German GP. The Armco inflicted terrible injuries to which Depailler subsequently succumbed. Scandalously, the catchfencing that might have saved him from serious harm lay rolled up close by; because it was 'only' a test session the organisers did not believe it necessary to erect it until the official meeting began.

A year earlier at Zandvoort Derek Daly had a monstrous shunt at the end of the main straight after a brake disc broke on his Tyrrell. The car hit the tyre wall and was launched 4.5m (15ft) into the air. In 1982 Rene Arnoux's Renault lost its left front wheel there and subjected him to something worryingly similar. In neither case did the cars actually reach members of the public, and both men walked away, but they were very close calls that could have put cars into the crowd. Shortly afterwards Jochen Mass and Mauro Baldi touched at more than 321kph (200mph) at Signes on Paul Ricard's Mistral Straight. Mass's March skittered through the catchfencing and rode the Armco. Though it missed going into the spectator enclosure, several onlookers had to be treated for scrapes and burns after a brief flash fire.

Gilles Villeneuve was killed at Zolder in one of those freak accidents as he tangled with Jochen Mass in practice. Then the spectre of fire returned as Italian racer Ricardo Paletti's Osella slammed into the back of Didier Pironi's stalled Ferrari at the start of that season's Canadian GP in Montreal. Paletti died, however, from impact injuries. Less than two months later Pironi himself lay critically injured after crashing over Alain Prost's Renault during rain-soaked practice at Hockenheim.

By the time that Martin Brundle flipped his Tyrrell on its side and crashed spectacularly at Monaco's Tabac corner in 1984, however, there were some who felt that many of the sport's safety issues had been addressed. After all, they postulated, Paletti's accident had just been one of those unfortunate things, and Brundle had walked away. Months later, however, a wall in Dallas accounted for the promising Briton's ankles.

Worse lay ahead, however. Four days after the Monaco GP in 1986 several F1 teams gathered to test at Paul Ricard, which at that time still used its longest extension, which ran down to a hairpin past the pits. A suspected rear wing failure at 290kph (180mph) pitched Elio de Angelis's Brabham-BMW over the barriers, and in a shameful episode which revealed once again the paucity of safety facilities at such sessions, the 28-year-old Italian was asphyxiated when the upturned car caught fire. World Champion Alan Jones was among those drivers who, horribly reminded of the tragedy that had befallen Roger Williamson at Zandvoort 13 years earlier (see Chapter 15), tried unsuccessfully to save Elio. It took eight minutes for the marshals to extricate him.

Retrospectively, much criticism would be applied to Imola's Tamburello corner after Senna's death, and in truth the hard lessons of 1 May 1994 had been there for the learning for at least seven years. Nelson Piquet had crashed heavily there in his Williams-Honda in 1987. Two years later Gerhard Berger did the same during the San Marino GP. Two years later still, Michele Alboreto's Arrows came to grief there after front wing failure.

The Williams team first knew how serious Piquet's 1987 accident was when Benetton driver Teo Fabi pulled up by its pit and said, 'You'd better get down there as quickly as possible. Nelson is out of the car, but he's lying on the grass ...'

The Brazilian had already set fastest time and had just begun his seventh consecutive lap of the qualifying session. He had just overtaken Adrian Campos's Minardi and had entered Tamburello, when disaster struck. On the exit to the long curve the FW11B suddenly spun and hit the concrete outer wall backwards at very high speed. Investigation later revealed that the left rear Goodyear tyre had failed.

The emergency services reacted very quickly and it soon became clear that Piquet was okay, though he was bruised and shaken. 'My memory is that the car spun round and went into the wall backwards on the left rear corner,' Williams's technical director Patrick Head remembers, 'but then the left front corner impacted on the wall as well. Certainly the suspension completely collapsed and the wheel shattered and it actually drove the upright through the side of the monocoque round about the footwell area where Nelson's ankles and feet were. But though it did go through the monocoque around about the suspension bulkheads towards the front, and displaced them a little, it didn't go through enough to damage his legs. It was a very, very big impact, but the main structure of the monocoque was intact.

'It was a period where basically, because we were running such enormous horsepower, we were able to run enormous wings on the cars and we were producing massive downforce. I'm not sure that either we maybe hadn't given Goodyear quite the scale of figures involved, or Goodyear hadn't been testing at the loading levels, but whatever the failure was it concerned the sidewalls of the tyres. It was basically a repeat of what happened to Nigel Mansell in Adelaide in 1986. And we had also had a couple of tyres fail on us over the winter.

The aftermath of the accident that befell Philippe Streiff during testing at Rio in 1989 was one of F1's least-publicised tragedies, and left the Frenchman paralysed. The damage to his AGS's rollover hoop is all too evident. (Sutton)

It wasn't until Nelson's accident at Imola that Goodyear realised the problem was quite as big as it was.'

Williams engineer Frank Dernie, now with Lola in ChampCars, did some calculations on the accident. 'It was a fairly shallow angle, similar to Senna's I should think. Like Nelson, Ayrton should just have been shaken; but he was unlucky.'

If Goodyear learned a lesson at Imola, nobody else appeared to. In 1989 Berger hit that same concrete wall. Going into the fifth lap of the race, his Ferrari simply didn't get round the second part of the Tamburello curve. Instead, it just kept running wider and wider until it struck the concrete outer wall at an oblique angle, then slid down it for 300yd (275m), shedding parts as it went. Its motion threw up a cloud of grass and dirt, which suddenly took on the orange hue of fire.

To their eternal credit the rescue workers reacted at fantastic speed and were actually going into action even as the Ferrari was slithering at high speed on to the grass. The fire intervention crew arrived within 15 seconds, dead-heating with three marshals – Bruno Miniati, Paolo Verdi, and Gabriele Vivoli, already known as the 'Angels of Imola' after attending Piquet two years earlier. This time they would save a life.

Within 23 seconds the fire had been contained. By the time the race had been red flagged, Berger had already been extricated and whisked away to the medical centre.

Again, Dernie had taken measurements and made some calculations. 'I measured the skid marks, relative to the wall, and he was at a sort of 30 to 35° oblique angle, so it was the equivalent to a head-on of probably 65kph [40mph] or so. You have to guess to a certain extent because you don't know how much he was decelerating. It could have been less. But we know that in a 65kph head-on accident into a concrete wall, you're dead. There's almost nothing that can be done for you. So these accidents at very, very high speed are luckily oblique angles and the car goes skidding down the track dissipating energy over a very considerable period of time. They look spectacular but the peak gs aren't that high. The very bad accidents are the ones that are over in fractions of a second.'

Thierry Boutsen later said he'd seen one of the Ferrari's front wings go flying off just before the impact. Ferrari technical director John Barnard made a painstaking analysis, and concluded that Berger had subjected the front wings to forces with which they had not been designed to cope. He suggested that one had sheared at its root as a result of continual impacts as Berger ran over kerbs. When the wing sheared as Gerhard was going through Tamburello, there was nothing he could do about the sudden, and terminal, understeer. Like Senna he would be carried into the wall but, unlike Ayrton, luck rode with him.

Within minutes of his miraculous extraction Berger was examined in the medical centre, undergoing the usual scans and X-rays. He was then transferred to the Maggiore Hospital in Bologna, having sustained nothing worse than a broken rib, a fractured shoulder blade, some painful chemical burns to his body, burns to his palms, and a severe shaking. Being Berger, he discharged himself in the morning.

'I remember thinking that a front tyre had failed, so I went hard on the brakes until I left the track,' he recalls. 'Then I took my hands off the wheel, tucked them under my armpits and pulled my legs up as far as I could. For the first few minutes after the impact I remember thinking: "I'm not sure I want to drive one of these again …", but by the time I was in the ambulance I began wondering whether I might be fit enough to race at Monaco …'

In Alboreto's case his shunt at

Tamburello happened in testing the week before the 1991 race when his Footwork-Porsche's nose wing broke off. 'The car arrived across the kerbs and hit the wall at a very shallow angle, and then ran along the wall, sort of destroying itself,' recalls designer Alan Jenkins. 'It was similar to Berger's accident, because we weren't sure whether Michele had run over a kerb prior to that, so we had to do a fair bit of looking around. The car stood up to it pretty well, but the accident went on forever. It was almost a true lateral impact. Certainly it was one where, if you take the new regulations introduced after Senna's accident, they would have helped. The photos show that Michele's body and head protruded a long way from the side of the car and it was only a matter of inches from the wall.'

Not until 1994 would something finally be done, by which time it was too late.

Perhaps the accident that most savagely demonstrated the folly on the lack of run-off area in the pre-Senna era was Martin Donnelly's at Jerez in 1990. The Ulsterman's Lotus broke something in its front suspension during practice for the Spanish GP. The author was an eyewitness as the car speared into the Armco barrier at undiminished speed and simply blew into fragments. The largest was the engine and gearbox and rear suspension package, but the biggest of the rest was the remains of the seat, which clung to Martin's shoulders like a schoolboy's rucksack as his prone form lay crumpled in the middle of the track. It was quite the most serious accident F1 had seen since de Angelis's, worse insofar as the whole car had simply flown to pieces. Everyone in the paddock was horrified as television screens suddenly flashed to Donnelly's image, for no driver had been flung from his car since the days before seat belts.

It was the disintegration of the Lotus that actually saved his life, however, for its absolute destruction absorbed the

Gerhard Berger admits that he considered quitting even while he was having his fiery accident at Imola in 1989, but after a very impressive rescue effort by the marshals the Austrian would soon think again. (Sutton)

fearsome kinetic energy. Thankfully he recovered after a long convalescence, but though he actually drove a Jordan in an emotionally-charged comeback some years later, his Grand Prix career was over.

Two other accidents stand out as signposts for the work F1 still had to do to get its house in order. Donnelly survived by the grace of God. So did Philippe Streiff, but the Frenchman's accident and subsequent lack of suitable treatment, at a test in Rio early in 1989, remains one of the most unfortunate episodes in the sport's chequered past.

Streiff actually got himself out of his upturned AGS after crashing it heavily, but had sustained a neck injury following the collapse of the rollover hoop. He actually walked under his own power to the medical centre, where he was fitted with a cervical collar and had a gash to his leg attended to under local anaesthetic. At that time his spinal cord showed full function.

Later he was transferred to hospital where doctors diagnosed dislocation of his neck. A number of unfortunate decisions, made with his best interests at heart, led to a delay in operating to rectify the dislocation. During the day Strieff gradually began to lose movement and feeling, and in one of the sport's most tragic incidents became an irreversible quadriplegic.

At Spa in 1993 Alex Zanardi discovered the shortcomings of Eau Rouge's run-off areas when he crashed his Lotus 107 following a malfunction in his car's active suspension. The impact was so hard that the Italian's head broke the dashboard where the stretch in the seat belts allowed him to move forward, and he was out of racing until the following season. But still Formula One rolled on, apparently satisfied that everything was under control. It would take Ayrton Senna's death to bring about overdue change.

* * *

Even today, speculation surrounds the precise causes of the accidents which claimed the lives of Ayrton Senna and Roland Ratzenberger at Imola that ill-starred weekend in 1994.

The Austrian was killed 17 minutes into the second qualifying session on Saturday afternoon when his Simtek went straight on into a concrete wall on the outside of the very fast Villeneuve right-hander which follows Tamburello. The corner was so-named after a sizeable accident that Gilles Villeneuve had there.

The Brazilian died on the seventh lap of the Grand Prix itself when his Rothmans Williams failed to negotiate the Tamburello corner itself, which in those days was an easy 305kph (190mph) left-hander that, despite its speed, posed no particular problem even for the least experienced drivers. The race had continued behind the safety car for five laps following a startline accident involving JJ Lehto's Benetton and Pedro Lamy's Lotus.

Senna's Williams understeered wide until it hit the concrete retaining wall before bouncing back and coming to rest minus its right-hand wheels. He was slumped in the cockpit and received prolonged medical attention by the side of the track as the race was red-flagged.

'We took his helmet off and he was alive and breathing,' Professor Watkins remembers. 'He had a good pulse. But there was evidence of serious brain damage. His pupils were fully blown and he had no reactions whatsoever. He was like a doll, really,' he added gently. 'I couldn't believe how light he felt when I lifted him.'

The accident happened around 2.07pm, but because of his copious bleeding and his other injuries it was 2.31 before Senna was finally taken to the air ambulance that had been landed on the straight between Tamburello and Villeneuve. He was then transferred directly to the Maggiore Hospital in Bologna. On the way he suffered a cardiac arrest. To all intents and purposes Ayrton Senna had died at the moment of impact, but though he was brain dead at the accident scene his heart still kept beating for another four hours. Finally, at 6.40 that evening, he was pronounced dead.

Ratzenberger was also slumped in the cockpit of his shattered Simtek when it finally slid to rest at Tosa, 200m (656ft) from the point of impact. As they had been at the shunt which befell the Brazilian driver Rubens Barrichello earlier that weekend, medical and safety services reached Ratzenberger's car virtually before it had come to rest. But though Roland received lengthy attention and was later declared dead at 2.15pm, eight minutes after reaching Maggiore Hospital, he too was clinically dead at the accident scene.

The left front wheel had come back into the cockpit, inflicting severe chest and abdominal injuries. He had also sustained a serious head injury and a thoracic spinal injury, and was kept alive by cardio respiration resuscitation the moment medics arrived at the scene. His heart was still beating in the helicopter, but he was dead on arrival at the Maggiore Hospital.

In the immediate aftermath of the Senna accident speculation flared that he had picked up debris from the Lehto/Lamy accident. There was widespread anger that the race had been allowed to continue under the safety car instead of being stopped to allow course workers to do a meticulous clean-up job. However, Goodyear representatives were later able to examine all four tyres from the Williams, and though there were many cuts they were able to rule out debris damage as a possible cause.

Other lines of enquiry centred on suggestions that the FW16's steering column had broken where it had been shortened and then rewelded, or that the car bottomed over the bumps on the inside of the corner and was thus thrown off line.

The evidence of the onboard camera on Michael Schumacher's Benetton, which was following closely, tended to support the latter theory. Schumacher said: 'I saw that his car was already touching quite a lot at the back on the lap before. The car was very nervous in this corner, and he nearly lost it then. On the next lap he did lose it. The car touched with the rear skids, went a bit sideways, and he just lost it.'

Frank Dernie, then with Benetton, pointed out that the laps run behind the safety car would seriously have affected

Shortly before Martin Donnelly's near-fatal accident in a Lotus in Spain in 1990, his teammate Derek Warwick escaped unharmed from this high-speed roll at Monza. (Formula One Pictures)

The worst weekend in F1's history began at Imola in 1994 with this horrific practice accident for Rubens Barrichello, at Variante Bassa. (Sutton)

the ride heights of the cars, since the tyres' temperatures, and therefore pressures, had fallen well below the intended set-up, which would have relied upon the tyres operating at full temperature. Other drivers also voiced their opinion that this could have been a crucial factor.

'Tyre temperatures and pressures are absolutely crucial on today's Formula One cars,' Senna's team-mate Damon Hill said. 'In fact, if for any reason we had to do so many slow laps in testing as we did behind the safety car, we'd come right back in for a fresh set of properly heated tyres. It's that serious. They should have stopped the race after that first lap.'

As Ratzenberger's Simtek exited Tamburello, televisual evidence indicated that it was okay; but just as he approached the advertising bridge that crosses the track before Villeneuve something could clearly be seen to fly off the car. There was speculation that it was part of a front wing, such as the endplate or the second tier of the wing structure, or part of a sidepod. However, Jean Alesi was spectating at that point and said that he thought a front wing dropped down and folded under the wheel. It was surmised by the team that Ratzenberger had damaged the wing running over a kerb the previous lap. Roland was a helpless passenger as his car ploughed into the wall at a sharp angle.

These accidents inevitably raised further angry protests about the lack of run-off areas, just as had Martin Donnelly's four years earlier, and the Tamburello incidents involving Piquet, Berger, and Alboreto. Since Berger's accident the grass had been replaced by a concrete strip, but with the Santerno river running behind the wall the organisers had always fallen back on the excuse that they had no room to develop a run-off area. At Villeneuve there was only grass before the concrete wall. There were no gravel traps.

There were other issues, too. One of the great mysteries in recent F1 history was what had happened to the errant wheel from Lamy's Lotus, which had struck the back of Lehto's stalled Benetton at the start of the race. In the midst of all the drama of Senna's death, that aspect tended to go unresolved. Some imputed a sinister motive to this lack of disclosure, especially since it was potentially an even more explosive aspect given the risk to the spectating public. Once the wheel had been severed from Lamy's car, it bounced on the track and actually cleared the main grandstand to the left before bounding into a group of people.

'It injured four people,' FIA president Max Mosley admitted during an interview for this book in February 2000. 'It seriously injured one man, who had to have brain surgery. That whole thing was more serious for racing. Senna knew he was taking a risk and everyone else knew that he was. But the man in the crowd who has just paid for his seat ought to be able to sit there in peace. The fellow was seriously hurt, but that was completely lost in the panic about Senna. I think he is all right now, but the other three people fortunately only had minor injuries.'

Then there was the incident in which, incredibly, the Larrousse team released a delayed Erik Comas from the pits even though the race had been red-flagged, so that the hapless Frenchman arrived at racing speed at the scene of Senna's accident.

Finally, there was the incident close to the end of the race in which Alboreto's Minardi had struck and injured Minardi and Lotus mechanics when it lost a wheel in the pit lane. That was the incident which ultimately led to the pit lane speed limits currently in force.

Back in 1994, in the aftermath of Imola, Mosley outlined his view of the specific aims of what was still at that time called the FISA. 'Our number one priority has to be the safety of the public; number two the safety of the drivers. There is an argument for us slowing the cars down in the corners; in fact I think it's an overwhelming one.'

He appreciated not just the need to be seen to be doing something, but also the need to put long-term changes into motion. 'The Technical Working Group was really just engineers working under the auspices of the Concorde Agreement,' he says, 'so that was already running on some form or other. But we set up a research group under Sid Watkins, called the Expert Advisory Group, to try to bring together the different elements. The task was to look everywhere: aerospace, the military, ground traffic, everywhere you could think of for elements that might be useful in improving safety in Formula One. Because the feeling was that the days of making obvious improvements were finished, and the thing had really to be done more scientifically. That really has

Forever fated to rest in Ayrton Senna's shadow, Roland Ratzenberger was killed when his Simtek crashed during qualifying on the Saturday afternoon. (Sutton)

worked very well. We've got all sorts of people involved. There are certain permanent members, but you can get anyone along who's an expert on something.'

Mosley rightly read public opinion, particularly in Italy where there had been the predictable outcry against racing that had last been heard after the Mille Miglia tragedy in 1957. But there had also been questions asked in the Italian parliament about the future of racing, and these made Mosley's ears prick up. Karl Wendlinger's accident in Monaco a fortnight later merely exacerbated an already tense situation.

'After Senna there was this tremendous "Something's got to be done" reaction. It was very annoying in a way, because I had always seen being a racing driver as being like a test pilot. There is a distinct risk in Formula One. I don't know what happened in Senna's case, but even if you took the Italian hypothesis that something broke, that the steering broke, so what? Things break all the time. We know perfectly well that cars break – and I'm not speaking specifically of Senna's now – because they are built on the limits of technology. And the objective is not to stop them breaking, which is impossible, but to stop anybody getting hurt when they do break.

'You know that cars are going to go off the road for whatever reason, driver error, mechanic's error, engineer's error, act of God. There are a lot of things that can cause a car to crash. Our job is to try and make sure that nobody gets hurt.

'So that reaction was completely irrational, but nevertheless it was no good saying that when we were dealing with the media. There was pressure from all sides. That was containable, and beginning to die down, until Wendlinger had

Moments before his fatal accident, Ayrton Senna leads Michael Schumacher and Gerhard Berger behind the safety car, which was deployed after an accident on the start/finish line. (Sutton)

his accident at Monaco two weeks later. Then it began to get more serious because a lot of the big companies behind Formula One were beginning to question their involvement. Not because the people that we see at the Formula One races were questioning it, but every big company that is in Formula One is spending a lot of money, and there are always people on the Board who are against it. And they then started to have much more ammunition. One or two of the big car companies were saying to me that we had better do something, or else. So that's why we came up with all the changes.'

The way that the FISA achieved this was to get all the teams to agree to these changes, and though he had to be careful to bear in mind the nuances and clauses of the Concorde Agreement, these were tough times so Mosley got tough. 'I told the teams that if they did not agree, then we would not run the World Championship. In those days I could do that under the Concorde Agreement. And that in the end got them to the table, and we then pushed through all the changes.'

There was a significant degree of opportunism in Mosley's actions, and many suspected that he seized a bad situation to force through longer term plans – that he might otherwise have had trouble implementing – to reduce cornering speeds. Not for nothing does he have a reputation as a consummate politician.

'The thing is that the teams were saying it was irrational, completely stupid, which I am fully prepared to agree that it was. But you had to do something. You had to be seen to be doing something. But at the same time, I was quietly pleased because I had wanted to do something to slow the cars down for some time. I started to see that it was really dangerous, and this gave me the opportunity to do that.

'What we did was to use the momentum of public opinion to push through a lot of changes that should have been pushed through already. The truth of it is that they were not because of Senna, necessarily, but because they were necessary anyway.'

It was the age-old situation, of course. The teams saw one picture, Mosley saw another, perhaps larger. The teams were involved day-to-day, Mosley, as the frontline recipient of the flak, could step back slightly. History indicates that in this particular instance, he took the right decisions. Who remembers now that questions were being asked in the Italian Parliament about the desirability of motorsport? By nipping that in the bud, by being seen to be doing something, Formula One kept its house in order and the sense of shock and outrage that had come in the wake of Senna's death gradually lessened.

There was another key point in Mosley's actions. Because he is a politician, he thinks like one, and was well aware of the way things were moving in the European Parliament. It wasn't that you needed genius clairvoyance to see the direction of the wind, but the teams were too busy being teams to pay heed to what might come along in five years' time. But Mosley could foresee a time when environmentalist lobbies started to give racing a rough ride.

'If the environmentalist lobby gets stronger, as it will, I think in the long-term motorsport has to be sold on positive benefits to the environment because it speeds up research and development,' he said in May that year. 'So long as the regulations are directed in the right way, or push research in the right direction, that's okay on the one side. On the other side, it creates an atmosphere in which it's not the thing to go quickly on the roads. If you want to go out and go fast, you compete. That ethos will gradually start to come across. Those are the two planks on which we can continue to justify motorsport in an increasingly environmentally conscious society.'

Chapter 10

Triumphs – and tragedies

If the safety facilities hadn't been so good at Imola, with Professor Watkins getting to the scene so quickly, Rubens would have been dead as well.

Gary Anderson

By the end of the 'seventies more attention was being paid to safety in F1 car design. Rules in 1976 called for safety structures around the dashboard bulkhead and the pedals, while pedalbox protection was more stringently defined a year later, and by 1978 cars were required to have a bulkhead between the driver and the front rollhoop, in order further to strengthen the chassis. Then 1979 brought yet bigger cockpit openings and further improved fire extinguisher systems.

These changes came as technological fertility continued to boost lap speeds. Ground effect and turbocharging made their debuts in 1977, the one dramatically enhancing cornering speeds, the other boosting engine power by an equally alarming rate.

When air moves under a racing car it becomes constricted, and therefore its speed increases and its pressure drops. This creates a low pressure area beneath the car. The higher pressure acting on the top surface thus exerts a downward pressure while the lower area creates suction, so the net effect is an increase in downforce. In the early days, designers sought to enhance this further by including longitudinal skirts between the side wheels of their cars, so that air was channelled the full length of the undertray before being carefully exhausted at the rear via the upturned tray known as the diffuser. Later, to take into account bumps on the track, designers came up with skirts that could move up and down with the car's suspension. The trouble was, from the safety point of view, that sliding skirts sometimes stuck in the up position. The first the driver knew of it was when he had bravely committed his car to some mind-numbing speed in a given corner, only to discover that his car was no longer generating the downforce it had the previous lap when the skirt was behaving properly. Accidents were frequent.

Eventually, in the early 'eighties, sliding skirts were outlawed, so designers sought to minimise pitch change of their cars by making the suspension rock hard. Eventually it would get to the stage where much of the flexure in a car was either in the sidewalls of the tyres or in the suspension arms themselves, rather than in any springing medium. This did not help from the safety point of view either, because it made some cars more nervous, especially in the wet.

The regulations called for yet stronger chassis for 1981, when the expression 'survival cell' first came into common parlance, and chassis had to incorporate an extension ahead of the driver's feet. Gradually, he was being relocated further back in the chassis, after some years in which some designers had sited him precariously close to the nose.

It could be argued that another enemy of safety was the qualifying tyre, so called because it lasted little more than the one flying lap a driver would need in qualifying to set his quickest lap. This had the effect of obliging drivers to make the most of their 'quickie', and in precisely the circumstances that he had so often predicted the French-Canadian star Gilles Villeneuve had been killed at Zolder in May 1982 while trying to go faster. Coming across Jochen Mass's slower March, Villeneuve made the split-second decision to go one way round it, to preserve his hot lap, at the very moment that Mass moved in the same direction to make room for him. Villeneuve's Ferrari took off over Mass's rear wheel.

The Ferrari landed nose-first, tearing off its footbox and catapulting out Villeneuve who was still attached to his seat. At one stage, either during the ejection or when he landed, he broke his neck at the base of the skull.

'He was flacid like a doll,' Professor Watkins recalled. 'There was a heartbeat and we ventilated him and took him first to the medical centre and then by helicopter to hospital in Liege. The X-rays showed that the neck dislocation was so high that there was not any possibility of recovery.' He was kept on life support until his wife Joanne arrived, and then it was switched off.

Later in that extraordinary season, Villeneuve's team-mate Didier Pironi had a similar accident after he somersaulted over Alain Prost's Renault in murky conditions in Hockenheim. Serious leg injuries ended his F1 career.

Both Ferraris used a method of construction that had become popular towards the end of the 'seventies, with

Robin Herd's McLaren M2B of 1966 was one of the first F1 cars to use composites in its chassis, the underrated designer choosing the Mallite balsa wood sandwich. (Phipps/Sutton)

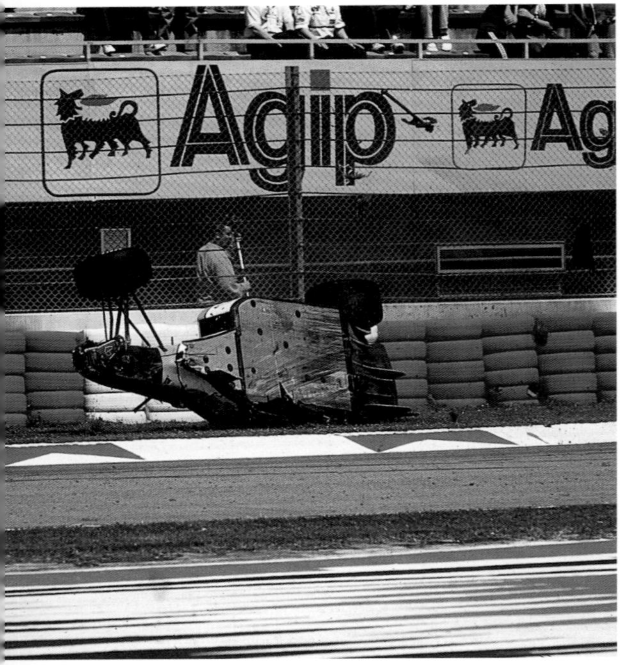

Barrichello's Jordan lies on its side after his fearful practice accident at the 1994 San Marino Grand Prix. (Formula One Pictures)

cars – such as the ground effect Lotus 78 and the McLaren M26 – which harked back to Robin Herd's Mallite composite McLaren M2A of 1966. Instead of sheet aluminium they made use of honeycomb aluminium. This comprised two sheets of lighter gauge aluminium which were bonded either side of aluminium foil honeycomb to form a light but extremely rigid sandwich. But even this had been superseded by another method which would revolutionise F1 design and safety: the carbon fibre composite monocoque.

Composite materials were hardly new by the standards of the aerospace industry, and indeed they had been used before in F1 applications. In the 'thirties, offbeat multi-millionaire Howard Hughes's infamous *Spruce Goose* flying boat had used a plastic-impregnated wood material. But the real development of composite materials gained momentum in the late 'fifties, partly as a result of the search by America's space programme for light, strong and stable materials. The composites that were created were then horribly expensive. But as the price fell they began to find their way into F1, where they had appeared by the mid-'seventies.

One of their first applications was in the rear wing strut on German driver Rolf Stommelen's ill-fated Embassy Hill GH1 which briefly led the Spanish GP at Montjuich Park in 1975. Unfortunately, that was also the component that broke, and which pitched the car over the barriers, where it killed a photographer and several spectators and left Stommelen with broken legs. Brabham designer Gordon Murray was also au fait with the benefits of such materials, and, having successfully introduced carbon brakes to the hefty BT45 Alfa Romeo-powered Brabham in 1976, began to use carbon fibre in other areas of the chassis. The BT49, which appeared late in 1979, used a fair bit of it.

The first pukka carbon fibre composite F1 cars were the McLaren MP4/1, which was designed by John Barnard and initially had its chassis built by Hercules in Salt Lake City; and Colin Chapman's ill-starred Lotus 88. The latter actually used two chassis – one for the driver, engine, and running gear, the other to carry aerodynamic control surfaces. Because its career was dogged by controversy that led to it being banned, it was often overlooked that the 88 was an all-composite design.

The McLaren MP4/1 weighed in at a remarkable 20kg (44lb), which was some 40 per cent lighter than comparable aluminium sandwich cars, and though it was a great deal more expensive it was also significantly stronger. This was proven time and again by the erratic second driver Andrea de Cesaris, who appeared to have taken upon himself the role of crash tester and endured an embarrassing number of accidents during a heady year without doing himself any noticeable harm. After a string of good results, John Watson brought his MP4/1 home first in the 1981 British Grand Prix at Silverstone.

The success of the McLaren prompted an immediate rash of emulation. By 1982 Gerard Ducarouge's Alfa Romeo 182 and Rory Byrne's Toleman TG183 were both composite chassis, and a year later Austrian designer Gustav Brunner made another small but significant breakthrough when his ATS D9 proved to be the first composite chassis whose panels actually comprised the external body panels. This enterprising step reduced weight further, to 17.6kg (39lb), and set a trend that is universal today. That same year Brabham, Ferrari, Renault and others switched to composite chassis, though it would be 1985 before Williams had enough faith in the new materials (and its understanding of them) to build its first.

At the end of 1982 FISA president Jean-Marie Balestre controversially outlawed ground effect aerodynamics and introduced new rules which called for cars to have flat undersides instead of shaped undercar venturis to create downforce. Skirts were also banned.

The new chassis designs created whole new areas of research for F1 engineering teams and stress analysis became an important new field. Working with composites is now done in-house by almost all the racing teams and they lead the world in such technology. Laminators lay carbon 'cloth' impregnated with resin in female moulds of the planned chassis. The cloths have to be laid in the correct orientation and at the correct thickness so that all the loadings, calculated by the designers, will be in the right directions. The laid-up chassis is then baked in a vacuum autoclave.

No amount of medical help could save Ayrton Senna, after his Williams-Renault hit the wall at Tamburello. (Sutton)

The inherent strength of carbon fibre, allied to ductile materials such as the Kevlar seen in bullet-proof vests, brought a massive step forward in motor racing safety. Now, by careful decision on lay-up methods and wall thicknesses, designers could create cars that would deform progressively, the way they wanted them to, in heavy impacts.

Since 1978 designers had helped to reduce fire risk further by siting all the fuel in a central tank behind the driver, where it was far better protected. The first car to do this was the ill-starred Amon AF101 of 1974, which was a dismal flop, but Chapman took up the idea for his super-successful Lotus 79 in 1978 and the idea soon caught on. By 1984 the FISA rules made a central fuel tank mandatory.

John Watson was the first man to win a race with a carbon fibre chassis, and he was also the first man to destruction-test one when he got his McLaren on to a kerb at Monza and separated its engine and chassis in a heavy impact. It was not just impressive that the Ulsterman could walk away, but also that the car did not catch fire. That was a tribute to another safety breakthrough, the one-way fuel valve. If a fuel pipe was torn away in an accident, the strategically placed valves would shut off fuel flow.

There were problems with composite chassis at times – notably in the 1984 Monaco GP when both new Renaults of Derek Warwick and Patrick Tambay crashed at the first corner and suffered serious chassis failures on relatively slow-speed impact with the barriers. Two years later, at Brands Hatch, Jacques Laffite suffered ankle-breaking injuries in accidents. But composite chassis improved as designers understood the materials better. And as we saw in the previous chapter, Nelson Piquet, Gerhard Berger, and Michele Alboreto all escaped relatively unharmed from heavy impacts with the Tamburello wall at Imola. Indeed, seeing drivers escaping from wrecked composite cars would become so routine over the years that it was easy to forget that in the old days of aluminium monocoques most of them would have become names on F1's roll-call of tragedy.

Colin Chapman's 1977 Lotus 78 was innovative not just for its ground effect aerodynamics, but also for its extensive use of honeycomb aluminium. (Phipps/Sutton)

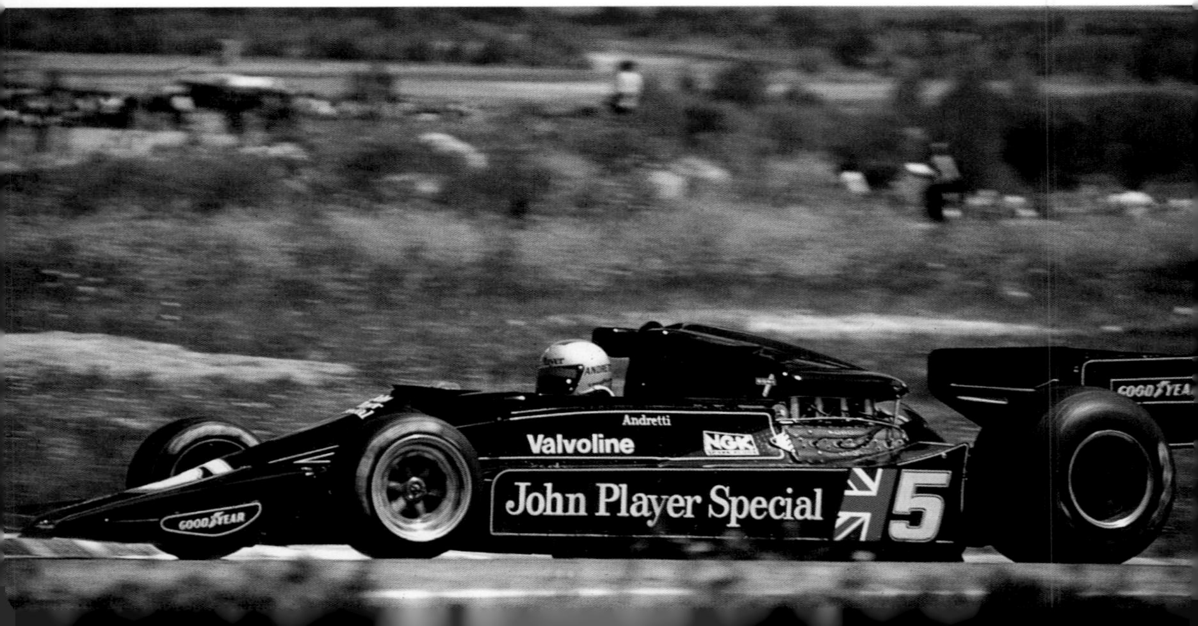

Alan Jenkins, the technical director of Footwork in 1991, gave a graphic insight into the incident where Alboreto's Footwork-Porsche crashed at Tamburello. 'The front wing snapped off and he went off into the concrete wall there quite heavily. The problem with side impacts is where the wishbones end up. We had one go through the tub but that's very difficult to do anything about. It went in and sliced underneath his thigh, just missing him. It helps that today we have all moved the driver back, which pretty much guarantees that the thighs are going to be okay. Michele had stitches in his leg, but he was otherwise okay. He is remarkably together, Michele, in situations like that. Certainly his head remained pretty clear. He got out of the thing himself, and there was a picture of him standing next to it. That to me was the most incredible thing! The last picture in the sequence is the most amazing one. There's this trail of destruction, and then there's the driver, out of the wreckage, looking at it!'

'I was knocked about a lot, but basically, apart from a couple of stitches in my leg, I just felt like I'd been beaten up,' recalled Alboreto.

'One single accident is pretty straightforward,' continued Jenkins, 'but the difficult part is always a secondary impact, whose further effects are almost impossible to plan for. There was a front and a rear impact because it broke the gearbox and there was a gearbox oil fire.

'It's the classic thing for a designer, isn't it? We've all had the odd car destroyed, and certainly in those days I was quite close to Michele. That's the worst part of the business, really. Being on the edge of that sort of situation. That's half the reason why us people on the Technical Working Group get hot under the collar, really. I think everybody has their own concerns about safety for such reasons, but after Ayrton's accident it would become a joint concern.'

Hand-in-glove with the breakthroughs in materials had come another revolution that shaped the F1 that we know today. Balestre introduced a mandatory frontal crash test in 1985 to help safeguard drivers in foreseeable accidents, and opened up the avenue to raise safety standards further. Most are conducted, under FIA supervision, at the Cranfield Impact Centre in Bedfordshire. The first test was made with a nose cone attached to a rig and crashed head-on at 12m/s (39ft/s) into a solid barrier. The purpose was to ensure that structures were strong enough to offer adequate protection to the driver's ankles and legs.

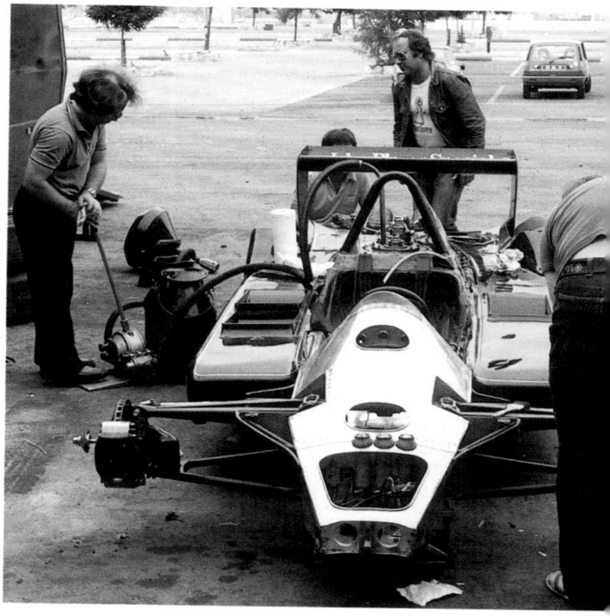

The 1978 Lotus 79 took the 78's concept another stage further forward. (Formula One Pictures)

In 1988 came the static load test on both sides of the survival cell, known in the business as the squeeze or crush test and designed to ensure that the monocoque will provide adequate protection against side impact. Over the years the tests have been extended to include a number of points along the tub, at the driver's hip level, at the front bulkhead, and on the underside.

Two years later came a static load test on the side of the nose, known as the 'push-off test', designed to make sure that the nose, with its energy-absorbing deformable structure, would remain intact during a glancing type of blow, as if the car has struck a barrier at a relatively shallow angle.

1991 brought a static load test on the top of the main roll structure, designed to assess the ability of the car to withstand inversion without its rollover hoop distorting or breaking under load.

All of the tests are assessed regularly, and are frequently revised in the never ending search for greater safety.

Despite all of this, the 'nineties began with Martin Donnelly's fearsome accident in Jerez, where his Lotus collided with an Armco barrier when a suspension component failed. There was an outcry over the way in which the carbon fibre composite chassis disintegrated, as described in Chapter 9, but Donnelly's friend Gary Anderson, who was Jordan's technical director at the time, offered a different view.

McLaren's Tyler Alexander and Mr Cosworth, Keith Duckworth, admire the lightweight structure that is McLaren's carbon fibre MP4/1 chassis. (Phipps/Sutton)

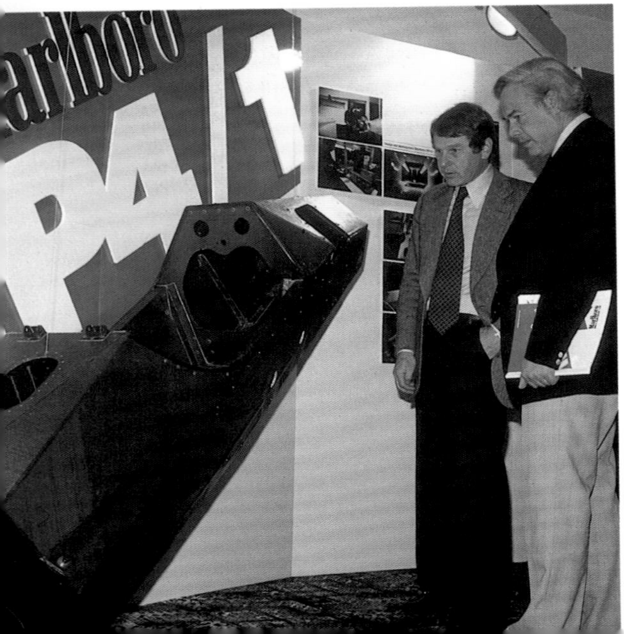

'If you looked at Martin's chassis,' he said, 'you could figure out that what happened was going to happen. That chassis was going to explode, because of its structure. Now the regulations have changed, and they're not far off what we proposed in the aftermath of that, via the Technical Working Group. I think the lay-up of that particular car's composites had a lot to do with it. I'm not saying they were wrong to do it like that, the regulations were like that and they went as far as they could.'

The Lotus 102 also used pullrod front suspension, where the dampers were mounted horizontally at the base of the chassis. This too attracted criticism because it is thought that Donnelly bottomed the car heavily a little earlier while hammering over the chicane, and that the resultant impact compromised the pullrod. This, it was suggested, failed as Donnelly turned into a right-hand corner that had no run-off area.

The fact that Martin survived lulled some into a false sense of security, and until 30 April 1994 the F1 world believed that cars had reached an acceptable ratio of performance to safety. It wasn't that they had become complacent, the way, perhaps, that they had become about circuit safety. But the pendulum had swung in favour of enhanced car safety and great strides had been taken. Many drivers had escaped nasty-looking accidents, and television cameras habitually seemed to capture them levering themselves out of shattered machinery and walking jauntily away after another brush with death. Designers felt that they were keeping pace with safety requirements, perhaps even keeping slightly ahead, because so much effort was being invested.

But it all goes back to the point about safety being a statistical science. Lessons had been learned since the last spate of serious accidents, and changes had been implemented. The ensuing statistics had suggested that the changes had been successful. They had reacted swiftly, sensibly and, it seemed, successfully. What else could they have done?

On 29 April Rubens Barrichello had done a 'wall-of-death' at Imola's Variante Bassa corner, having lost control after slightly misplacing his Jordan going into the corner. He was fortunate to escape with little more than a shaking and a broken nose. There was widespread relief throughout the paddock, and not a few words of congratulation that F1 was now such a safe sport that a driver could make a mistake like that and get away with it. And they were right. It was a safe sport.

It took the death of Roland Ratzenberger, the following day, to highlight that it was not safe enough. The Austrian had driven heavily over a kerb and damaged the front wing of his car, but decided to carry on rather than stop in the pits to have his Simtek examined. The wing broke as he turned in to the very fast Villeneuve curve, which swept right just prior to the Tosa hairpin. He had no chance as the car failed to make the corner and crashed at very high speed into the outer wall. The impact tore most of the left-hand side out of the Simtek chassis. Ratzenberger thus became F1's first fatality since Elio de Angelis.

F1 is a sport that focuses on the successful and the famous. The Ratzenberger tragedy left the circus quiet and introspective, but nobody was reaching for the rule book to start changing the regulations. It may be a harsh comment, but had there been but one tragedy at Imola that weekend, nothing would have changed. Roland's death would have been put down to his own misfortune in deciding not to pull into the pits.

Everything changed the next day, when Ayrton Senna was killed on the seventh lap of the San Marino Grand Prix. What made his death even more shocking than Jim Clark's 26 years earlier, was that millions of television viewers the world over had seen it happen, 'live' on their screens. The sport lost its yardstick, a man who had seemed superhuman. As with Clark, it was completely unthinkable.

The Simtek's chassis had been severely compromised by the impact, which occurred at close to maximum speed, yet ironically the Williams withstood its impact extremely well. What killed Senna was not the impact, but the way that the right front wheel remained attached only by the steering arm, and was swept back up into the cockpit where it struck him on the head. In another irony, it was almost exactly what happened to BRM F1 driver Mike Spence while he was testing a Lotus turbine car at Indianapolis in May 1968.

Chillingly, Anderson believes that Barrichello might also have become a victim, but for the fast reaction of the rescue teams. 'If the safety facilities hadn't been so good at Imola, with Professor Watkins getting to the scene so quickly, Rubens would have been dead as well,' he said. 'He'd swallowed his tongue and was choking to death, but Sid got there and helped him.'

Prior to the blackest weekend in the sport's modern history, it seemed that F1 had beaten the old spectres, but Imola forced it to subject itself to the most searching scrutiny. The Italian authorities launched an immediate investigation that would grind on inconclusively for years, and as Brazil went into mourning the shockwaves began to ripple through the motorsport world.

Though the 'eighties had seen tremendous steps forward on the technological side, Formula One was now on the verge of the greatest investigation into its safety philosophies that it had ever known.

Chapter 11

Gallic bombast

Balestre was altruistic. He was always keen on safety;
I think he really minded when people got hurt.

Max Mosley, FIA president

As befits a man who went on to carve a reputation as one of the most controversial figures in motorsport, Jean-Marie Balestre was a colourful character.

Having enlisted in the French Army as a volunteer at the age of 19, he joined the Resistance after the fall of France in 1940, and his undercover work posing as a member of the French Waffen SS was to create a great deal of confusion following his return to France at the end of the war. It was always a very touchy subject with him, but he could boast of appropriate Resistance decorations, including initiation as a Chevalier of the Legion of Honour.

He began his career as a sub-editor at *Sport et Santé* and *l'Auto Journal*, the car magazine that he helped to establish with his friend Robert Hersant. He also worked as a layout artist for the latter. But his abiding interest in politics was reflected by his secretaryship of the LICA, the International League Against Racism. In time he moved on to become sub-editor and reporter at *Droit de Vivre*, LICA's own journal.

He and Hersant built an impressive publishing empire. Soon he appointed himself chief editor of *l'Auto Journal*, and later general manager. Subsequently he became administrator and then director of a range of titles, such as *Semaine du Monde*, *l'Oise Matin*, *Cahiers du Yachting*, *l'Eclair du Nates*, *Nord Matin*, and *Sport Auto*. Eventually he rose to become a director of Publiprint, an advertising agency; director of AGPI, the Press and Information Agency of the Press Group; and eventually managing director of the Hersant Press Group, which boasted 45 publications, 12 printing houses, a press agency, an advertising agency, and 50 radio stations.

Politics soon beckoned again, however, and by 1952 Balestre, a keen motorsport enthusiast, had founded the French Motor Sport Federation (FFSA). In 1959 he laid claim to founding the French national karting authority, which would soon be followed by Europe's International Karting Commission (the CIK), of which he made himself the founder and honorary president. Within seven years he had also founded a National Motorists' Association, the

Syndicat National des Automobilistes, and installed himself as its secretary general.

His career in publishing ran alongside these political diversions, and for the next 15 years he acted as president of the French National Weekly and Periodic Press Federation. He became secretary-general of the FFSA in 1968 and ascended to its presidency in 1973, but his greatest coup was to found the Federation Internationale du Sport Automobile (FISA) in 1978. As president of the FFSA he had become increasingly frustrated that the senior managers of the Federation Internationale de l'Automobile (FIA) appeared to have little interest in motorsport, which it governed at that time via the Commission Sportif Internationale (CSI). In 1978, therefore, he proposed the foundation of the FISA, which would be a sporting authority independent of the FIA. Naturally, he was its first president.

Balestre played his role to the full, revelling in his influence over the sport. And when he was elected president of the FIA itself in 1985 his pleasure knew few bounds as he lorded it over the 92 national automobile clubs that constituted its membership, together with their 72 million paid-up members.

Within two years of setting up the FISA, he became embroiled in a lengthy battle with Bernie Ecclestone and Max Mosley. The sport was in a state of flux, and Ecclestone and Mosley at the Formula One Constructors' Association (FOCA) quickly realised that the Frenchman's agenda centred upon wresting complete control from their hands and back into the governing body's. But when they proposed an independent series to the FIA's, to run outside the control of the FISA, they discovered that Balestre had strong allies in France.

The major sponsors, meanwhile, were becoming disquieted by the deteriorating relationship between the FISA and FOCA, and made their views clear. For a while Balestre laid low, but as 1980 came around, so the battle lines became ever more clearly drawn between the rival factions. Balestre and the FISA were on the side of what Enzo Ferrari and Balestre liked to refer to as the 'grandee' teams, those which manufactured their own chassis and engines: that meant Ferrari, Renault, Alfa Romeo, and Toleman. Ecclestone led the constructors

Tough, autocratic and frequently argumentative, former FIA president Jean-Marie Balestre was a passionate advocate for safety. (Formula One Pictures)

who made their own chassis but used proprietary engines and gearboxes. These, the grandees caustically dismissed as 'garagistes'. Even then, however, the handful of winning garagistes had more World Championships and GP victories to their credit than all of the grandees put together. This was partly because the British designers' development of ground effect aerodynamics had allowed them to keep pace as the grandees' powerful turbocharged engines rendered their faithful off-the-shelf Ford Cosworth DFV engines obsolete.

Nobody needed a war, but Balestre was determined to do away with the downforce-inducing skirts that were decimating lap times year after year. He argued that they posed a safety risk if, as frequently happened when a driver ran over a kerb, they stuck in the up position and thus dramatically reduced download. He also sought to emasculate FOCA further by taking control of television's growing interest in motorsport. After a bloody battle – and FOCA's unsuccessful attempt to stage its own South African GP with fully skirted cars on 7 February 1981 – the two sides sat down around a table under the watchful eye of Enzo Ferrari, and peace was finally hammered out. Both sides realised that they needed each other, and face-saving measures abounded.

Balestre succeeded in maintaining his ban on skirts; Ecclestone, ever the shrewd and far-sighted businessman, retained control over the lucrative television rights. Under the terms of the compromise document which ushered in the peace, the Concorde Agreement, Ecclestone and Mosley guaranteed that the FIA would get considerable revenue from the sale of these rights, but these would be marketed under a long-term agreement by Ecclestone and FOCA. It was partly because the sums involved impressed the FIA so much that Balestre succeeded ageing Prince Paul Metternich as its president within four years of the peace deal being finalised. 'I am now more important than Kennedy. I am the world's only triple president,' announced Balestre.

By the end of the decade, however, serious questions were being asked of his dictatorial handling of headline issues, such as the collision in the 1989 Japanese GP at Suzuka of McLaren team-mates and World Championship rivals Ayrton Senna and Alain Prost. The latter retired on the spot after he and Senna had come together at the chicane; Senna rejoined, pitted for a new nose, and then fought his way back past new leader Alessandro Nannini. But in the very hour of what seemed to be his greatest victory yet, the Stewards disqualified Senna for rejoining the race in an improper manner by missing out the chicane, even though he had clearly derived no benefit from standing still for some time before rejoining. Prost went on to seal his third title in the final race in Adelaide.

Senna was furious, and openly accused Balestre of manipulating the championship in the favour of his fellow countryman. As a result the Brazilian was only granted the superlicence that he needed to race in 1990 after 'apologising' to Balestre.

Despite such incidents, Balestre continued to rule the FISA with an iron fist until Max Mosley emerged to challenge him at the end of 1991. Unknown to Balestre, Mosley had long been running a covert campaign to win votes from smaller clubs all over the world rather than relying purely on the support of the big European bodies. In the big showdown, Balestre was outmanoeuvred and defeated by 43 votes to 29.

He was 70 years old and had already suffered a heart attack in December 1986 and had since undergone a number of heart operations. His defeat marked the beginning of the end for him as a key player on the international motorsport stage, though he remained FIA

President until 1993, when he offered no opposition to Mosley's plan to merge the FIA with the FISA. Indeed, he gave Mosley his support. Mosley reciprocated by bestowing upon him the face-saving presidency of the FIA Senate, a role which allowed him to withdraw with dignity.

Balestre's unsuccessful fight against Mosley had highlighted the man's view of himself, and his penchant for rambling. 'Formula One is part of the Star System,' he declared. 'This is not my fault but that of the media. Formula One beats all the records, with 17 billion television viewers.

'It is the locomotive of international motorsport and glorifies the FIA World Championship. Therefore Mr Mosley will permit me to paraphrase good old Henry IV of France who, although a Protestant, declared: "To be King in Paris is worth going to a Catholic mass." I say for my part that the success of Formula One is worth a few sacrifices – let's not be jealous of this.'

Egged on by the majority of Colin Chapman's rivals, Balestre waged war against the highly controversial twin-chassis Lotus 88 in 1981, seen here during another fruitless attempt to race at Silverstone for the British GP. (Phipps/Sutton)

There was more. 'I will not say – as my opponent did with immodesty – I am the right man for the job, because, with the exceptions of a few new presidents, you all know me. You have all given me your confidence and esteem.

'We cannot accept that in his letter of candidature Mr Mosley treats the president of the FIA and the FISA with contempt and accuses him of being incapable, of trading on his influence, and of incompetence.

'I owe my fortune neither to inheritance nor to marriage. I am a self-made man and I ended the essential part of my professional career as the head of one of the most important press groups in Europe, with 12,000 employees including 2,000 journalists. Believe me, examining the accounts of 42 different companies, handling difficult conflicts with workers of journalists' unions, was a domain infinitely more complex and demanding. In comparison with the triple presidency of the FIA, the FISA and the FFSA, it seems like a croquet match.'

One of the foundations of Mosley's successful bid for the presidency of the FISA and the FIA had been his contention that Balestre got too involved. 'Balestre goes to Grands Prix and gets involved in whatever controversy there is,' Mosley said. 'If there is a row, he's there, and I think that is quite wrong. The Stewards should handle any disputes, any refereeing of questions. The president has no business at the Grand Prix, other than as a pure spectator.

'Out of those controversies come these great rows: he's had a great row with Senna, a great row with Prost, he's had great rows with so many people. It's not a president's function to have rows but to smooth them over, to eliminate them. You've got to try and maintain a position outside, a balance. It's obviously a lot of fun to get involved, but the object is not to have fun, it's to try and do the job properly.'

Balestre trumpeted: 'I do not know if I am indispensable, but I have just read in the English press that I am "the most important man in world motorsport", and in an important Japanese magazine that I was one of the most popular sportsmen in Japan. The champions of sailing have stated that they would like to have a president like JM Balestre at the head of their federation. To them I am the model of a "strong" man.'

You get the picture. Balestre thought much of himself.

But when he transformed the CSI into the FISA in 1978, motorsport was completely sectarian. Only 20 countries were members of the World Authority, which at the time was directed by a very exclusive group of only eight people. Balestre opened up the FISA to the rest of the world, and 75 countries had become members by the time of his last presidential battle. The World Council boasted 22 members.

Behind all the bombastic nonsense there was a good story about the man. In the opening round of the 1979 F1 season, in Argentina, he lost no time in stamping his mark and astounded drivers with his hard-hitting response to a first-corner accident. Funnelling away from the starting grid, John Watson felt a bump at the rear of his McLaren, and suddenly he and Jody Scheckter's Ferrari were tangled at the side of the road. Behind them Niki Lauda and Nelson Piquet were involved in their Brabhams, together with reigning World Champion Mario Andretti's Lotus, Patrick Tambay's McLaren which went over the top of it, Didier Pironi's Tyrrell, and Art Merzario's eponymous machine. The race had to be red-flagged as Piquet was trapped in his crumpled car. The young Brazilian sustained toe injuries and bruising, while Scheckter, to his immense chagrin, was deemed unfit to take the restart after spraining a wrist.

Balestre took a dim view of all this, and with scarce recourse to complete assessment of the facts imposed a fine of 10,000 Swiss francs on the astounded Watson. If his purpose had been to get the full attention of all the drivers, Balestre certainly succeeded. Nor did it escape their notice that poor Watson was an Ecclestone man, even though he had just quit Brabham to take up the late Ronnie Peterson's place at McLaren. Thus from the very start Balestre had laid down his marker.

This incident was a stark contrast to the other end of Balestre's reign, when Ayrton Senna deliberately drove Alain Prost off the road at the start of the Japanese GP at Suzuka in 1990. The move was the unpalatable product of a fit of temper that had its roots in Balestre controversially denying Senna his dramatic 1989 victory at the circuit, and then refusing this time to let him choose which side pole position should be on. Faced with starting on the dirty side, Senna vowed: 'If he [Prost] gets off the line ahead of me, he ain't gonna make it [to the first corner].'

This time, Blalestre took no action whatever against what many observers (even those at McLaren) saw as the most outrageous act of piracy in the history of the World Championship. By punting Prost off the track at more than 193kph (120mph), with 24 other fuel-heavy cars thundering into the first corner in their wake, Senna assured himself of that season's title.

There had been many controversial incidents in between these remarkable career book-ends. Colin Chapman was another to discover that you tangled with the volatile Balestre at your peril, though the English design genius would have the last word. Enraged that his innovative twin-chassis Lotus 88 was banned from racing for the third Grand Prix in a row in Argentina early in 1981, he issued a coruscating press release which ended with the words: 'When this is over I shall seriously reconsider with my good friend and sponsor David Thieme of Essex Motorsport whether Grand Prix racing is what it still purports to be: the pinnacle of sport and technological achievement. Unfortunately, this appears to be no longer the case and, if one does not clean it up, Formula 1 will end up in a quagmire of plagiarism, chicanery and petty rule interpretation forced by lobbies manipulated by people for whom the word sport has no meaning.'

As if this was not enough, he added a rider. 'When you read this, I shall be on my way to watch the progress of the US Space Shuttle, an achievement of human mankind which will refresh my mind from what I have been subjected to in the last four weeks.'

Balestre was apoplectic. He was supposedly in Argentina merely to spectate, but grabbed the limelight and immediately responded to Chapman's criticism with another of his now famous fines. This time it was $100,000. But he had reckoned without Chapman's standing among his peers, who rallied round him with strident voices of support, not for the car they all feared and wanted banned but against the high-handed manner in which Balestre had handled the press statement he made about the Lotus affair. Within ten days, the fine had quietly been rescinded.

Those who recall their first sighting of Balestre usually carry an impression of an irate man spouting off in French while simultaneously banging the table for extra effect. When the mood took him, however, he could be equally charming and polite, especially since he was a sufficiently shrewd politician to know whom to butter up, and when. His undoubted grandiloquence was a powerful weapon that he used to overcome rivals and enemies, and his powers of advocacy and penchant for the dramatic made him a compelling speaker who used his innate intelligence to its maximum effect to win arguments.

He also had a sense of humour.

Drivers tell the story of how he was once watered down by Nelson Piquet, for whom he openly admitted that he had a soft spot. The Brazilian was tiring of yet another of the lectures on driving etiquette which Balestre habitually made during the mandatory pre-race drivers' briefings, and to the amusement of his colleagues sidled up to him and nonchalantly poured a bottle of water into his blazer pocket. Balestre continued his harangue, until he could contain himself no longer and had to give vent to his own laughter.

Balestre was also smart enough to recognise sound logic when he heard it. Up until the early 'eighties the medical centres at many GP circuits were temporary structures erected and dismantled just before and immediately after a race. Professor Sid Watkins then suggested to Balestre, at one of the FISA Executive Committee meetings, that all international race circuits which staged FIA events should be required to have a permanent, fully-fledged medical centre. At the time Balestre dismissed the idea out of a hand, as an expensive dream.

Some months later Watkins arrived at the Jacarapagua circuit in Rio for the Brazilian GP to discover that erection of the medical centre had been delayed by poor weather. In fact, Balestre was actually helping Bernie Ecclestone to get it ready in time, though practice had to be delayed while workers made the electricity supply function. When Balestre issued one of his habitual summonses to Watkins to explain why the medical centre had not been ready, and why such problems arose, the Prof gave it to him with both barrels and reminded him that he himself had turned down the idea of permanent medical facilities. To his

Balestre's administration was responsible for introducing the mandatory chassis crash tests which did so much to enhance safety standards throughout the sport. (Formula One Pictures)

credit Balestre agreed that this was so. 'I remember and we must do it,' he replied, 'so this problem does not happen again.'

It didn't. Balestre subsequently issued an edict that all circuits holding FIA-sanctioned events must have permanent, fully-equipped medical centres. Watkins was wryly amused to see his own idea so astutely appropriated, but at least another crucial step forward had been taken.

Despite his manifest failings, and his sometimes questionable handling of the politics of the job, Balestre's love of motorsport was not in question. He banned ground-effect and turbocharging from F1 because the cars had to be slowed down, and he cancelled Group B rallying with immediate effect after the death of Henri Toivonen. His policies were never overturned, despite considerable opposition.

This was not all. Balestre also pursued a relentless agenda to improve safety. Perhaps his greatest legacy was the series of mandatory crash tests (see Chapter 10), the first of which was introduced in 1985. It was thus poignant that he was so shattered by Martin Donnelly's accident in practice for the Spanish GP in 1990. To some he appeared like a lion tamer who had invested hours in controlling his capricious beast, and who simply could not accept that it had turned upon him. He took the Ulsterman's misfortune as a personal slight, an affront to everything he had sought to bring about in the name of safety.

Balestre was much maligned during his days as the president of the FISA and the FIA, frequently with good cause, but was instrumental in pushing through changes that would have far-reaching effects. That Donnelly should be injured after so much progress had been made was just another illustration of the harshest fact of motor racing: no matter how hard people try to make it safer, there may yet come that collusion of fates which creates a freak combination of circumstances to defy their best efforts.

'He tried very hard on safety,' his successor Max Mosley willingly admits. 'Like Louis Stanley, he was altruistic. He was always keen on safety; I think he really minded when people got hurt, and he did a tremendous amount.

'I don't think he could have carried it on into what you might call the scientific age. I don't think that was his area, but within the limits of what was possible, he pushed it forward. And, of course, the technology went in the right direction. The teams all the time were working steadily on things like non-puncturable fuel cells, and carbon fibre composite materials made a big step, as did the crash tests that Balestre started. His was really the era and administration that began all that, because up to the end of the 'seventies it was just the teams doing the best that they could. There were no rules, and the fact of the matter is that when there are rules, people try harder. With our crash tests now, people quite often fail, and I think that shows how effective they are.

'He made a big contribution. A lot of it was bedevilled by the controversy about things like skirts. That wasn't really a safety thing. It was the Brits, who were good at aerodynamics, versus the Continentals, who were good at engines.

'Fundamentally he was very pro-safety. And he did a lot generally. He was the one who understood that we needed to separate sporting control from financial control, and that's what the first Concorde Agreement did. Here we are 20 years later, and other big sports, like the Olympics, have this same problem. How do you deal with it? And we actually dealt with it 20 years ago. Balestre must take a lot of the credit for that.'

When his own day of reckoning came as he was ousted from presidency of the FIA, Jean-Marie Balestre could stand up to be counted on the strength of what he had done in the name of safety. And he was entitled to hold his head high.

Chapter 12

Eliminating the red bits

If you marked the part of the circuit where they could get killed or injured in red, then it would be virtually red all round. Then in the 'seventies we started, fairly haphazardly, shrinking the red bits, and that process accelerated during the 'eighties and further during the 'nineties.

Max Mosley

Prior to that fateful weekend of the 1994 San Marino GP, Formula One thought it had most safety issues licked. Designers and the FIA alike were not being complacent. It was more a case that most people believed they had taken sufficient steps on the safety side. There had not been a fatal accident at a race meeting since Paletti's death in Montreal in 1982, and in any sort of F1 accident since de Angelis died at Paul Ricard four years later. True, accidents had accounted for the careers of Philippe Streiff and Martin Donnelly, but both men had lived, the latter despite his massive impact.

But the drivers were worried by the removal at the end of 1993 of many of their electronic 'gizmos', such as computer-controlled active suspension, traction control, and anti-lock brakes. Senna himself was not at all happy. 'I hope I don't have to push to the absolute limits this year,' he said at the beginning of his last season, 'but if necessary I will do it. Certainly the risks are higher, with refuelling coming back, but how much greater they will be remains to be seen. But I tell you this, there are gonna be some big accidents this year, for sure ...'

Two accounted for JJ Lehto and Jean Alesi, who missed races after injuring their necks in shunts well before Imola. Then, less than a fortnight after Senna's death, Monaco felt the chill wind that was blowing through Formula One when Karl Wendlinger crashed his Sauber-Mercedes at the chicane. It happened towards the end of Thursday morning's free practice session, and gradually the news filtered back to the paddock. But at first people just shrugged, assuming he'd merely bent the car. Later, as the news came through that he was in a coma, it became apparent just what had happened.

Going into the chicane the Austrian had braked a fraction too late. The Sauber had gone sideways and struck a water-filled butt, designed to act as an absorbent safety device in just such a situation. But Wendlinger struck it at cockpit level, and though the impact was estimated at only 50kph (30mph), he suffered severe head injuries as the force threw his helmet into contact with the butt.

In time Wendlinger recovered, after many weeks in a controlled coma, and he raced again. Out of old-fashioned loyalty Peter Sauber kept a seat open for him in 1995, but it was clear that he had not recovered fully. Later he would return again, racing cars in the GT category.

Less than another fortnight later, chirpy Italian Andrea Montermini caused hearts to flutter in practice for the Spanish GP when he lost control of his Simtek exiting the last corner in Barcelona, and smashed into the one section of concrete wall that was poorly protected by a single layer of tyres. As the amethyst car spun back on to the track, its driver slumped in the cockpit and his legs exposed at the shattered front end, it looked for terrible moments as if recent history was repeating itself. In the pits, more than one driver was deeply affected. It transpired, thankfully, that Montermini had sustained a broken ankle and concussion, but it was another dark moment.

There was yet another during a test at Silverstone in May when the Portuguese driver Pedro Lamy crashed his Lotus very heavily at Abbey Curve after the rear wing had snapped off and the car got sideways.

Peter Wright, now a technical delegate at the FIA but at that time the technical director of Team Lotus, was there that day. 'Pedro's car took off, cleared a wall and went through the fence, which was supported by big hawsers,' he recalls. 'One of these took the engine off, and the engine ended up back on the circuit. The car did a complete barrel-roll and went into a tunnel by the earth bank of a

Two weeks after the tragedies of Imola, Karl Wendlinger is taken to hospital following his accident at Monaco. (Sutton)

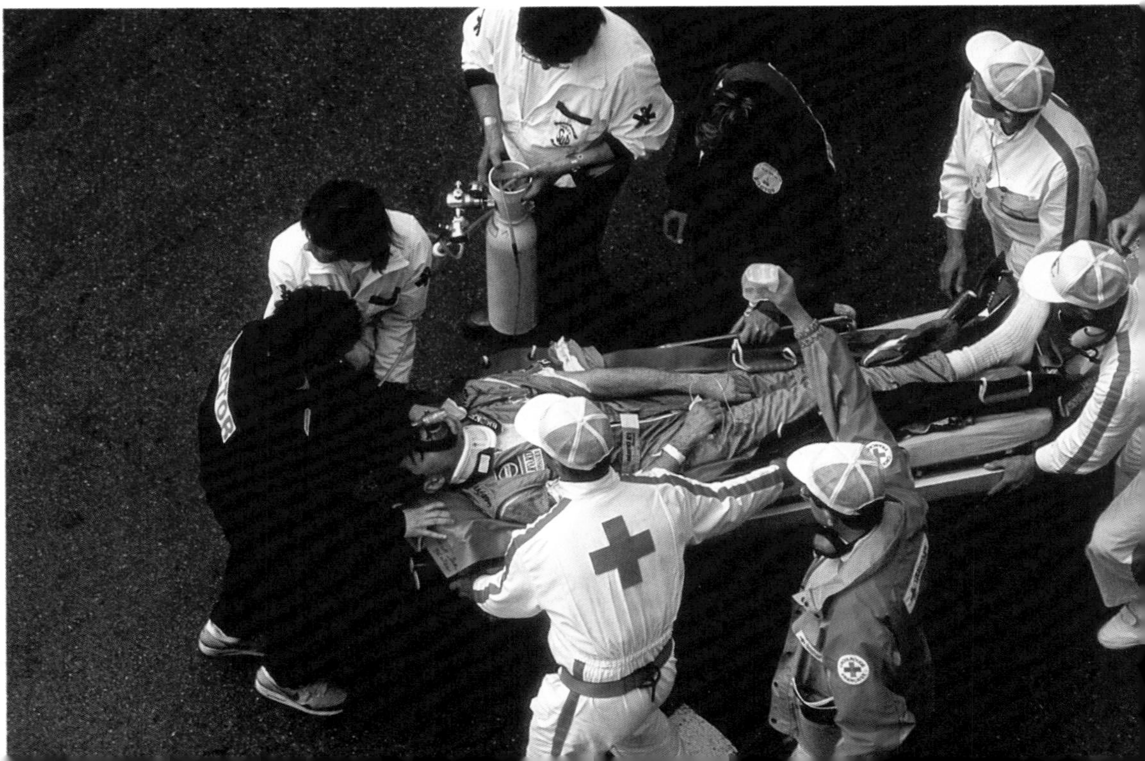

Wendlinger struck water butts similar to these, which had come on to the scene in the early 'nineties. (Mike Theobald)

bridge, and caught fire – not seriously, but a flash fire because the engine had been torn off and there was a hole in the oil catchtank. A fence post went through the monocoque and broke Pedro's legs.

'It was all a complete freak, but the poor Silverstone guys were completely shattered. They did something about Abbey, and reacted incredibly fast. But always they had the thought in mind that had that been race day … But in all fairness there was *no way* that you could have predicted that the car would end up in a spectator tunnel.'

Lamy recovered from broken legs and raced again, albeit not in F1, while the legacy for Silverstone was radical change at what used to be one of the Northampton track's fastest corners.

Formula One had never seen such an intense crusade as that launched in the immediate aftermath of Imola, and lent further impetus by the Wendlinger, Montermini, and Lamy accidents. Not even Jackie Stewart's campaign in the 'sixties had aroused such a willingness to listen and to act. The world had changed, and these were completely different times. The sad fact is, however, that the immediate manifestation of this took some decidedly less than credible forms.

The drivers took swift action. By Monaco they had banded together for the mutual cause, and reformed the Grand Prix Drivers' Association. Michael Schumacher, Gerhard Berger, and Martin Brundle took leading roles.

The unification was understandable, for it was the public echo of the drivers' own private thoughts and fears. They were unhappy about the way in which they had been treated at Imola. In particular, they were furious with one official who had taken it upon himself to tell Senna that he had no business visiting the scene of Ratzenberger's accident. This enlightened blazer had even threatened to fine the Brazilian.

Even before Senna's death moves had been afoot to revive the GPDA. Now they attempted to speak with one voice, and it was indeed a vocal majority that faced down the governing body at the Circuit du Catalunya for the Spanish GP. They insisted that they would not race until a chicane had been installed on the back straight where drivers faced hard braking just before an immovable wall. They stood firm and won that round. At the time, Brundle explained some of their thinking with his usual clarity.

'The drivers' meetings were really originated by Schuey and me after Imola. It's something I've felt really strongly about for some time now, and it came up again during the Saturday Six media thing at TI Aida for the Pacific GP. I said to him then that the last time I could remember the drivers getting together was in March 1987 in Rio, and that was about superlicences, not safety.

'At Aida there were mumbles even then about the latest regulations, without electronic controls, and we agreed that the drivers ought to have a common voice. Schuey agreed, but I don't know what Ayrton thought. I'd have to say that the meetings have been very successful.

'Of course Imola was a massive, dreadful shock. In the immediate aftermath I put together an agenda for a meeting in Monaco, and every driver turned up, plus a few from outside F1 who wanted to show support. We had a four and a half hour, properly structured meeting, and we covered an awful lot of ground. I've felt for a while now that the guys in Formula One are probably as sensible a bunch as I've ever seen in my ten years. There are some very intelligent young men. A lot of the big egos have gone. I don't think this could have happened three years ago, because the egos were matched by the bank balances. We couldn't have had such a constructive meeting as we had in Monaco.'

There was talk of the drivers electing Niki Lauda as their spokesman, as there was a strong feeling that if they were led by somebody who was a current driver there were too many emotional strings that could be pulled by either the teams or the governing body. In the end Lauda simply lent his emotional support, but the accident made a big impression on the tough Austrian. He and Senna had talked in the paddock at Imola and agreed to call the drivers together at the next race, in Monaco, to talk about safety. 'Two hours later,' Lauda said, 'he was dead.'

'In the past we've trusted others to look after safety,' Brundle continued. 'But now nobody accepts the death of a racing driver or a sportsman. With respect to the others, and because Ayrton was much more than just a racing driver, people focused on his death. It was very bad for our sport. And we don't want to be killed, either.'

Brundle took on responsibility for inspecting Montreal and Silverstone, Schumacher for Barcelona and Hockenheim, Erik Comas for Magny-Cours, and Berger for Monaco. Each was allocated a role and was to report back at Barcelona with their findings. The drivers felt it was particularly important to put their recommendations not from

A month after Imola hearts again leaped into F1 mouths when Andrea Montermini endured this unpleasant ankle-breaking shunt in a Simtek during practice for the Spanish GP. (Sutton)

individuals, but from the GPDA itself. They were completely united.

'I have to say,' Brundle affirmed, 'all the circuits have been extremely welcoming, they want to be seen to be doing their best. Money hasn't been mentioned, and nobody wants to be the next Imola.' But there was a serious threat of a drivers' strike in Barcelona when it transpired that the chicane they had requested had not been installed. Brundle was not the only one who firmly believed the omission was a deliberate means of testing just how determined – and united – the drivers were.

'The confrontation we had in Barcelona was because they had done most of the work apart from an area we felt strongly about, the exit to the fast Nissan corner,' Brundle said. 'The wall there is at a bad angle and we go through that corner at 240kph [150mph]. It could have been Tamburello all over again. The circuit organisers either didn't want to, or had been told not to, change the corner. Maybe somebody wanted to see how much the drivers were going to stick together. We said, "Okay, we don't race". I was very impressed that we were unanimous. The chicane that subsequently appeared wasn't an elegant solution, but we wanted the race to be as safe as possible. The drivers were very sensible, and nobody touched it in the race.

'In Barcelona, one of the best things was to see changes to Montreal and Silverstone signed off by the FIA, and to see people being refocused. When I went to Montreal I took a speed trace from the previous year, to show them what the car was doing and where it might end up. The guys there were terrific, and they said they'd never had that kind of input before during a safety inspection. Going into the hairpin there at 300kph [186mph] and going round it on foot are two different things, believe me …

'It takes time to come to those conclusions, but we've had a lot of sensible input. I'm the chairman of the GPDA, and we make sure that in meetings there is only one conversation, so things don't degenerate. It's why they're so productive.

'In the short-term there are changes being made. We're having a chicane put in at Montreal. It's in that fast sweep which is like Tamburello; demanding on the car, not the driver. No skill involved. But if you go off there you're in trouble, and Formula One can't afford to lose another driver.

'We all signed a statute in Monaco, and the GPDA is properly set-up and properly defined. We don't want to meet every race, and I don't want to be walking round standing in gravel traps all the time. We've been obliged to do that as the more experienced guys, but standing there as a driver and seeing what you might hit is not good news … But it had to be done.'

The drivers acknowledged that it would be difficult to keep the balance between something being a challenging track and a safe track, and none wished to adopt the pretence that motor racing could ever be completely safe. But they felt a fresh need to make it as survivable as possible.

'As drivers, we don't want a combative role in safety,' Brundle stressed. 'We want to drive. But we also want to be set up so that when the engineers and the FIA come to us we can give one opinion. In the short-term everyone has become a safety expert, in and outside Formula One. We're all focused. And whilst the drivers stay together we've got a lot of clout. Everybody wants to be seen to do what the drivers want. The crunch is going to come if somebody is hurt in a corner where the drivers asked for changes, because then we may become open to political manoeuvres. We just have to see what happens in a year.' He paused for a moment, as if considering the true prospects, then added, 'But this is not a particularly democratic society we live in …'

Besides the potential strike in Barcelona, Mosley also had to deal with a high-powered meeting between the FIA and the teams in which he outlined his ideas to engineers who had already had to modify their rear wings and diffusers at short notice. Several media representatives were present at the Benetton motorhome when team principals Flavio Briatore and Tom Walkinshaw returned from the meeting to declare roundly: 'Mosley is finished.'

History relates that reports of his demise were greatly exaggerated.

'It just shows how politically naïve they were,' Mosley says today with a smirk. 'In fact, I was too nice. I sort of sat around, and when they started to have that abortive strike, I should just have got in the car and gone home and said get on with it. You knew you didn't even have to do anything. I shouldn't really have been nice enough to talk to them. But I was much more conciliatory in those days. That was the kind thing to do. But it was wonderfully naïve to imagine that that was somehow going to result in a big change in the power base. Quite the reverse, actually.'

In Montreal the old flat-out sweeps down by the Olympic rowing basin were broken up by a silly chicane marked out by orange and white rubber traffic cones, and a new infestation of chicanes broke out. At Spa, the glorious and very quick Eau Rouge corner had already been put on a black list following the accident that befell Alex Zanardi there in 1993. There were plans to modify the corner to create significantly greater run-off areas, but the work could not be carried out in time so another chicane sprang up. Concerned purists (several of the drivers among them, if the truth be known), feared that the greatest corner still left in motor racing had been struck from the calendar. But in an indication of just what can be achieved when the will exists, the FIA

Jean Alesi leads JJ Lehto and Damon Hill through one of the makeshift tyre chicanes that blighted circuits in the immediate wake of the Imola accidents. (Sutton)

and the organisers kept their word and liaised brilliantly to recreate the corner for 1995. Somehow they managed to accommodate the required run-off area, without diluting the challenge of one of the last Great Corners.

At Monza, meanwhile, arguments raged with environmentalist parties who were outraged that the organisers proposed to cut down trees to create larger run-off areas at the second Lesmo corner, even though the authorities pledged to plant more trees elsewhere than they needed to remove in the name of safety. A deal of horsetrading ensued, and it took a threat by the FIA to cancel the race before a sensible compromise was achieved.

Up to the task: Max Mosley resisted serious challenges to his authority to lead the sport through one of its darkest hours. (Formula One Pictures)

At Estoril, which would disappear from the calendar by the end of 1996, the second corner had always been deemed highly dangerous because its two-tier Armco barrier would barely protect errant cars from a steep drop. But while this remained untouched, a ridiculous chicane entitled the Corkscrew was installed on the back straight. It hit the headlines during practice for the 1995 Portuguese GP when Eddie Irvine inadvertently tipped Damon Hill on to his head after they collided at low speed. Neither driver was hurt. There were minor changes at other circuits, too.

None changed more than Imola itself, however. New chicanes at Tamburello and Villeneuve left the Autodromo Enzo e Dino Ferrari a pale shadow of its former self, and only a more sensible Acque Minerali corner redressed the imbalance. Jacques Villeneuve, who had raced there in Formula Three, said in 1997: 'It's not a very nice track anymore, with chicanes everywhere. It doesn't feel like there's a natural rhythm to it. It's a very modern track, basically. I guess Piratella is a nice corner, but …'

Harvey Postlethwaite, Tyrrell's managing director of engineering, had only part of his tongue in his cheek at the launch of the team's new 024 in 1996. 'We have analysed the characteristics of all the circuits hosting Grands Prix and found the most common F1 corner is second-gear at 120kph [75mph],' he said. 'Accordingly, we have optimised our car for second gear 120kph corners.'

Max Mosley denied wholeheartedly the persistent suggestions that there was an 'official' FIA handbook for circuit design, or that countries with new circuits who aspired to stage a Grand Prix had to have their proposed designs vetted. According to popular rumour, it was more important that they be vetted to ensure that they flattered advertising locations and opportunities, rather than that they should create an interesting configuration with plentiful overtaking opportunities. 'That is definitely untrue,' he said. 'What we would like is some magician to find a way of building a circuit that was both safe and where you've got overtaking and thrilling racing. Do that, and circuit advertising looks after itself, because people watch it if it's exciting.'

But there was a definite agenda for identifying and eliminating what the FIA deemed to be 'dangerous' corners, as Mosley admitted in 1995. 'We identified 16 in the first instance,' he said, 'and have now whittled that down to eight.' But he declined to be specific. 'I can only tell you some of them, and it would be invidious to do that! And it raises the question that eventually you are going to end up with a few – three or four – where you can't solve the problem because if you slow the cars down enough to make those corners safe, you'd definitely be interfering too much with the performances of the cars. You know, there's a mountain or a cliff or a lake or something that stops you changing the corner. We are almost getting to that point, so that raises a very interesting question of principle that is going to get raised at the World Council. Is it acceptable that there is the odd dangerous corner?

'I've always felt that the governing body should push safety to the point where the drivers are saying, "We want to take more risks". It shouldn't be the other way round. It's completely wrong if the drivers should be put in a position where they are saying, "This is dangerous", and the governing body is saying, "It's all right". I want to discuss this basic philosophical point with the World Council, and also it's one of those things it's quite interesting to talk to the drivers about.'

The principle that the FIA employed was the speed through the corner, the length of the corner, and the lateral g – typically, a corner where drivers pulled 4 to 5 lateral g. 'We whittled it down eventually, I think, to three, and then of course the grooved tyres dealt with those,' Prof Watkins said. 'But as cornering speeds go up, they can come back.'

Peter Wright was later delegated to have a look at 'dangerous corners' when he joined the FIA in 1995. 'Most of them disappeared under chicanes,' he says. 'Eau Rouge was one of the biggest because of the lack of run-off area, which had been highlighted the previous year with Alex's accident. Since then they have had a number of accidents there, but though they have been very spectacular they have not been serious. Eventually they got the number down to four, either by inserting chicanes or modifying the line of the corner, until improved car performance upset the balance again.

Bernie Ecclestone: always a powerful presence behind the scenes of F1. (Formula One Pictures)

Peter Wright: F1 designer turned FIA technical guru. (Sutton)

'In 1999 Bridgestone's monopoly tyres were hard compound, which displeased the drivers but generally helped to contain lap times. But once Michelin's planned return happens compounds will inevitably soften, and so lap times will again begin to fall as they did when Bridgestone and Goodyear battled on grooved rubber in 1998, when lap times were supposed to remain constant under the new regulations. At the same time car designers are inevitably clawing back any downforce lost to regulation changes, and they and the engine designers are always making little chunks of progress, so the whole thing becomes a moving target.'

Even with the safety campaign, there were still accidents, some potentially fearsome, some actually serious. In the Japanese GP in 1994 Brundle saw his life flashing before his eyes, together with a Suzuka marshal. Brundle crashed in the rain when his McLaren aquaplaned. He remembered every detail, as if a slow motion movie film was running in his head. 'The car just swapped ends so quickly. And as soon as I touched the grass it just accelerated. It was very clear I was heading for a nasty situation. There was a red Honda Accord Estate reversing out of the way. Then I was heading for a caterpillar tractor 5m [16ft] away. I can see it now, a blue caterpillar, out of the right side of my cockpit, looming up. And I'm going at enormous speed still. I really thought that I was going to die. What's amazing is that I wasn't scared, which is really scary in itself. But I saw this one coming up, and it was the first time I really thought: "You've had it, you're not going to make this one."'

At the last minute he missed everything by brilliant use of his brakes and superfast thinking, employing a trick from his days racing in America's International Race of Champions. But by the time he next raced, in Adelaide, he had already put the incident out of his mind.

A year later, during practice for the Japanese Grand Prix at Suzuka, Brundle's replacement at McLaren, Mark Blundell, crashed at the infamous 130R corner. This was one of the corners still on the FIA's blacklist, a sweeping left-hand bend taken as close to maximum speed as the car's behaviour and the driver's courage and commitment will allow. Blundell lost control of his McLaren, which spun, skipped across the protective gravel bed which should have arrested its progress, and slammed almost head-on into the old tyres that were positioned in front of the metal barriers.

Blundell was a hard boy, well able to look after himself, and he managed to climb out of the cockpit unaided. The car had done an extremely good job of protecting him. But he was shaken and retched violently, partly through sheer reaction, partly because the impact had left him badly winded, as he stood by the side of the track. But he had survived what seemed like a very unpleasant accident. As recently as ten years earlier, he would have been another statistic. But while the accident was confirmation of the strength of the current breed of cars at that time, it was worrying insofar as the gravel bed had done little or nothing to arrest the McLaren's progress.

One race later Blundell's team-mate Mika Hakkinen narrowly escaped death when his McLaren crashed in Adelaide as a result of a puncture, but since the incident had such a significant impact on the design of the cars it is dealt with in a later chapter (Chapter 14).

Human nature being what it is, it was not long before there was a backlash against the steps taken in the aftermath of the Senna accident. Three years on the drivers were complaining that their cars were no longer fast enough to be interesting, and that the circuits had no decent fast corners left.

Perhaps, given his bloodline, it was inevitable that 1997 World Champion Jacques Villeneuve was the most vocal complainant, especially after the switch to grooved tyres for 1998. But the response from Mosley was trenchant and personal. 'If the latest specification cars are not "fun" to drive, then I can only say sorry. When Jacques claimed that slower drivers would find it easier on grooved tyres to stay close to the most skilled drivers, all the evidence is to the contrary. Indeed, if you believe that you wipe out the history of motorsport. In effect, Jacques suggests that all racing drivers were mediocre until he came along ...'

Villeneuve responded in kind when someone asked him if he had talked the

Martin Brundle has never forgotten the 1994 Japanese Grand Prix, where only the grace of God saved him from what he believed at the time was about to become a fatal accident. (Sutton)

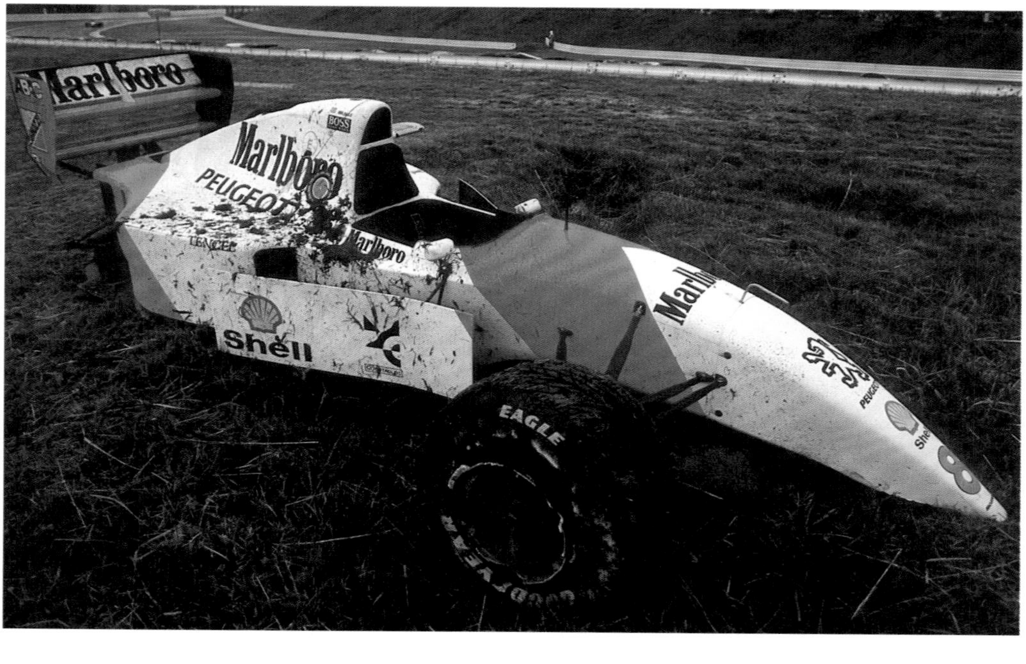

situation through with the FIA president. 'Talking is one thing,' he said, 'but listening is another.'

Two years later Villeneuve, now with BAR, spelled out his feelings loud and clear. 'I haven't changed my mind about these cars, or the racing today. It's not fast enough – there's not one high speed corner now where you tell yourself that that was almost too fast – I couldn't make myself go quicker. It's very rare – maybe Eau Rouge and 130R, but that's it – just these two – most of the rest of the tracks don't feel fast enough for you to decide to slow down. The cars are very safe.'

It seemed that much of the rapprochement betwixt drivers and governing body, which had been a feature of the post-Senna months, had evaporated. But in Bernie Ecclestone, Villeneuve appeared to have found an unexpected ally. 'I think there will always be accidents and we need to look after the drivers when the accidents happen,' said the FIA's vice-president of marketing. 'And that's what we've been doing for the last 20 years. Steadily improving every year. Villeneuve doesn't say that motor racing should be dangerous, he just says we want more challenging circuits. I agree with him 100 per cent. Since the accident at Imola, I think the FIA panicked a little under pressure from the media and went a bit over the top with chicanes all over the place. Which was proved at Barcelona, the next race, where we had chicanes everywhere, which was completely wrong and unnecessary.'

Ecclestone, who is most definitely a racer, was firmly in favour of quicker corners. 'Sure we want them. You don't want to tempt people to have accidents, but a lot of these drivers like big balls corners. They don't want the slow stuff. The fast stuff sorts the men out from the boys, and that's what it's all about, after all. Nothing says you have to go flat out. You can always go nine-tenths. In particular, when the new circuits are being built, we should be a bit more careful, rather than saying let's put a chicane in there. But you couldn't really keep corners like the old Boschkurve at the Osterreichring, could you? That would be a bit naughty.'

Mosley, a racer himself up to the level of Formula Two, knew only too well that risk is a part of the attraction for drivers. 'I remember asking Berger about something once at Monza, and he said to me, "Well, what do you think?" And I said to him, "I don't have to drive the car". And that really is the difference. Yet if you said to mountaineers, "We're going to let you climb that north face of the Eiger, but you've got to have safety ropes attached all the way up and you've got to take the following precautions so if you slip you can't hurt yourselves", they probably wouldn't like it.'

Mosley's accompanying gestures summarised the difficulty of living in a society that likes to protect adventurers from themselves. Such moral judgement can be difficult, especially when it comes to circuit safety and deciding what is and what isn't acceptable.

'If you go back to the 'sixties the main objective was to make sure the spectators didn't get hurt,' he continued, 'and really the drivers knew damn well they were doing something really dangerous and if they didn't like it, they didn't have to do it. If you marked the part of the circuit where they could get killed or injured in red, then it would be virtually red all round. Then in the 'seventies we started, fairly haphazardly, shrinking the red bits, and that process accelerated during the 'eighties and further during the 'nineties. And then really after Senna we set out to eliminate the red bits altogether. Now maybe we shouldn't be doing that. It's a question to discuss with the drivers, because in the end they've got to take the risk. And, to be honest, I think it is true that the wish to eliminate the red bits diminishes the further we get away from Imola.'

Chapter 13

Barriers to progress

Where people get hurt are the 'unexpected' corners. And anything is unexpected until it happens. So the big question is, is there anything we can do to start to predict places where people could get hurt?

Peter Wright

As part of the wholesale investigation into enhancement of F1 safety in 1994, Max Mosley asked Professor Sid Watkins to set up what became known as the FIA's Expert Advisory Group. Behind the scenes it continues its long-term investigation into all manner of subjects as far-reaching as barrier design and materials, and systems to arrest errant cars.

The FIA is now able to apply standardised circuit safety criteria across the globe, though naturally specifications change in accordance with lessons that are learned. Today the principal weapons deployed to slow down and arrest errant cars are: the metal Armco barrier; the run-off area; the gravel bed; and the tyre wall.

As an indication of the progress that has been made with Armco barriers, Johnny Herbert walked away from a hefty accident at Monaco in 1997. In wet conditions he had lost control of his Sauber-Petronas and eventually hit the barrier head-on at the Ste Devote corner, at very high speed. Three years earlier David Coulthard had struck metal barriers head-on at around 50kph (30mph) at the Hungaroring, and recalled: 'That hurt far more than the accident I had later that weekend when I ripped two wheels off the car.' Yet Herbert barely mentioned the incident later in the day, such was the improved design that had allowed the barrier to 'give' without arresting the car instantly.

Since 1995 run-off areas have been increased significantly, though, as we have seen, this is often a trade-off between safety requirements, ecological interests and the satisfaction of spectators. They don't want to be moved so far back from the action that they might as well not be at the track. There is a fine line to be drawn.

In the first Australian GP to be held in Melbourne, Martin Brundle had reason to be thankful for the run-off area in the third corner. When the teams gathered Down Under they did so against a backdrop of moderate anxiety after protestors had threatened to take disruptive action. This came to nothing, however, and the race was memorable instead for Brundle's phenomenal escape from a huge accident on the opening lap.

The British driver's Jordan-Peugeot was launched over Coulthard's McLaren-Mercedes when cars ahead produced a funnel effect under braking for the third corner. The Jordan landed briefly on the back of Herbert's Sauber-Ford, crushing its rear wing, then barrel-rolled into a gravel trap at terrifying speed. The engine hung from the chassis by a few pipes and wires, but Brundle was able to extricate himself from the upturned cockpit. With commendable coolness, he arrived back at the pits and drew applause by running to find Professor Watkins. Once he had received medical clearance, he lost no time getting strapped into the spare car for the restart!

'I had my eyes closed most of the time,' he said, 'and when it all stopped I realised I was still alive. But I could feel something wet and I was terrified that it was fuel. Fortunately it turned out just to be water from the ruptured radiator. I suppose it made good TV, me running to find the Prof, but if there hadn't been the amount of run-off area that there was, I would have been in big trouble.'

In 1998 the irrepressible Jacques Villeneuve taxed the run-off areas at Spa's Eau Rouge to their limit when trying to get through without lifting. The first time the French-Canadian had simply pushed his Williams-Supertec too hard and too fast into F1's most demanding corner and had lost it at 298kph (185mph). 'I think that was my best crash yet!' he grinned as he walked away unscathed. The Williams had registered its protest by spinning sideways, then slid across the road and over the gravel bed before hitting the tyre wall on the outside of the corner, at the top of the hill.

In 1999 both he and team-mate Ricardo Zonta came to grief at the Belgian track in their BAR-Supertecs. On Friday morning the front suspension of Villeneuve's car broke at 322kph (200mph) as he braked for the Les Combes right–left–right flick. The car spun and clipped a barrier, but stopped without too much damage. Then came qualifying on Saturday, when both Villeneuve and Zonta crashed heavily at Eau Rouge. The Brazilian hit the outer tyre wall hard enough to remove all four wheels, while the French-Canadian went in backwards before rolling dramatically. Neither was hurt, but the value of the gravel traps was once again called into question.

'That was way better than last year. I got a roll in this time!' Villenueve enthused. But looking at Zonta's wheel-less hulk, he confessed, 'Mine wasn't as good as yours, though.'

Only two months earlier, on the opening lap of the British GP at Silverstone, the whole philosophy not just of run-off areas and gravel traps, but also of tyre walls, had been called into question by Michael Schumacher's heavy accident at Stowe corner.

As Hakkinen and Coulthard led off the line in their McLaren-Mercedes, Schumacher had made a poor start and seemed irritated when team-mate Eddie Irvine refused to concede third place to him on the run down to Stowe. There, he tried to dive through on the inside line, which even in normal circumstances would have been a likely prelude to a trip into the gravel. But a rear brake bleed nipple on the Ferrari was loose and therefore leaking, and with brakes only on the front wheels the German was suddenly in serious trouble. The red car skipped precariously over the gravel run-off, before embedding itself nose-first into the two-layer tyre wall. As the front end of the chassis cracked and broke away, Schumacher sustained double fractures in his right leg.

Irvine was in the vanguard of criticism of the way in which the gravel bed did not appear to have slowed

Martin Brundle launches over the back of David Coulthard and Johnny Herbert on the opening lap of the Australian GP in Melbourne in 1996. The Englishman was fortunate to escape unharmed, and ran back to take the spare car for the restarted race. (Lewry/Sutton)

Schumacher very much. 'The GPDA has been campaigning for months to have gravel beds that slope upwards, because the ones we have right now just don't do the job they are supposed to.' Perhaps surprisingly, he had an ally in Bernie Ecclestone, whose view was diametrically opposed to Max Mosley's.

'It has been my opinion for years that gravel beds are quite useless,' Ecclestone said at Hockenheim as he bounced back from heart surgery. 'They do not brake the cars effectively. Michael's Ferrari could not dig into the gravel because it was up in the air most of the time.' Hakkinen's McLaren appeared to have traversed one in similar manner after its spectacular exit from the German race.

Ecclestone's criticism focused further attention on what was becoming a growing problem. 'What we need,' he continued, 'is a run-off area with an extremely rough asphalt surface, and the track surface itself should be rougher too so that the cars don't slide as much. We need a very, very abrasive material. That way they could get more grip and be slowed down more efficiently.'

Ecclestone said the technology existed to detect – and punish – any driver using such run-offs to gain track advantage, and on a more flippant note revealed that he had also suggested the idea of a bed of nails, 'that would tear at the tyres and slow the car down. They didn't seem to like that idea.' No mention was made of what might happen if a car went in upside down …

The FIA's technical delegate Peter Wright took a long view of the whole situation, early in 2000. 'I've just done an analysis on which corners in F1 are still dangerous,' he revealed, 'to try and predict which are going to become worse, taking into account g and such factors. Under the current F1 regulations the highest g load in the fastest corners is probably just below 4g, while the grooved tyres have also rendered the 6g spikes under braking a thing of the past. Today the highest retardational loadings are around 4g too. Still plenty, when it makes you four times your normal weight.

'I have been studying the criteria for judging corners, to assess whether it is still right, and part of this has entailed looking at all the ADR (Accident Data Recorder – see Chapter 14) data to see whether there were any trends there. You get certain corners where a lot of people fly off every year, and there are certain of those corners where when they do fly off it ends up with a big impact. 25g or such. So those are the ones, and there are a few of them, but they are totally different corners to the ones that are high g and high speed. If you look at the people who have been hurt or killed in the last ten years, none of their accidents have been on any of those "dangerous" corners. So the simple conclusion came, after talking to Max, that the corners that are obviously dangerous are being handled. Where people get hurt are the "unexpected" corners. And anything is unexpected until it happens. So the big question is, is there anything we can do to start to predict places where people could get hurt? But it isn't obvious. We have got a very complicated set of criteria which is: the car flies off like this, and there is so much run-off area and then a barrier; but there are things you cannot predict. Michael's accident was one of those unpredictable things.'

Wright calculated that Schumacher was doing 193kph (120mph) when he braked and left the track, and he was still doing 80kph (50mph) when he'd been through the tyre barrier and had used up most of the crushability of the Ferrari's nose. 'Basically, a front wheel came round and hit the side of the monocoque, which buckled. But that structural collapse gave him another metre for deceleration, which probably saved him. He was going a bit quick for the barrier.'

There were plenty of tyres at Stowe,

but they weren't tied together with conveyor belting because nobody was expected to go off there. 'It's exactly that case, where you don't expect something to happen at a specific point,' Wright admits, 'and when it does, your reaction is, "Oh, shit!"'

The easiest thing in the aftermath of any serious incident is to ask the age-old question: 'Why did nobody think that might happen?' The answer is far more complex than the question.

'With Schumacher's accident,' Wright says, 'I could see the bullshit from the start. By Monday I had on Max's desk a plot of what the car did, particularly through the gravel bed. He checked it was okay with Ferrari, and we released the numbers to the press. That just damped down the crap that we could see was beginning to build up.

'The gravel bed slowed the car as well as the car was slowing down on the track. The car was down to 1.3g when it left the circuit, and had only got front brakes. The front tyres were down to the canvas. It was categorically said by Ferrari that there was a rear brake failure. I saw my trace and Ferrari's trace, and there was nothing that contradicts that.

'The most spectacular accidents are the ones you don't have to worry about. The worst ones are when the car goes in and appears to be hardly damaged. When Schumacher went into the tyres you could tell it was quite bad. Okay, he was in the tyre barrier, which made a big difference, but it's the ones where not a lot of stuff appears to have been knocked off the car that you worry about. He went in at 106–109kph (66–68mph), having left the track at 193kph (120mph) and decelerated across the gravel at an average of 1.1g, which was about what he would have done if he had stayed on the track, the state he was in. That's the problem; there has been a lot of talk about changing gravel to tarmac, but the time when things go wrong is when the car hasn't got any wheels, the throttle is wide open; those are the times when gravel can work quite well. Ron Dennis came out in favour of gravel and said don't rubbish it too much, it's the best we've got. It's certainly better than catchfencing.'

The big problem is that gravel beds work very well with heavyish cars with reasonable ground clearance, such as GT cars and touring cars. The only thing you have to make sure of is that they don't roll. The mechanism by which gravel beds work is basically fluid dynamics. The tyres will aquaplane. They do even with racing trucks, and they are very highly loaded tyres. And even if the tyre engages with the surface, there is usually only a small clearance to the undertray, and then the vehicle will start to toboggan.

'We know the right type of gravel,' Wright insists. 'The problem is getting everyone to use it. There are two things that matter: the gravel specification and the depth of the amount of gravel. The ones where it doesn't work are where the drivers just drive straight over them! The easy way to tell is just to go and try to walk on them. If it's easy to walk on, it won't be very effective; if it's difficult to walk on, then it probably will be.

'The whole thing about gravel beds is that if there was anything better to do, then we would do it. Simple as that. You've got a certain amount of space; what do you do with it to stop the cars? The ideal thing is something like a cornfield which doesn't make the car bounce but takes quite a high force to shear it off. Cars used to spin into cornfields and come to a halt without any problems. But then you had the problem of repairing the field. So there isn't obviously something that is a lot better.'

One of the underlying considerations is that no driver wants a minor mistake, say a slight misjudgement under braking, to be penalised by getting stuck for good in the gravel. Such is the type of pebble used today that most drivers can regain the track if they do transgress, provided that they can maintain their momentum. But equally, none of them wants to toboggan across gravel without slowing down when they are in real trouble.

The FIA maintained strongly that the gravel bed at Silverstone performed as it should. 'This was a worst-case scenario,' a spokesman said, 'and it did what it needed to do. There are no simple answers to slowing down a car that is out of control.'

Irvine is a big fan of the sloped gravel bed. The FIA does not agree. 'If you go up a gravel bed,' Wright says, 'the load on the car is no greater. The only time you get the load greater is when it's curving, so it's got to continuously curve upwards, like a quarterpipe or a halfpipe in a skateboard park. It's got to go up two or three metres, and you've then got to put your barrier at the end. That means the spectators aren't going to see anything!'

Mosley agrees with Wright. 'A sloped gravel bed is not the sort of panacea that Eddie thinks it is,' he says. 'If something is obvious, we do it. This is why it is difficult for the drivers. When they come up with an opinion the press tends to listen. 'He must know, he's a driver.' The truth is that it has gone way beyond that. You wouldn't ask a test pilot now about the aerodynamics of the rear elevator flap. He can tell you what happens when you pull the lever, but even then you are probably better off looking at the onboard data recorder than you are listening to the pilot. On the other hand there are certain things they can tell you that no-one else can, particularly about anything to do with human reactions. It's quite irritating, something like that, Eddie's ideas, because if you had a big engineering problem, much as I like him, he wouldn't be the first person you'd go to.'

But, since the driver or the test pilot is the man who takes the ultimate risk, the man who can lose his life if others get their calculations wrong, he at least deserves the respect of having his opinions and ideas listened to. That's a point that the FIA in general, and Mosley in particular, occasionally appears to overlook. And just because the man in the can chooses to take the risk in the first place does not deny him that basic respect. If anything, it should strengthen the validity of his claim to it.

Mosley also chuckles at the recollection of Ecclestone's outburst against gravel beds at Hockenheim in 1999. 'Bernie's got this theory that we are better off with tarmac, which is true in certain circumstances. But in Schumacher's case, for example, he would have been worse off because he was through to the canvas, had no brakes at the rear, and couldn't make the thing spin. The answer really is that Bernie is like everyone else in Formula One, he's got his ideas and his theories but it has gone beyond that. It's all scientific now.'

'It's all very well people saying all you've got to do is this, all you've got to do is that,' Wright continues, 'but they should put a damper between their thoughts and their words. There are no instant answers where safety is concerned. After any accident, people want instant cures. There are none. It is a very slow, steady process, changing circuits.'

One of the most significant changes in the post-Senna period is the attitude towards safety. It's all a very far cry from the days of Jackie Stewart's original crusade. 'Circuit owners want to do the best job that they can,' Wright affirms. 'We are down to one or two what you would call serious injuries a year. I define a serious injury as being if the driver is not passed medically fit to drive. So in 1999 there was Ricardo Zonta and Michael Schumacher. It's been bubbling along, statistically, as one or two really since 1994. It was down to less just before that, and it sort of sits there.

That's a very difficult number to do much about. You get about 100 incidents in a year, so you are talking 0.1–0.2 per cent of people getting hurt. And the accidents that do that are all slightly freakish. Zonta lost control over a bump when he crashed at Interlagos.

'The worst thing that can happen is when, as in that accident and in Greg Moore's ChampCar accident at Fontana, the driver tries to regain control over the car and goes off at a funny trajectory. If you lose control of a car it will go off at a tangent, which is exactly what you would expect it to do. But if the driver suddenly fights back, gets some control back and makes the car generate whatever g that it will generate, it will send the car in a different direction and will accelerate it somewhere you don't expect. And maybe he goes flying off and hits a barrier where there are no tyres, as happened with Zonta in Interlagos. In Montreal in 1997 Olivier Panis hit one side of the track and bounced into the other. It's always terribly easy to know what should have been done, after the event. The really hard thing is to look and see where nobody else is looking. These things can be predictable, but it's an awful lot of work to look at a circuit and see what could happen.'

For years Tamburello was deemed safe, despite the number of drivers who walloped the outer concrete wall when something went wrong. 'Tamburello was like a corner on an oval, which is why concrete was not a bad solution. Berger, Piquet, and Alboreto, for example, all hit it and got away with it. Senna hit it at the wrong angle, and the wheel came back and hit him.'

In the aftermath of the Schumacher accident there was also criticism of the fact that the tyres in the wall had only been two-deep, not three, and had not been tethered together. Accordingly, they flew in all directions as the Ferrari speared into them.

Stewart, the champion of safety, has thrown in some critical observations of his own. 'The idea of the deformable tyre wall was great, until everybody forgot that the tyres have to be changed regularly because in inclement weather they get hard,' he says. 'So they no longer had the same deformable rubber cushion effect. Then they were putting things round them, and bolting them together to such an extent that they

With a single-layer tyre wall protecting the Armco barrier, Michael Schumacher was able to race home to a wet victory at Spa in 1996, despite the apparent severity of this shunt in practice. (Reporter/Sutton)

weren't as effective. You need to keep up with that sort of stuff. Just because you put in a tyre wall made of rubber doesn't mean to say that it will stay as effective as it was initially. In European winters water gets into the tyres and freezes, and expands the rubber. That's why I say that safety is a never-ending progression of looking for new benefits, new technology.'

* * *

Mike Theobald was deeply affected by Ayrton Senna's death. The proprietor of Advanced Wear & Safety in Ashford, Theobald had been on the racing scene a long time as a supplier of protective clothing, and resolved to do something to prevent a similar occurrence.

'Ayrton and I were very close, almost like brothers, and he often dropped in to see us at AWS. He was always very interested in safety matters, and was considering coming in with us on some projects. So I felt it very personally when he was killed, and I was determined to try and do something to stop that sort of thing ever happening again. If you like, it was my way of paying a tribute. I was going to call my idea the Senna System.

'What he envisaged initially was a rubber-coated barrier made from elastomeric polyurethane foam, within the matrix of which were suspended Microcel E-SORB 2.5 hollow ceramic spheres. Microcel claimed that its hollow sphere composites had the ability to absorb more energy per unit of volume than conventional materials. At the time the FIA was seeking a "thin" barrier to augment the Zolder method of bolting old tyres together, which offered the best levels of impact attenuation, longevity, ability to withstand repeat impacts, and ease of assembly and maintenance. Two rows accounted for a depth of 3m [9.8ft], but the FIA also wanted a thinner barrier of 1.5m [5ft] for specific applications.

'But we soon realised that it would be far too expensive to put our original idea into production,' Theobald says. 'That was our impractical idea. A company I talked to wanted £30,000 for the tooling to manufacture a prototype. That wasn't silly money, but it was money I didn't have for that sort of project.

'Then after talking to Prof Watkins and Ian Brown of the Safety Committee, we hit on the idea of installing the hollow sphere composites in the tyres themselves, in the sidewalls. That was much more practical, and effectively gave you two energy absorption systems in one. If you then had a plastic in the middle it could be stronger still.'

This was a far more practical proposition, for all circuits on the F1 calendar already employed the Zolder method to help restrain errant cars. 'There was a huge possibility of making this work. In the very early days we just tried filling the insides of the tyres themselves with foam, without the hollow spheres. This was so simple. Really, just like a belt and braces system. Once you've got the system, it looks after itself. The sidewall is filled with the foam and perhaps the hollow spheres, and the centre of the tyre is still open so it can collapse but spring back to shape. We carried out some tests, but then apparently Bosch came up with a couple of better ideas and modifications.'

Theobald put his ideas before the FIA's Expert Advisory Group in 1995. He believes that it was tested, but if it was he never saw a final result. 'Gerhard Berger and, ironically enough, Michael Schumacher, showed interest in the Senna System on behalf of the GPDA,' Theobald says. 'But then the whole idea just kind of died off. I still have no idea why. I never even got a feel for the politics of the situation. I was never privy to what was going on and what was being discussed, but I knew that the idea of a giant airbag was never going to work because of the reaction time that was necessary.'

To this day Theobald remains in the

dark, his attempt to do something in the name of safety apparently going without any acknowledgement. 'I tend to speak my mind, so perhaps that's why I was kept out of the politics of it all. I don't know; the logistics of putting everything together may also have come into play, because there are hundreds of thousands of tyres used as tyre walls all round the world. But all you needed to do was ship the hollow spheres to the relevant circuits and let the organisers put them into the tyres themselves. If the FIA had made the system mandatory, a way to do it would have been worked out.

'In the end you just have to draw back, and accept the fact that sometimes it's not going to go your way. But somebody said to me after the Schumacher accident, "Where was your barrier? That would have made a difference, wouldn't it?" Well, I like to think it would have.'

Had Schumacher been killed, there would have been an outcry not just against the lack of adequate run-off area and the lack of adequate tyre wall protection, but also against the fact that potentially superior protection systems had been developed yet had not been employed at that particular part of the circuit. What the Schumacher accident highlighted was just how easily – despite all the changes that had happened after Imola, after all the thought that had gone into making the sport safer, after all the heartache and the soul-searching – a

Three years later the German came off a little worse after his much-publicised accident on the first lap of the British GP at Silverstone in 1999. But despite the extensive damage to his Ferrari he could count himself lucky to escape with nothing worse than a broken leg after the high-speed head-on collision with the tyre walls and the barrier. (Sutton/Collins)

fatal accident might still have been possible.

'We've had something in the order of 100 different ingenious and interesting proposals for safety barriers, and something less than that for retardation systems, as in gravel traps and so on,' Mosley reveals. 'The most spectacular one was four vertical rockets which the driver would fire by pressing a button when you went off into a gravel trap, which would push the car down into the gravel so that it would stop really quickly. I think it was John Barnard, at the relevant meeting, who asked what was the temperature of the propellant. That was about 2,000°C! You name it, somebody had it written down. Retarder hooks, all sorts.

'Speaking firstly of gravel traps and barriers, if you could specify the accident you could improve greatly on what we've got. The problem is that you can't specify the accident. And even with the gravel trap, even in the worst case, like Schumacher's, it's still retarding at one g. Schumacher arguably, once he was off the road, could have put the steering on to full lock. At the least that would increase the drag, and at the worst cause the car to spin. When you ask him about it, which I have at least twice, he said he had no steering on the track, which is understandable because he had no brakes at the rear but full brakes at the front where he had the tyres through to the canvas. But I think he acknowledges that the best procedure in those circumstances is to put on full lock, but it's very easy to talk about these things.'

That may be the full essence of much of the talk about safety. The thing that those tasked with improving situations must bear most in mind is that it is all too easy to talk about it afterwards, to be smart in hindsight. Everyone has an answer afterwards. The trick is to have one before the event, and one that can stand up to any eventuality. And the men who really know what they are talking about on safety matters will willingly tell you that such an answer does not exist.

'When you are talking about the actual barrier, the best all-round retarder that we have so far is the tyre stacks with plastic tube in the middle,' Mosley insists. 'In all the various circumstances, they are the best, better than the really sophisticated systems that have been proposed and tested. Sooner or later somebody will come up with something really sophisticated, which even if it was expensive, we could use in really sensitive places where we couldn't, for some reason, move an obstacle further back. But that is the sort of question which Sid's group, which has now matured into the Safety Commission (an evolved version of the Research Group), looks into.'

Wright remains protective of the steps the FIA has taken. 'One of the biggest things that has happened in motor racing safety over the last ten years is the work that FIA technical delegate Charlie Whiting and Professor Sid Watkins have done, particularly Charlie, to raise the standards. We've worked out a lot of what we want on circuits, and Charlie has done fantastic work in making sure the standards have been brought up to the best. We have done a lot of work on tyre barriers, and we have begun to understand how best we should build them. Should they be strapped together, or bolted? Now we can go around the world and say, "That's the way it should be".

'You've got 16 or 17 circuits – that's how many kilometres of tyre barrier? And they're going to be put together by Australians, Brazilians, Japanese, Italians, all sorts of nationalities. So that's the biggest thing that we have done, taking what we have learned in the laboratory and putting it on to the circuits, and knowing that it is the same wherever we go.'

The FIA does much of such lab testing at Transport Research Laboratory

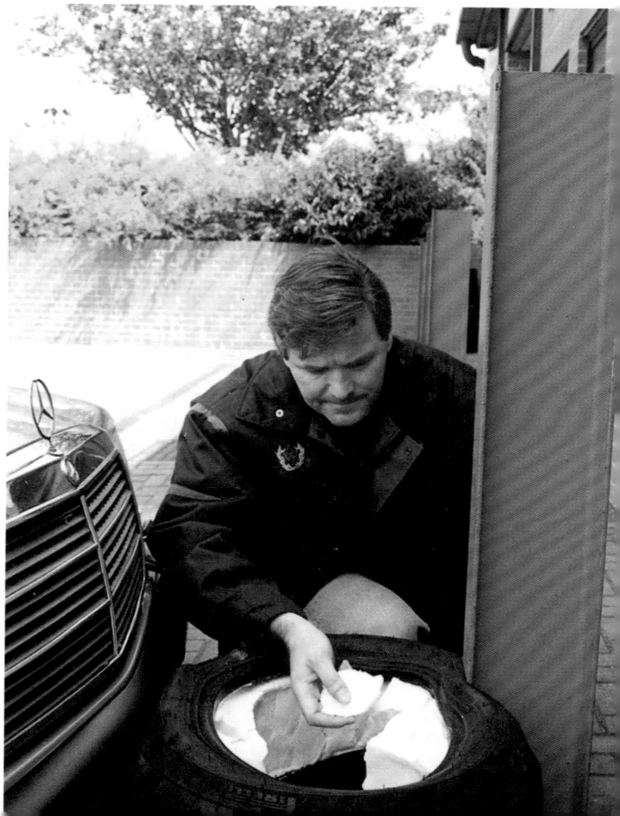

Mike Theobald indulged in a little empirical research of his own while investigating alternative barriers following the death of his friend Ayrton Senna. Initially Theobald envisaged solid rubber-coated barrier blocks made from elastomeric polyurethane foam, within whose matrix would be suspended Microcel E-SORB 2.5 hollow ceramic spheres. Subsequently, however, research indicated that foam-filled tyres were just as effective, and much cheaper and more practical. (Mike Theobald)

(TRL) at Crowthorne, where a lot of the impact testing was conducted in its early days. Their work is among the best in the world.

Watkins and even Max Mosley himself, do not seem to know precisely what happened to Theobald's Senna System, probably because it is outside their immediate field of expertise. But Wright offers an explanation. 'We have looked at a lot of different proprietary barriers,' he admits. 'There have been lots of suggestions. But tyre barriers have a limit. Basically a good tyre barrier will absorb 40kph [25mph]. In our barrier testing we found a way of raising that to 80kph [50mph], and that was by putting plastic tubes into the tyres. That correlates well with work they have done in the States as well. It's polyethelyne tubing, and is used on roads in America. It's gas pipe, with quite a thick wall. You jump on it and you think, "Bloody hell, I wouldn't want to hit that hard!" But you look at it after an impact and it takes it really well. And it's weather resistant, which is also very important. It's very practical.

'Somebody once commented that Porsche did some research into filling tyre barriers with foam, and the Brazilians replied: "That would be great, because the mosquitoes wouldn't breed in them." And you think, "Oh, really; I hadn't thought of that!" Look at all those tyres round Interlagos; they all get filled with water when it rains, and they're the perfect breeding ground for mossies.

'As far as the Senna System is concerned, our research has shown that you don't need to fill the tyres with foam, even foam with air bubbles suspended in it. People have done research with barriers that look like air bags, a series of large cells with vents on them. But the big problem is that an F1 car is a bloody stiletto. There's this very sharp, quite stiff nose, which is very good, and the way that we have tyre barriers now is that we use up the barrier and the car goes through it, then the nose starts working. The nose is your contingency. The regulations call for the front of the nose to be much softer, so that it blunts itself quite quickly and is not so likely to go through any conveyor belting that holds a tyre wall together. But it would burst air bag type barriers quite easily.'

At Imola in 2000 a new type barrier was tried out. Known as the Impact Protection System (IPS) it was the brainchild of former F1 and ChampCar racer Fabrizio Barbazza, and was being marketed by former ChampCar owner Antonio Ferrari. Testing had shown the IPS set-up to have strong potential, with the possibility to absorb 90 per cent of a car's kinetic energy upon impact. It relied upon a mix of PVC and rubber honeycomb, which would deform and compress when struck to absorb energy and reduce the impact of a car on the unyielding wall in front of which the IPS would be located. Like the simpler tyre wall, the beauty of the system was that it would simply regain its shape after the impact, ready to do its job again without any maintenance. Both Formula One and CART are currently looking further into the system.

It is doubtful, given its shortcomings, that catchfencing will make a comeback, though John Surtees remains convinced that it still has much to offer. 'The main problems were the posts, and the fire risk, and the need for constant maintenance. I acknowledge all that. But my own thinking is that there has never been enough work done to utilise the *principles* of catchfencing. I'm sure that if you could apply a bit of modern technology you could solve the problem with the posts and flying debris, maybe using technology from aircraft carriers, that sort of thing. Tyre barriers have their limitations, and you can't keep pushing the public back and back and back. I'm sure with modern technology, catchfencing could still be one of the answers.'

Time will tell whether fast corners do reappear in F1. But Professor Watkins' words, written as the foreword for the author's book *Echoes of Imola*, are as valid today as they were when he penned them, one year after the Ratzenberger and Senna tragedies.

'Given a retrospective choice between a Tamburello or a Senna,' he said, 'I do not believe any sane person would now select the wall.'

In today's more enlightened Formula One, nobody would disagree with him.

Chapter 14

Restraint in all things

I hear Max is saying that my accident at Spa would have been fatal if I hadn't had a safety cockpit …? You know, I guess he's probably right!

Jos Verstappen

The aftermath of Imola brought far-reaching change to Formula One's cars as well as to its tracks. At a stroke the FIA reduced downforce by mandating sizes for the diffusers and front wing endplates, and by insisting on a skid block plate to increase ride height and thus further reduce the grip generated beneath the car. Engines had to run on pump fuel and, in one of the sillier changes, engine airboxes had to have holes drilled in them so that the effectiveness of ram air at high speed, which boosted engine power, was impaired.

Those were the immediate changes. In the slightly longer term came a reduction in cubic capacity from the 3.5 litres that had been introduced in 1989, to 3 litres. Side impact crash tests were introduced, the impact speed was increased for the frontal crash test, and the side load was increased in the nose push-off test. The minimum height of the monocoque survival cell increased 10cm (4in), the cockpit opening was subject to specific (and larger) dimensions, and a protective headrest located at the back of the driving compartment became mandatory. Seat belts, widths were increased from 5cm to 7.5cm (2in to 3in) to provide better chest protection in an accident, and the race weight limit of the cars now had to include the fully dressed driver.

There was nevertheless a curious paradox, and the FIA's refusal to drop refuelling was the subject of much debate when Jos Verstappen's Benetton was engulfed in flame in the pits at Hockenheim after as little as a litre or two of fuel had escaped during his routine stop.

'That was a very small amount of fuel,' Mosley agrees. 'One never wants a fire in the pits, but if you are going to have a fire somewhere, that's about the best place to have it because all the gear is there to fight it. The car is static, everybody is dressed for it, the driver hasn't just had an enormous bang on the head. Nobody is allowed in the pit lane unless they are dressed for it. Touch wood, it shouldn't happen. We haven't had one now since Diniz in 1996. Since Berger at Imola, where the car really caught fire, there have only really been

Verstappen, Irvine, and Diniz after refuelling. And they don't really count, especially Diniz, because that was a refuelling equipment failure.'

But they would have counted had any of the drivers been injured.

One of the most important changes was ready for 1996, and this was the lateral head protection for drivers. This had been prompted primarily by the Wendlinger accident at Monaco in 1994, when his spinning Sauber-Mercedes had suffered a sideways impact with a water butt at the chicane at little more than 50kph (30mph). Deeply shocked as his driver lapsed into a coma for 18 days, team owner Peter Sauber had immediately initiated his own research into enhanced cockpit protection, and his cars raced with it later that season. Now, after working closely with Professor Sid Watkins's Expert Advisory Group, designers had come up with protective padded cockpits. The rules called for higher cockpit sides, so that the drivers' shoulders and necks were no longer visible, and the special collar that was fitted to the edge of the cockpit at head height was made from Confor foam. Extensive rig testing had been conducted to determine the best material and the optimum thickness.

Following Karl Wendlinger's 1994 accident at Monaco, Peter Sauber responded immediately by creating higher cockpit sides on his eponymous cars long before the FIA introduced the regulation two years later. (Sutton)

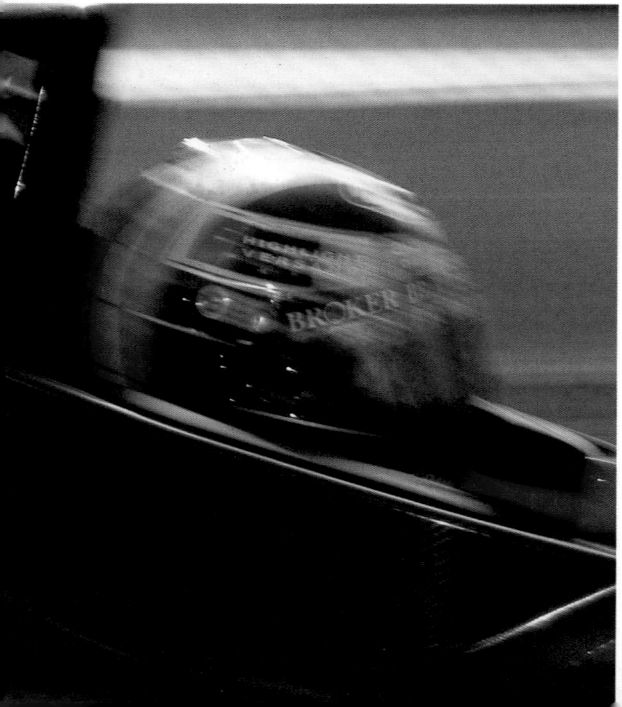

'Limited movement is good,' says Peter Wright, 'because it limits the velocity at which you hit something. Christian Fittipaldi hurt himself during a rear impact accident in CART, and they couldn't figure it out because it was not a particularly serious accident. Then they got the onboard video and he was looking over his shoulder where he was going, and it put a twist on his neck in the impact. It's little tiny things like that that make the difference, how you present yourself to the safety equipment.'

By this time there had been two further heavy accidents, one of which focused attention not just on the need for the safety cockpits, but for something more. By pure chance both accidents involved McLarens, and the first came with Mark Blundell's previously mentioned crash at Suzuka's notorious 130R left-hander. This was one of the 'dangerous corners' left on the FIA's list, a bend taken at as close to maximum speed as the car's behaviour and the driver's courage and commitment would allow. Blundell lost control and his McLaren spun before hitting the barriers on the outside of the corner almost head-on.

'I looked at the data later and I was doing 288kph [179mph] on the grass,' Blundell revealed. 'The car took off about 32kph [20mph] of that when it spun, but from that point on it was airborne anyway. I went in at a slight angle, because I sustained 6g frontal impact and 6g lateral at the same point. There was quite a lot of force …

'They reckon I hit the barrier at

around 249kph [155mph]. So considering, I think we did fairly well. I was winded and didn't run in qualifying because my vision was slightly burred, and I didn't feel 100 per cent fit. It was the best option to actually walk away. But I can assure you, that was a harder thing than going out there and doing it.' The following day he raced to a brave seventh place finish.

Blundell's accident was typical of the sort of risk a racing driver runs, but his team-mate Mika Hakkinen's accident at Adelaide, during practice for the next race, was even more serious. When a rear tyre deflated suddenly the Finn was sent crashing very hard into a concrete wall protected by two layers of tyres. He struck his head on the steering wheel, such was the force of the impact, and suffered a skull fracture. His life was only saved by an emergency trackside percutaneous mini-tracheotomy, performed at Professor Watkins' request by a local doctor, an anaesthetist with suitable experience who was among the team at that part of the circuit. After months of recuperation, Hakkinen was able to return to racing in time for the start of the following season, apparently none the worse for the experience, and subsequently went on to win the World Championship.

The Finn's miraculous deliverance was in its own way a confirmation of the progress that safety had made even since Senna's death, but at the same time it was an horrific illustration of the work that remained. The protective cockpits were certainly a major step forward, and work was already very well advanced at the time of the Adelaide incident, but it prompted even more serious consideration of air bags for the cockpits of F1 cars.

'Mika hit his head on the steering column, so you can appreciate just how far the safety belts stretched and how far his body elasticated,' said McLaren chief Ron Dennis. 'It's a long way from where

The message says it all, as the McLaren team in Adelaide wishes Mika Hakkinen a speedy recovery from the accident that would have been fatal but for an emergency trackside tracheotomy. (Sutton)

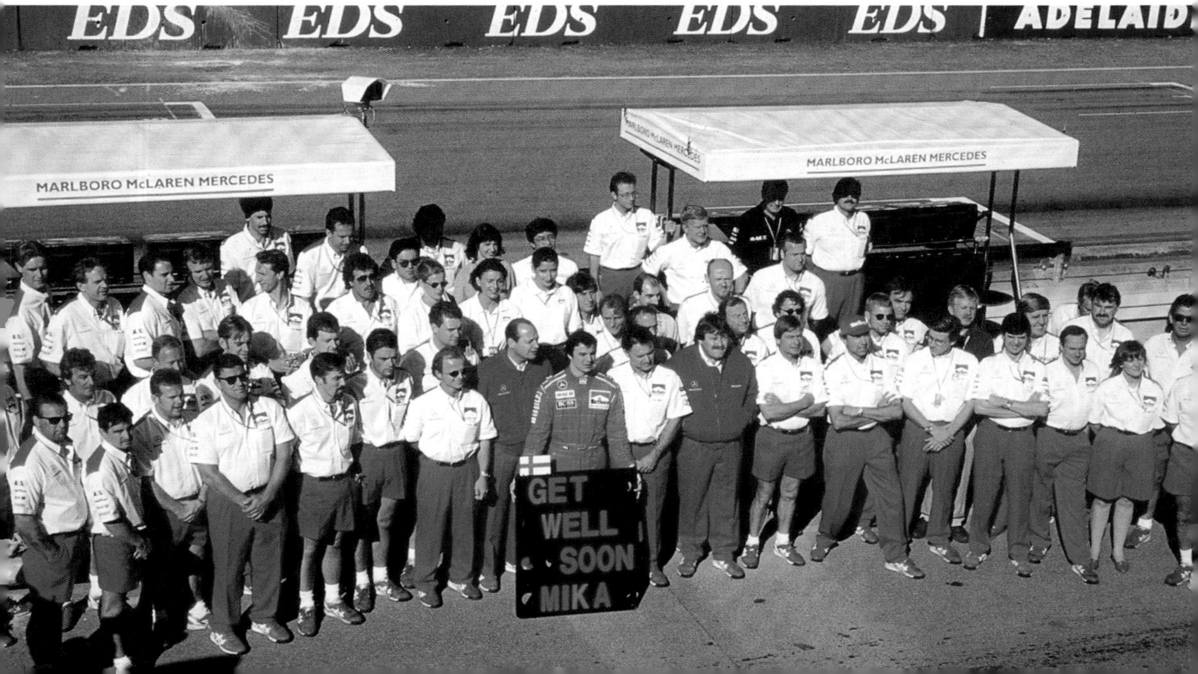

his head started and where it struck. I'm told by Prof Watkins that the forces required to fracture a skull in that way, are very, very high.'

At the time, air bags seemed a promising avenue of investigation. Meanwhile, however, protective cockpits continued to hold the fort. The Dutch driver Jos Verstappen escaped from a very heavy accident during the Belgian GP in 1996, when his Arrows suffered a stub axle failure. Because the incident was not shown on television its severity went largely unnoticed, but FIA president Max Mosley brought the subject up at Monaco in 1997 when discussing safety matters.

'You may be interested to know what we have learned about the cockpit padding that we required on F1 cars at the beginning of last season,' he said. 'After the accident we studied both Verstappen's helmet and the padding on his Arrows. We now have conclusive scientific evidence that without the cockpit padding, his accident would have been fatal.'

Verstappen himself was amused by this revelation, as only racing drivers can be. 'I hear Max is saying that my accident at Spa would have been fatal if I hadn't had a safety cockpit?' he inquired with a smile. And he thought for a moment or two, before adding: 'You know, I guess he's probably right!'

'I think that safety cockpits are one of the biggest areas of safety that we've had,' Jordan's technical director Gary

The spectre of fire returned briefly to F1 during the Argentine GP in 1996, when a faulty fuel valve during a refuelling stop resulted in Pedro Diniz's Ligier catching fire. The Brazilian vacated his hot seat in a hurry after spinning deliberately into a gravel bed run-off. (T.Melzer/Sutton)

Anderson said. 'I felt that the sides could be narrower and closer to the driver's head, all that sort of stuff, like IndyCars, but ... It's better if the guy is taking load vertically, down through his head, through the spine rather than through the neck.'

* * *

Another highly significant, but little appreciated, breakthrough came in 1997, when it became mandatory for all cars to carry Accident Data Recorders (ADRs).

'It's very, very rare to have a big accident where you actually know what the forces are,' Max Mosley points out. The biggest accidents outside F1 involve trains or planes, and often there are few survivors. Now we get an awful lot of basic information that we never had before.'

The F1 ADRs are made by Delphi (formerly Delco) and located just below the driver's spine, as near the centre of gravity as possible. Basically, the current ADR has built-in sensors that provide what data investigators require of any accident: high and low-g accelerometers. 'The first thing I did when I came to the FIA was to say to Max that I didn't believe that we had no data on Senna's accident,' Wright continues, the incredulity evident in his voice. 'In this day and age we had to do something about that, so I laid down the specification of what I wanted to know:

Having vaulted over Jean Alesi's Sauber Petronas and Heinz-Harald Frentzen's Williams during the dramatic start of the Canadian GP at Montreal in 1998, as the field concertinaed in the tight first corner, Alexander Wurz's Benetton then made heavy contact with Jarno Trulli's Prost before rolling into the gravel run-off area. Despite the terrifying ferocity of the accident, none of the drivers was injured. (Sutton)

Everything from the point at which the driver loses control, to the point where the dust settles.

'It's different to aircraft systems. Conventional crash recorders, which were already running in CART, just measured the impact. They didn't tell you anything about the speed of the car. The crash recorders in aeroplanes tell you nothing about the impact, and everything about what happened before. The ADRs in F1 are kind of a combination. They tell you what happened before and what happened during. The box of electronics with the sensors built in has got to be bolted hard to the car, which means that it's subjected to all the vibration. That can scramble the electronics. That's why all the normal electronics black boxes on racing cars have been mounted on rubber. You can't do that with the crash box, because it wouldn't measure the crash. The vibration from the engine looks remarkably like an accident all the time, plus or minus 80g, 250–300 Hz. So it's just *waaah*. Noise!

'Fortunately, the drivers tend to come off the throttle before they hit things. Not always. When they go in with full throttle – which does happen – or with their foot on the throttle, you don't get a crash path. It's just swamped by the engine vibration.

'What happens is that the crash looks like that,' – he scribbles on a piece of paper to indicate the graphic representation of the impact – 'which you then filter to get the crash pulse, and then the engine does that,' – he scribbles again. 'You can't separate the two. If you had a signal from the engine, you could probably synchronise that and pull it off, but we don't.'

The latest ADRs include rotation sensors to detect yaw, and thus provide a better understanding of the trajectory of the car. They also have a port which connects into the network of the car and can thus collect data from the car: the lap marker, car speed, steering input and throttle opening. 'Initially we had other things too,' Wright says with a rueful laugh. 'But that would have allowed us to look for traction control, and the teams spotted that!'

The system has the potential to record all sorts of other things; in America, for example, CART is measuring seat belt loads in accidents. It is an extremely hard task to make the systems work because of the unfriendly environment in which they are asked to operate, but Wright is full of praise for Delphi.

'What this means,' he enthuses,' is that as well as looking at the accident from beginning to end, the system also stores enough data that you get all or most of the previous lap, so you can see what happened that was different between the two laps. I have seen accidents that aren't necessarily predictable, and you can see that the car has bottomed on that lap and that the driver has lost control as a result. You can see the difference between what the driver does and what the car does, and say that that is the cause of the loss of control.'

This is the sort of data that would have made an immeasurable difference in the investigation into Ayrton Senna's accident, the precise cause of which remains a mystery all these years later. 'I've talked to Patrick [Head] about it,' Wright says, 'and the only thing you can say is that the steering column was broken by the end of the accident. I would be very interested about the car bottoming on cold tyres, with low pressures. It doesn't half upset it when a car bottoms. It's just enough, usually, to unload the wheels, and the car starts to run wide.

'What I really find unacceptable is that we couldn't just go into it all and say, "Right, that's what happened". At least we could have had an effect on the legal process, set people's minds at rest. In this day and age we should be able to do that. And now we have that in place. It's a lot of work running this, and a big task at the circuit, making sure it all

Chaos reigned on the downhill run from La Source after David Coulthard spun his McLaren on the opening lap of the 1998 Belgian GP. Of particular concern to FIA officials was the number of wheels torn off as half the field collided. (Mazzi/Sutton)

works. We never got Panis's crash pulse when he broke his legs in Montreal, because something didn't work. We struggled a bit to start with. But we got a lot of data, and it was enough to start doing a statistical analysis.'

The FIA had also introduced a rear impact test in 1997. Most teams came up with something incorporated into the rear wing support. The Italian driver Giancarlo Fisichella was unwittingly the first to test the structure empirically, and the value of the ADR, when he lost control of his Jordan-Peugeot at Silverstone during a test early in 1997. He left the road backwards at Stowe corner in a similar accident to the one which had damaged JJ Lehto's neck in 1994, or Jean Alesi's mirror repeat for Ferrari at Mugello around the same time. The Jordan was fitted with an ADR, and the figures make interesting, if chilling, reading. The Jordan went from 227kph (141mph) to zero in 0.72s, with an impact speed of 50g and a deceleration of 12g. But the new rear impact structure saved him from any serious injury, and the cockpit structure also did its bit.

'It helped Giancarlo enormously,' Gary Anderson said, 'and he was able to get himself out. He did a couple of circles, found out he'd hurt his knee, then lay down. For that to be the end result of that sort of accident was pretty impressive. We'd also have done the gearbox there, no problem, without the structure. But we were actually able to use the same gearbox casing in Brazil the following weekend.'

Fisichella had actually fractured his knee, but the team kept that quiet at the time otherwise he would not have been allowed to race in Brazil. The very fact that he could, after such fearsome deceleration, spoke volumes for progress. As with so many 'nineties accidents that tended to get shrugged off because the driver walked away, ten years earlier it would probably have been fatal.

★ ★ ★

In the aftermath of the oft-overlooked Pedro Lamy/JJ Lehto accident at Imola the FIA had also set in train an investigation into ensuring that wheels sheared off in accidents rather than being retained by one link and thus swinging back dangerously into the cockpit. They almost came too late. On the wet opening lap of the Belgian GP in 1998, David Coulthard spun his McLaren-Mercedes exiting the La Source hairpin and triggered Scheckter-like carnage on the run down to Eau Rouge as car after car became entangled. As chassis tobogganed down the hill, errant wheels flew everywhere.

'I think probably the single biggest step in the last ten years is the wheel tethers,' Peter Wright says. 'It was just pure statistics with the amount of wheels bouncing around, that sooner or later one was going to hit something or someone. Prior to the 2000 Italian GP at Monza the last person to be killed in F1, Senna, was because of a wheel and suspension component. They have the same problem in the States. They had a couple go into the crowd and hit people, and they put wheel tethers on so fast it was untrue.

'It's not unlucky, it's just statistical inevitability. If you look at a wheel separately, and the amount of energy stored in it, they are going to end up in places you can't stop them going unless you put a lid on it. The first thing I was told in F1 is that if you see a wheel rolling slowly down the road towards you, don't try and stop it. They have a lot of rotational energy, so that if they hit anything it can set them off on trajectories that you are not expecting.'

The author can vouch for that, after a wheel lost from New Zealander Paul Radisich's F3 Ralt at Zandvoort in 1986 passed over his head at no more than 3m (10ft) before whirling madly into the paddock.

'A wheel came off a car at Castle Combe in 1999 and hit David Richards's helicopter, which was half a mile away,'

Wright continues. 'It broke the tail off and caused £500,000 worth of damage. And obviously he had been told to park it in what was thought to be a safe place …

'We were incredibly lucky at Spa in 1998, because somebody was killed by an errant wheel in a minor race there a year later. It happens. You've only got to look at *La Source* at that time, to see the number of wheels flying around. It was pure luck that somebody didn't get hit.'

Sadly, that luck was absent at Monza in 2000 when fire marshal Paolo Ghislimberti died after being hit by debris – possibly a wheel – thrown from a multi-car accident in the second chicane.

Single tethers were introduced in 1999, and immediately proved their worth when Mika Hakkinen lost control of his McLaren in practice in the first race, at Melbourne. He did a fair bit of suspension damage, on all four corners, after going into the wall exiting the final corner. But all four wheels stayed attached and the spectating public remained perfectly safe. A race later, Ricardo Zonta lost control of his BAR over a kerb in Interlagos, and hit a wall hard enough to damage his left foot, which was fractured, and some of the tendons which were cut by penetration of metal through the cockpit side. But once again the wheels, though they did not stay attached, did not travel. The problem was that the tethers were occasionally doing serious damage to the monocoques, but it was only later, when wheels started coming off again during impacts, that the FIA's engineers were obliged to have another look.

'The thing is, the tethers have 5,000kg [1,1023lb] breaking strain, and you can generate forces greater than that, never mind any cutting action or what have you. So under certain circumstances they are going to fail, and there's not much you can do about that. If you trap a wheel against a barrier or something, and then drag it, you are basically not going to stop the car from tearing it off itself. I really liked what IRL and CART did, which was to use two tethers. That makes lots of sense, so that's what we did for 2000.

'The trouble is deciding where the tethers should yield. Where IRL is going is putting one at 50 kiloNewtons, and the other at 100. So you have a belt and

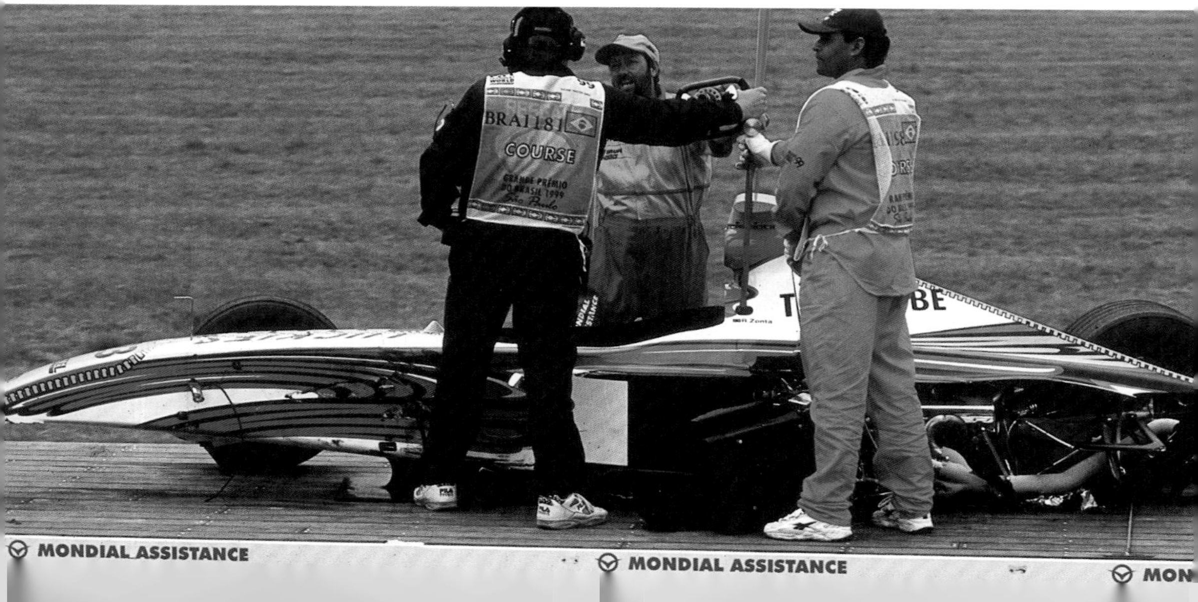

Wheel tethers proved one answer to the errant wheel problem, but as Ricardo Zonta's accident during practice in Brazil in 1999 indicated, the problem was a complex one. (Sutton)

braces thing. The great thing is that when you break the first one it absorbs a lot of energy, so the second one, which is stronger in any case, has a much better chance of hanging on.'

At Suzuka, two months later, another significant step was revealed when Jackie Stewart, Prof Watkins, and Charlie Whiting unveiled the Lear Extractable Safety Seat.

For some time Watkins had been concerned about possible spinal injury to drivers while they were being extracted from damaged racing cars. 'You will have seen us practising the removal of drivers from cars using a spinal splint,' he said. 'This has always been a difficult undertaking.

'At every Grand Prix we now deploy two or three fully trained extrication teams, comprising both marshals and doctors, who are trained in the use of the spinal splint. In any racing accident in which the driver is rendered unconscious there is no way of knowing whether he has fractured his spine, and of course there is no way of knowing where such an injury has been sustained. It may be in the lumbar region, in the dorsal region, or in the neck itself.

'If at all possible, it is important not to move a patient who has fractures, because the movement may well dislocate the fractured areas, making the injuries much worse. In the past, using the standard seats and cockpits, the dilemma that may arise has been the necessity to move the driver forward from his seat, in order to insert the spinal splint. Although this has been done successfully, for the past five years we have been seeking a better solution. This appeared to be the development of a seat, configured (as modern seats are) to the measurements of each driver, in order to provide him with a perfectly fitting seat which will itself also serve as a spinal splint.'

The difficulty lay in designing and manufacturing a seat which could be removed from the cockpit in one easy movement. Watkins and the FIA's race director and safety delegate Charlie Whiting had, via the Expert Advisory Group, been pushing for this for the past three years, and with the help of Stewart and one of his team sponsors, the Lear Corporation, the breakthrough had finally been made. Watkins and Whiting had passed on the expert analysis and recommendations to Lear, who then produced the required seat.

Watkins summarised the three stages of driver extraction. First, the driver's head is secured and his neck is supported while his crash helmet is removed; then the car's head and neck protection is removed from the cockpit lip; and finally, marshals lift the driver via four ropes whose hooks attach to inbuilt loops on the seat. Like so many inventions, it is ingenious.

'Even before I heard about a seat development that was taking place at Lear, our chief engineer Alan Jenkins had also informed himself,' Stewart said. 'In fact, it was Alan who suggested that I might visit Lear. Safety in motor racing has made immense progress in the past few years, and much of that must be attributed to Professor Watkins. It is very satisfying to know that no matter what technology man devises to improve car performance, there are constant improvements to be made in safety, too. Here is an example that provides ample hope not only that drivers will survive accidents but that they may be able to walk after crashes that would otherwise have left them paralysed.' The Lear seat proved that where safety is concerned, you keep going on until you discover inadequacies in whatever system has been developed, and then make the apposite changes.

That same month the FIA World Motor Sport Council met to discuss further means of enhancing the structural safety of F1 cars. Many teams had started using advanced composites of

After a kerfuffle in the first corner during the 1999 GP of Europe, Pedro Diniz found his Sauber Petronas looking at the sky the wrong way. Though the rollover hoop structure failed, Sauber's unique cockpit design continued to protect the Brazilian's head. (Sutton)

extremely high modulus which were very light yet still provided sufficient torsional rigidity. However, there were concerns about the materials' ability to handle lateral impacts. So from 1 January 2000 the outer skin laminates of the cockpit survival cell had to be a minimum 3.5cm (1.4in) thick, and incorporate 2.5cm (1in) thick Kevlar-laminated panels to reduce penetration, as in Zonta's accident. There was also a new side test, alongside the driver's legs, introduced to supplement these rules.

To further improve side head protection and ensure that energy-absorbing foam came up to the top of the cockpit sides, a new three-dimensional cockpit entry template was introduced.

The frontal impact test speed was upped from 13m/s to 14 (42.6ft/s to 46), and the regulation of rear impact structures was tightened to ensure complete integrity in off-centre impacts. A minimal cross-section of 90sq cm (295sq in) was introduced. And after a number of different ideas on seat belt mounting had been encountered in 1999, a standardised securing system was developed.

'There is a lot of crushable structure around the cars now,' says Wright. 'There is a very strong survival cell, stronger still for 2000 with the Kevlar side panels which really armour plate the sides of the monocoque. That should stop wheels coming in through the side of the chassis. It was helpful for Schumacher that that happened at Silverstone, but it's better if you achieve that give in another way.' It's a little like specifying the gauge of aluminium that had to be used in monocoque chassis in the old days. It's likely that these panels will in time have their own crash test requirement.

'The speed of the frontal impact test goes steadily up each year. It goes up around 1kph (0.6mph); that's about 16 per cent of energy. The side impact test will be much more stringent from 2001.

Jacques Villeneuve demonstrates the new raised cockpit regulations on his 1996 Williams FW18. (Formula One Pictures)

These things are all going to help. All these things are trying to cover the one or two cases where somebody gets hurt. The things that are in place now have got it down to one or two per cent, but that's still there.'

In the GP of Europe at the Nürburgring, Brazilian driver Pedro Diniz had been involved in a spectacular accident when his Sauber Petronas was flipped over by Alexander Wurz's Benetton. The rollover hoop on the Swiss car had sheared on oblique impact with the kerb, despite having passed the mandatory crash tests at the beginning of the season. This was obviously a serious matter, but Diniz was fortunate that the design of the Sauber C18 brought the rear of the cockpit up above head height even before the rollover hoop was fitted, and he was lifted out of the upturned car by the extraction team without injury. For 2000 the FIA also introduced advisory regulations for a stronger rollover hoop structure, with the intention of making them mandatory by 2001.

While all this was going on the Expert Advisory Group had looked at, but ultimately rejected, the idea of inflatable seat belts. The study had concluded that while they might work in a road car, they were not best suited to F1. Nor, it seemed, were air bags.

Back in Adelaide in 1995 they had seemed the perfect salvation, following Hakkinen's accident, and at the time GPDA safety representative Gerhard Berger was among those who had seen what the Expert Advisory Group had been looking at to restrict driver movement in an accident. 'They've shown me some of the work they have been doing, and it certainly impressed me,' he said.

Ron Dennis, however, was sceptical all along about air bags. On the face of it they are relatively simple devices designed to expand rapidly in an accident so that the vehicle's occupants are

Charlie Whiting, Prof Watkins and Jackie Stewart launched the new Lear Extractable Safety Seat at Suzuka in 1998. It became mandatory for 1999. (Sutton)

effectively protected from the impact by a large balloon-like bag which has sufficient 'give' to prevent them striking a solid object. They were already fitted on many upmarket road cars and the results had been impressive, but there had been problems. The explosive charge that detonates the bags, for example, could damage the interior of the car. Then there was the problem of precisely where the bags should be installed.

In road cars neither problem was particularly significant, but when the situation was transferred to the tight confines of a race car, some serious considerations arose. Not the least of them concerned precisely where to locate the bag, and the potential risk that the detonation might harm the driver.

There were further problems safeguarding against premature or accidental deployment, such as when a car might be jolted over sharp bumps or collide with another vehicle. Choosing the g-loading at which the bag would be triggered would also be critical, and the dangers of accidental deployment when the driver was travelling at maximum speed were self-evident.

'The speed of these accidents is so much higher than anything experienced on a production car that our engineers believe there is no system that could inflate fast enough to accommodate this sort of impact,' Dennis said. He believed that the sport should look to other areas, among them things such as more progressively deformable crash barriers.

Ross Brawn, then technical director of champion constructor Benetton, was more optimistic. 'What you are trying to do is decelerate the head, and there is a very arbitrary figure arrived at for the average human being which gives a critical impact figure for cranial deceleration. If you decelerate it too quickly, you will extrude a driver's brains through his ears, and we don't want to do that. So what we try to do is slow the head in a progressive way; but if you let it move too far laterally you then start to risk neck problems. It's a juggling act between deceleration rates, duration, and size of impact. You can have a relatively low impact but if it's sustained for a long time that can do a lot of damage. Or you can have a higher impact for a much shorter period.'

Brawn, like all designers, favoured increased deformable structures on the cars themselves, for in any impact getting rid of a car's kinetic energy is vitally important. 'We need to be able to get more information to verify that any trigger mechanism can react quickly enough,' he continued when discussing the possibility of air bags in Adelaide in 1995, 'but the people who make the air bag believe they can come up with one that will be viable.'

Watkins harboured no doubts about the desirability of air bags, and believed then that they could be seen as soon as 1996. 'Naturally we want them to inflate as soon as possible but not to hinder a driver's escape or extrication from the cockpit. They also need to be small enough so that if they did go off accidentally they would not be a hazard.' He envisaged then a small bag mounted in the steering wheel.

Though air bags were not, after all, deemed ready for 1996, nor even 1997, investigations went on. At Monaco in 1997 Mosley said, 'Our research is continuing, in collaboration with Daimler-Benz, and we have learned some very interesting things. It would be premature to discuss details, but we will not impose any regulations until we can be sure that they are entirely safe.'

On 23 October 1996 a joint venture between the FIA, Mercedes-Benz, and McLaren International in Stuttgart defined the requirements of a driver protection system to cope with frontal impacts. The new system had to be satisfactory in frontal impacts and in an oblique frontal impact with a realistic angle of up to 30°. A Formula 3000 monocoque with the 1998 Formula One cockpit dimensions was employed as a suitable crash test environment. The tests investigated the latest developments in air bag technology for racing cars, and a separate system known as HANS, an acronym for Head and Neck Support. The latter proved a particularly effective driver protection system.

HANS was conceived in 1991 by Dr Robert Hubbard, a biomechanics professor at Michigan State University. His initial research was intended primarily for car racers, but then Mod-VP powerboat racer Andy Anderson survived a flip without life-threatening injuries because he was the only driver wearing the HANS system. That prompted Hubbard to switch his research to powerboaters.

In crash sled tests with HANS at 65kph (40mph), the dummy's head was subjected to 453kg (1,000lb) of neck load. With HANS, that figure was dramatically reduced to 59kg (130lb), with reduced head motion.

The FIA's joint venture refined Hubbard's concept into a rigid, collar-shaped carbon fibre shell which slips over the driver's shoulders and is held there, once he is in the cockpit, by the safety belt shoulder straps. The collar is then attached to his helmet by appropriate tethers.

In a heavy frontal accident we have seen that even a driver restrained by seat belts can suffer serious forward movement as the belts stretch, as they are designed to in order to prevent internal injury to the driver. But Zanardi proved with his accident at Spa's Eau Rouge in 1993, and Hakkinen partly demonstrated in Adelaide in 1995, that movement could be so great as to allow the driver's

Schematic shows how the Lear Extractable Safety Seat operates. (Lear)

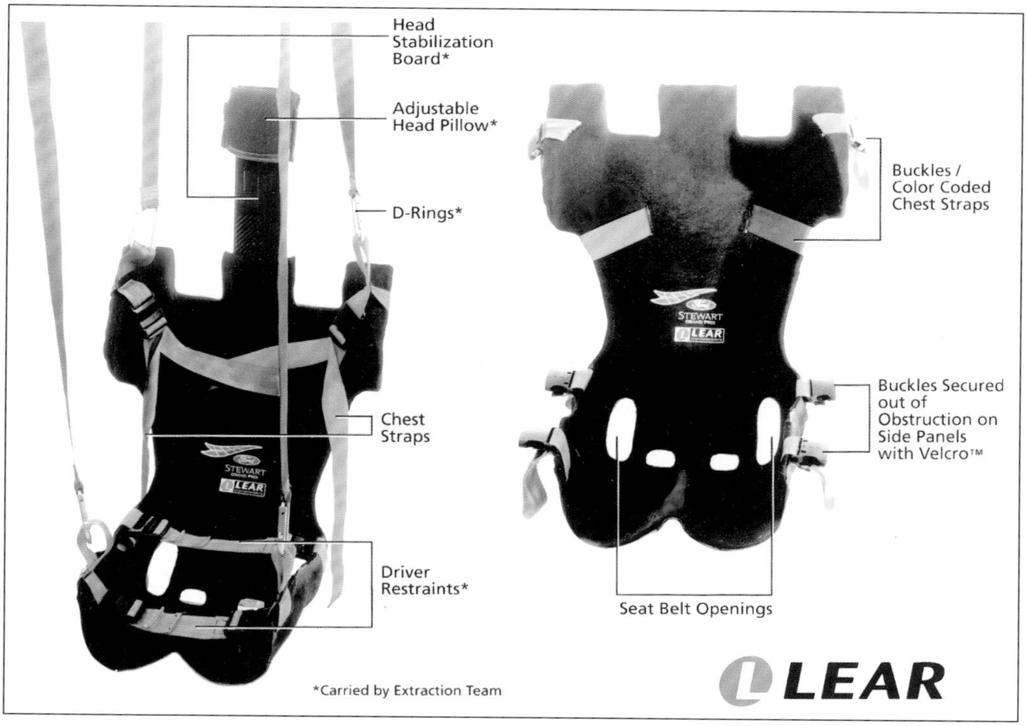

head to come into contact with the dashboard. In Hakkinen's case, the situation was exacerbated by the Finn's dislike at that time of having his belts done up really tight.

The HANS system prevents this. It minimises the head's extreme accelerated movement and therefore dangerous neck strain, because the belts hold the driver to a reasonable degree, and therefore anchor the HANS collar on to his shoulders, while at the same time the helmet tethers prevent further forward movement of his head.

At the San Marino GP of 2000, Mercedes-Benz, McLaren International, and the FIA presented the results of their testing in the form of a light HANS prototype in composite material, which weighed less than 700gm (1.5lb).

Jurgen Hubbert, a Board member of DaimlerChrysler, said: 'We are happy to take up the suggestion from the FIA of bringing our knowledge and our many years of experience of safety engineering for production vehicles to the HANS project, and possibly also to further research projects. We consider this to be a significant contribution towards making the fascinating sport of Formula One even more safe.'

Max Mosley backed that view. 'This is a major step forward in the search to introduce ever improved safety standards,' he said. 'It is particularly significant that this research has been carried

The HANS system, effectively a special collar to stop a driver's head moving too far forward in a head-on accident, has been deemed a superior answer to the air bag. (Mercedes-Benz)

At the DTM Championship round in May 2000, Bernd Schneider demonstrates the HANS system. All drivers in the race wore it, but in F1 drivers still have reservations about head and neck mobility while wearing the design. (Sutton)

out jointly with one of the world's major car manufacturers. This shows how motor sport is a research medium for the motor car industry not only for performance, but also for safety.'

HANS effectively spelled the end for the air bag, at least for the immediate future. 'We had a big programme going on with Mercedes for an air bag, and obviously if you have an air bag in Formula One it has to fire very violently,' said Mosley. 'And you usually have more than one impact in an accident. To cut a long story short, it was shown that the HANS system is superior to an air bag in just about every circumstance. So that's obviously the thing to do. But because it's awkward and uncomfortable the drivers say that if you are going to have it you will have to make it compulsory.'

'Air bags are a different thing altogether, and pose greater problems,' Wright agrees. 'That is much of the reason why research into their usage effectively stopped once HANS began to deliver such promising results.

'The air bag design was pulled out over the steering wheel by one explosive device, and was then triggered and inflated by another. And it worked. But there was two years of development needed to solve further problems and make it totally safe. What happened if there was a second impact; if you hit something and fire it, and then hit another barrier? Or if it triggered off because of loading from running over a kerb? All those sort of things had to be considered. It became very clear that HANS was so good that it was the way to go. It does everything that an air bag does, and it's passive.'

HANS had several immediate advantages. Impact loads are transmitted evenly across the driver's forehead with

HANS, instead of to the chin as would be the case with an air bag. Furthermore, since the driver's seating position is almost horizontal in the modern F1 monocoque, an air bag cannot cushion the head and chest simultaneously, as would be the case in a road car application. Consequently the low neck strain achieved with an air bag system could not be guaranteed in an F1 application. The same problem was eliminated with HANS, which was the principal reason why it proved superior.

Michael Andretti and one or two other ChampCar drivers were among the first to try HANS, while in Formula One the role fell to David Coulthard, who tried it in a McLaren MP4/13 during pre-season testing.

Both Hubbert and McLaren chief Ron Dennis admitted that the prototype was just that, while Mosley agreed that though the intention was to make HANS mandatory for the 2001 season, a degree of customisation would be allowed as some drivers complained that the system was not entirely comfortable. The same thing was the case in powerboating, where drivers occasionally complained that lifejacket collars restricted their head mobility and thus created some problems with all-round vision. Many young karters are also irritated by anti-whiplash safety collars. All drivers, however, appreciate the safety issues and the sense in wearing such protection, and there is an ongoing commitment in all quarters to refine systems to make them as comfortable to use as possible.

Drivers who have tried HANS have expressed their belief in its ability to save them in a head-on shunt, but they have reservations. 'It's uncomfortable,' said one. 'I would be worried if the FIA made it mandatory, without some changes being incorporated, because the collar definitely restricts your head movement.'

The future seemed to hold great promise of even better safety facilities, but life has a way of throwing out warnings, and motor racing is nothing if not a microcosm of life. During a pre-British GP test at Silverstone the unfortunate Ricardo Zonta was involved in another shunt. The front suspension broke as he approached Stowe, scene of Schumacher's crash the previous year. Zonta's BAR-Honda went end-over-end, vaulted the tyre wall and ended up just in front of the grandstands on the outside of the corner. It was enough to panic anyone, and for the British Racing Drivers' Club, which owns and runs the track, it was another uncomfortable reminder, like Pedro Lamy's shunt six years earlier, that nothing can ever be taken for granted no matter how many precautions may be taken.

'When the accident happened it was raining, it was my fourth lap of the morning,' Zonta recalls. 'I just touched on the brakes and called for fourth gear and suddenly the wheel went away. I knew it was going to be a very big shunt! I just held the steering wheel really hard, rather than have my arms flap around and maybe get damaged on the sides of the cockpit. When I opened my eyes I couldn't believe where the car was …'

It was a further tribute to the far-reaching investigations instigated by the FIA in 1994 that Zonta walked away unhurt. But it was another alarm call to the designers and safety delegates never to lose sight of the fact that motor racing was still a knife-edge sport.

Mosley has several times professed his personal aim to ensure that it will no longer be one that might kill its participants. While others might privately have thought that that was an impossible aspiration, given its very nature, none of them was going to draw back from trying to achieve it. But for every step forward that they took, they were acutely aware that all progress brings in its wake a different set of problems. The trick is not to introduce more than you solve. And never to feel complacent.

Chapter 15

International rescue

LORENZO BANDINI, MONACO 1967

I think Lorenzo just got tired. That Ferrari was a big old car to be hauling round Monaco all afternoon.

Denny Hulme

Lorenzo Bandini was one of Italy's most promising young race drivers when, midway through 1966, he had leadership of the Ferrari team thrust upon him by the dramatic departure of number one driver John Surtees.

This came about as a result of autocratic team manager Eugenio Dragoni's desire to create an Italian champion. The man he had in mind all along was Bandini, who found himself in an invidious position. He liked Surtees, and Surtees in turn liked him. But when Dragoni made life so awkward for Surtees when forming driver pairings for Le Mans in the middle of that season, the Englishman finally quit and switched to Cooper.

Bandini took pole position for his first race as Ferrari team leader, at Reims, and led comfortably until the 38th lap. Then, at the Thillois hairpin, his throttle cable broke. He finished sixth in the outclassed car at Zandvoort, a result he repeated in the wet German GP. More was expected of both Bandini and his car in the Italian GP at Monza, where he sprinted to the lead from the second row of the grid. But then a fuel line broke on the second lap, leaving team-mates Lodovico Scarfiotti and Mike Parkes to vie for victory.

Watkins Glen hosted the final race of Ferrari's season, the US Grand Prix. Bandini qualified third and led for the first ten laps until Jack Brabham overtook him, but soon retook the initiative. He stayed in the lead for another 24 laps, until an internal failure silenced the V12.

Much was expected of him in 1967. In sports cars he was a genuine star; in F1 he was a man on the move. He proved a point at the non-championship Race of Champions at Brands Hatch in March. After a misfire had held him back in the two heats, he charged through the field to hound winner Dan Gurney's Eagle-Weslake to the line.

Bandini had only ever won a single Grand Prix, in Austria in 1964. But now he was ready to rectify that as the circus moved to Monte Carlo in May. The Monaco GP was scheduled for 100 gruelling laps round the Principality, and he shared the front row with Jack Brabham, whose more nimble Brabham-Repco circulated half a second quicker than the heavy Ferrari. However, it was Brabham's partner Denny Hulme with whom Bandini would have to contend in what was to be his last race.

The Italian took an immediate lead, but after Brabham's engine had blown up on the opening lap Hulme and Jackie Stewart displaced him in their more wieldy cars. Stewart led for 15 laps until his BRM broke its transmission, which promoted Hulme to first place. Bandini gave chase.

Hulme was driving the race of his life and the Brabham was clearly faster than the Ferrari. But Bandini plugged on. The responsibility he felt resting upon him was enormous, not only to uphold Ferrari's honour, but Italy's.

For a while he fell back, but then he got his second wind and began to push after Hulme again. But the heavy Ferrari was a handful round the tight course. As Bandini headed towards the waterfront chicane for the 82nd time, he made a mistake. He clipped the inside wall with his right front wheel, and that was all it needed to throw the red car across the road. Today such an incident would be trivial. Back then, however, it was fatal.

The Ferrari hit the straw bales on the outside edge of the track by the harbour. Its left rear wheel was torn off, and the car landed upside down, partially blocking the track. The impact, though relatively small, proved devastating. Ferrari still employed a spaceframe chassis at that time, albeit strengthened by stressed-skin aluminium panelling. The fuel tank was ruptured, and immediately a fire broke out.

Bandini was trapped. The feeble rollover hoop had failed, and one of his arms was caught between the lip of the cockpit and the road. Though conscious, there was no way that he could help him-

Monaco, 1967. Chris Amon passes the scene of Lorenzo Bandini's fatal accident by the harbour. The Ferrari team leader lost control and overturned after striking straw bales. (Phipps/Sutton)

self. At the same time, the marshalling at Monaco was woefully inadequate.

Rescuers used ropes to try and drag the Ferrari back on to its wheels, but rather than injure Bandini's arm further by trying to pull the car in the easier direction, they tried to overcome the handicap of the remaining right-hand wheels and pull it over that way. Precious time was lost, and as the fire raged poor Bandini suffered terribly. The rescue operation was badly organised and lacked any real direction. Panic ensued. The situation was further exacerbated by a helicopter, from which the whole tragic incident was being filmed, which flew so low that its downdraught fanned the flames of the fire.

By the time the Ferrari was righted and Bandini was finally extracted, his condition was critical. He was taken across Monte Carlo's harbour by boat and thence to hospital, where his injuries included serious burns, a broken arm and a damaged lung. He survived for three days.

As in so many cases, Lorenzo Bandini's accident highlighted a myriad of shortcomings in the way in which marshals were dressed, equipped, and trained to react to accident situations, and to fight fires. And once again precious little was done that made any difference, as Jo Schlesser's accident a year later would all too chillingly prove.

JO SCHLESSER, ROUEN 1968

That car was bloody scary, lad. It looked absolutely awful, a real handful!

Innes Ireland

Much was made of Jo Schlesser's shortage of experience at F1 level, but the 40-year-old Frenchman was a perfectly capable journeyman racer who had shown well at Formula Two level on

In a team run by Honda France mechanics, the ill-fated Jo Schlesser prepares to practise Honda's air-cooled RA302 at Rouen in 1968. (Phipps/Sutton)

many occasions. He had also competed in the 1965 Race of Champions, and in the F2 section of the 1967 German GP. The root of his death was seen to lie with Soicihiro Honda's extraordinary decision to overrule John Surtees's counsel and insist that Honda's experimental RA302 air-cooled V8 car be raced at the 1968 French GP at Rouen.

Surtees had joined with Honda in 1967, and together with Lola had developed a more competitive chassis for the Japanese company's bulky V12 engine. But back in Tokyo, Soichiro Honda had also set in motion the air-cooled project, since most of Honda's products at that time used air cooling. To Surtees's surprise, the RA302 appeared one day at his factory in Slough, with instructions that it should be tested and raced as soon as possible. Surtees tried it at Silverstone, where he voiced strong concerns over its behaviour and turned his focus back to the increasingly competitive V12-engined RA301. The late Innes Ireland watched Surtees test that day, and said in later years: 'That car was bloody scary, lad. It looked absolutely awful, a real handful!'

Surtees made his views clear to Tokyo and headed to France with the RA301. There, to his complete surprise, he was confronted by the sight of the RA302 in the paddock at Rouen. Tokyo had insisted it be raced, partly because Soichiro Honda was in Paris negotiating a deal to import his production cars. The nascent Honda France company was recruited to enter and run the car for Schlesser. Engineer Yoshio Nakamura felt so strongly that the car should not be raced that he refused to sign the entry form. Both he and Surtees, however, were overruled again by Soichiro Honda, who personally oversaw the entry. Nakamura then advised Schlesser that the RA302 was still very much a prototype, and should be treated as such. Schlesser appeared to take the advice to heart.

While Surtees placed the 12-cylinder car seventh on the grid, Schlesser was cautious and started from the back row. It rained prior to the start, making tyre choice a critical factor and the first lap a matter of exploring where the grip lay. Schlesser did not appear to be pushing too hard and came round a long way behind the leaders.

On his second lap he arrived at the Nouveau Monde hairpin, where witnesses reported that his engine cut out. The unwieldy Honda slithered up a bank, scattering spectators, before crashing heavily and bursting into flames. Much of the chassis was made of magnesium in the interest of lightness, and it burned fiercely.

Journalist Ed McDonough was less than 15m (50ft) from the corner, and has no doubts that he heard the engine cut out. Several friends confirmed his opinion. 'I could see fire marshals standing at the corner in asbestos suits but without gloves or protective helmets,' he reported, 'and making no effort to get near the car. Throughout earlier races they did not wear full equipment, nor did they pay much attention to the track.' McDonough also noticed that the fire extinguishers were defective, emitting only a trickle of extinguishant, and that the water poured on to the blaze merely exacerbated the magnesium's burn rate.

'The fire marshals appeared to have no idea as to how they should deal with this type of tragedy,' he said, struck more than anything by their callous nonchalance.

ROGER WILLIAMSON, ZANDVOORT 1973

I was trying to get people to help me, and if I could have turned the car over he would have been all right, we could have got him out.

David Purley

In motor racing's lengthy and often tragic history, few incidents have left such an indelible stain on its character as the accident in which 25-year-old Roger Williamson was the needless victim of fire at Zandvoort during the Dutch Grand Prix of 1973.

He had quickly worked his way up to 13th place by the eighth lap, running just ahead of fellow Briton David Purley, who was running a similar car under the private LEC Racing banner. A star in F3 and F2, Williamson was gaining experience prior to graduating full-time to F1 in 1974 with a McLaren M23 entered by his mentor Tom Wheatcroft, the Leicester builder and developer later to become famous for resurrecting Donington Park and its enviable collection of historic racing cars.

Then, going into the first of two very quick fifth-gear right-hand curves out on the back of the circuit, the left front tyre exploded.

Purley saw the red March veer left, strike the kerb and then hit the Armco barrier at an angle of around 45°. It rode along the top of the rail, which had been incorrectly installed in sand, not concrete. The barrier leaned backwards, and became a launching ramp. Williamson's March flew for perhaps 73m (240ft), then landed upside down on the opposite side of the track. As it slid along the road for another 100m (330ft), fuel leaked out. There was a momentary eruption of flame, but as the car came to rest, just on the apex of the second fast right-hander, the fire temporarily died down.

Purley had witnessed the whole thing. Later he would shrug off the hero status that his ensuing actions attracted, explaining that his training as a paratrooper had simply kicked in. Unlike any of his fellows, he immediately stopped his car on the left-hand side of the track, and sprinted to the accident scene. There he found Williamson alive,

On the last afternoon of his life, Roger Williamson leads David Purley round the dunes at Zandvoort during the 1973 Dutch GP. (David Tremayne Archive)

but trapped in the cockpit of the upturned car.

Around him, marshals stood transfixed, unable to impel themselves to go near the smoking car. None of them was wearing the correct fireproof clothing, though it was never clear whether this was because they had none, or simply because they chose not to wear it. A little further round the track, no more than 46 to 92m (150 to 300ft) just beyond the right-hander, the crew of a firefighting vehicle stayed in position, refusing to travel against the flow of traffic. They did not consider reversing, or undertaking a complete lap to get to the accident, even though for two laps the fire was fairly subdued. Meanwhile, another firefighting truck moved slowly from the paddock area in the direction of the accident, with no warning to approaching drivers.

'You would have thought that with double-waved yellows, you would have made the original fire truck go back to the scene,' Mosley says trenchantly. 'The whole thing was a fuck-up that wouldn't happen today, because we have sensible people running the races, and sensible people in the medical and emergency cars. It wouldn't have happened. In the end it always comes down to the same thing: it's not the cause of an accident that matters, it's the consequence.'

Aghast at the apathy all around him, Purley attempted alone to push the car over on to its wheels, all the while aware of Williamson pleading for help to escape. Purley would single-handedly strain so hard that he ruptured blood vessels in both arms.

For agonising moments – perhaps two or three vital minutes – there was sufficient time for a group of strong men to have turned the car over and helped Williamson out. But nobody came forward to help Purley. Then after other cars had completed a further two laps the fire began to take hold once more.

His March covered in fire extinguishant that arrived far too late, Williamson lies dead after cowardly marshals failed to act in time. (Phipps/Sutton)

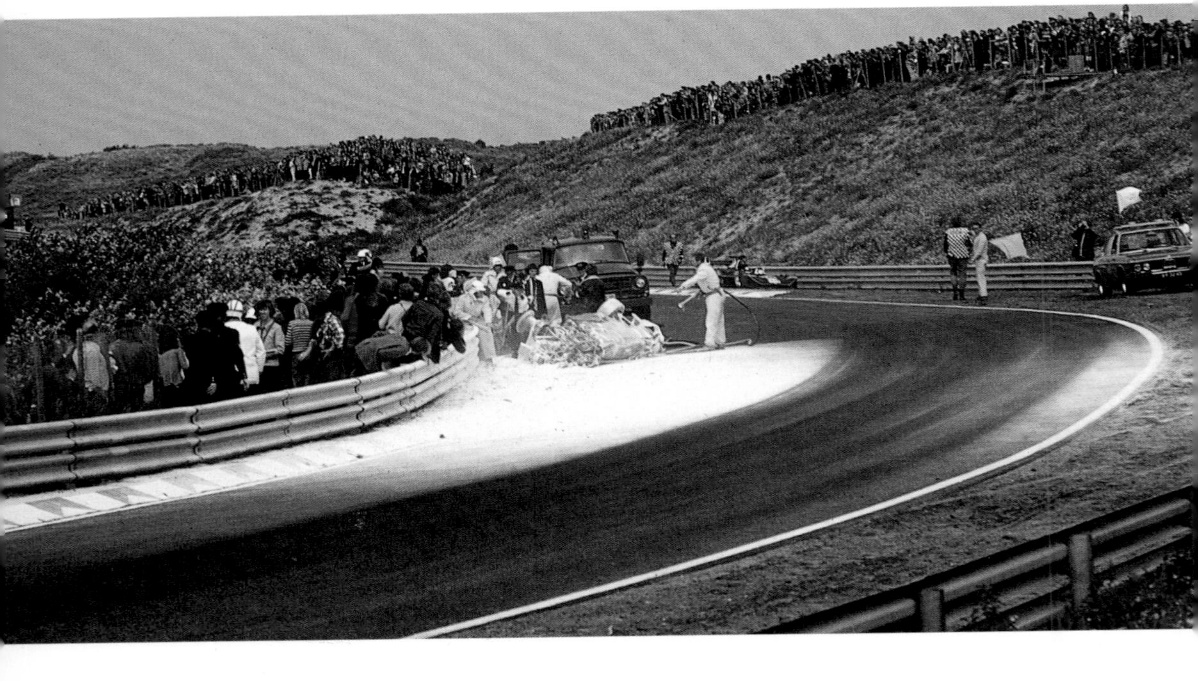

He ran across the track to grab an extinguisher, only to find that it didn't work. Finally, one marshal came forward with another, which also malfunctioned. Purley implored other marshals to move forward and help. None did. By now the fire had gained hold again, and was simply too strong. The marshals let it burn.

Assaulted by exhaustion and haunted by a terrible sense of inadequacy, Purley could still hear Williamson's cries as the marshals finally shook off their torpor and ventured forward to pull him away. Angrily, he shrugged them off and staggered away, crying his own tears of frustration. Elsewhere, police with dogs occupied themselves restraining any spectator brave enough to move to Purley's aid.

'I just couldn't turn it over,' Purley said. 'I could see Roger was alive and I could hear him shouting, but I couldn't get the car over. I was trying to get people to help me, and if I could have turned the car over he would have been all right, we could have got him out.'

All this while the race continued, and none of the other drivers stopped to render assistance. White smoke would obscure the track by the accident scene for several laps, and several drivers reported that they could feel their throttle slides sticking every time they passed the smoking wreckage. In it lay the body of man who would surely in time have challenged any one of them. Some, among them GPDA safety representative Denny Hulme, signalled angrily that the race should be stopped every time he passed the pits. But in those days there was no precedent for doing so.

In later years both Denny and Mike Hailwood, who had rescued Clay Regazzoni from his burning BRM earlier in the season at Kyalami, admitted that they were ashamed they had not had the courage to stop and help Purley. And later, like Hailwood, Purley was awarded the George Medal for gallantry for his brave efforts.

'Had the car not been upside down, Roger would have got out of it,' Mosley suggests. 'The marshals were, I think, very cowardly. If that had happened opposite the pits, everybody would have turned it up the right way whether they were dressed properly or not. It was possible to do it.'

The Dutch organisers deliberately put about a story that Williamson had died in the impact. The official report later confirmed what Purley already knew; Williamson was alive and uninjured, and died of asphyxiation. The organisers also made no comment on the fact that, since Piers Courage's fiery death three years earlier, only yards from the scene of the Williamson accident, its marshals appeared to have learned nothing. When Courage died, his de Tomaso had been left to burn and marshals had simply thrown sand on to it, leaving Courage's body aboard until the sacred race had run its course. In Williamson's case, they simply righted the car and then threw a sheet over it until the race had finished.

'All the organisers did for Roger was to get the car back to the garage,' Mosley recalls, 'then come to ask if a couple of us would go down and get the cadaver out. That was their only real concern. It was all so unnecessary. It could and should have been avoided. Roger was a good driver, sensational. He would have been a big star.'

TOM PRYCE, KYALAMI 1977

Stuck was the one who avoided the guy who ran across the road, and he did it so quickly that Tom was left out there. He wouldn't even have known about it, I'm sure of that.

Alan Rees

Like Williamson, shy 27-year-old Welshman Tom Pryce was a future champion in the making, as his performances for the Shadow team had demonstrated on numerous occasions. But the Northampton-based team's fortunes had fluctuated along with its budget, and in 1977 light had appeared on the horizon as the DN8, introduced the previous season, finally received some overdue development.

In the rain during practice at Kyalami, when raw talent could make its mark, Pryce had been in his element and was comfortably quickest, but qualifying dried out and he fell back. At the start of the South African GP he dropped inexplicably to last place, then began tigering back. By the 22nd lap he had caught a group comprising Jacques Laffite, Gunnar Nilsson, and Hans Stuck, fighting for 11th.

The previous lap, his team-mate Renzo Zorzi had coasted to a halt opposite the pits, just over the brow of a hill on the main straight. Wisps of smoke emanated from his engine bay as he climbed out, where a faulty fuel metering unit was pumping petrol on to the hot engine. That prompted two marshals, on the pit wall, to do the unthinkable. Against all reason they decided to run across the track. As they did so, a small dip hid three cars that were almost abreast.

The first marshal just made it. The second, a 19-year-old ticket clerk from Jan Smuts airport called Jansen van Vuuren, did not. He was lugging a heavy fire extinguisher. By pure reflex, Stuck was able to jink around him. But Pryce was trapped on the left-hand side of the track, with Nilsson to his right. There was nowhere to go. His Shadow struck and killed van Vuuren, tossing him into the air like a rag doll. But the extinguisher hit Pryce full in the face at 290kph (180mph). He, too, had no chance.

Its driver already dead, the Shadow

Charging through after a poor start, Shadow driver Tom Pryce was the victim of a needless accident during the 1977 South African GP at Kyalami, dying instantly when a young marshal ran across the track in front of him. (Phipps/Sutton)

careened down the straight to Crowthorne corner, where it collided with Laffite's Ligier before going into the catchfencing and a concrete wall at almost undiminished speed.

'There was only one more in that pack that Tom had to overtake, and that was Stuck,' Shadow team manager Alan Rees said. 'Stuck was the one who avoided the guy who ran across the road, and he did it so quickly that Tom was left out there. He wouldn't even have known about it, I'm sure of that.'

* * *

All of the foregoing accidents could have been avoided, or need not have been fatal, had the marshals been better trained or better equipped. Much of the progress that has been made since had its roots in such incidents.

Along with former racing driver Dennis Poore, Louis Stanley developed a new firefighting backpack in the 'seventies that left both hands free, and then set in motion training so that marshals learned how to fight a fire in tests carried out at Stansted.

As early as 1970 the GPDA had called for a professional body of travelling marshals, but the idea met with strong opposition and, as is often the way with these things, the lobbying died down. It flared up again after Williamson's death, and yet again after Pryce's. On the latter occasion one of the strongest voices belonged to reigning World Champion James Hunt. The blond Englishman had very definite ideas on how he wanted to dress long before he captured his crown, but while his sartorial philosophy might have offended some, he was deadly serious about motor racing safety.

'It makes me extremely angry when we lose drivers of the calibre of Tom,' Hunt said in the aftermath of the Welsh star's accident at Kyalami. 'People do not listen enough to the drivers, yet we are the ones who take the greatest risk. The system let Tom down, and it is time that

At the 1991 Spanish GP, marshals move into action to alleviate an oil spillage. (Sutton)

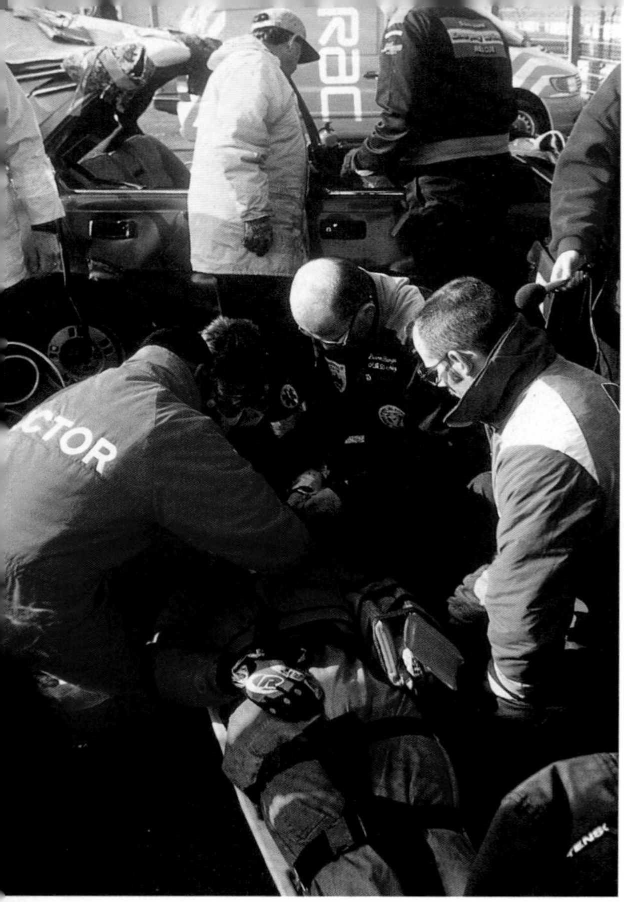

something was done to prevent the possibility of a recurrence. I strongly believe that creating a squad of professional marshals who travel to each and every Grand Prix, is the only sensible way to go for the future.'

Hunt was so serious that he proposed that this elite squad should initially be financed out of F1 drivers' pockets. 'Why not? We can afford it, and it is we who would benefit most. I cannot see why any of us should object to paying out whatever small amount it would cost to get the ball rolling, and then once the thing was up and running it could ultimately be carried on by the sport itself.'

In a similar way, drivers such as Max Papis and Jimmy Vasser tried to interest their fellows in contributing to have their own safety inspector on the

British marshals remain the class of the world, thanks to rigorous training and a high degree of professionalism and dedication. (Sutton/David Tremayne Archive)

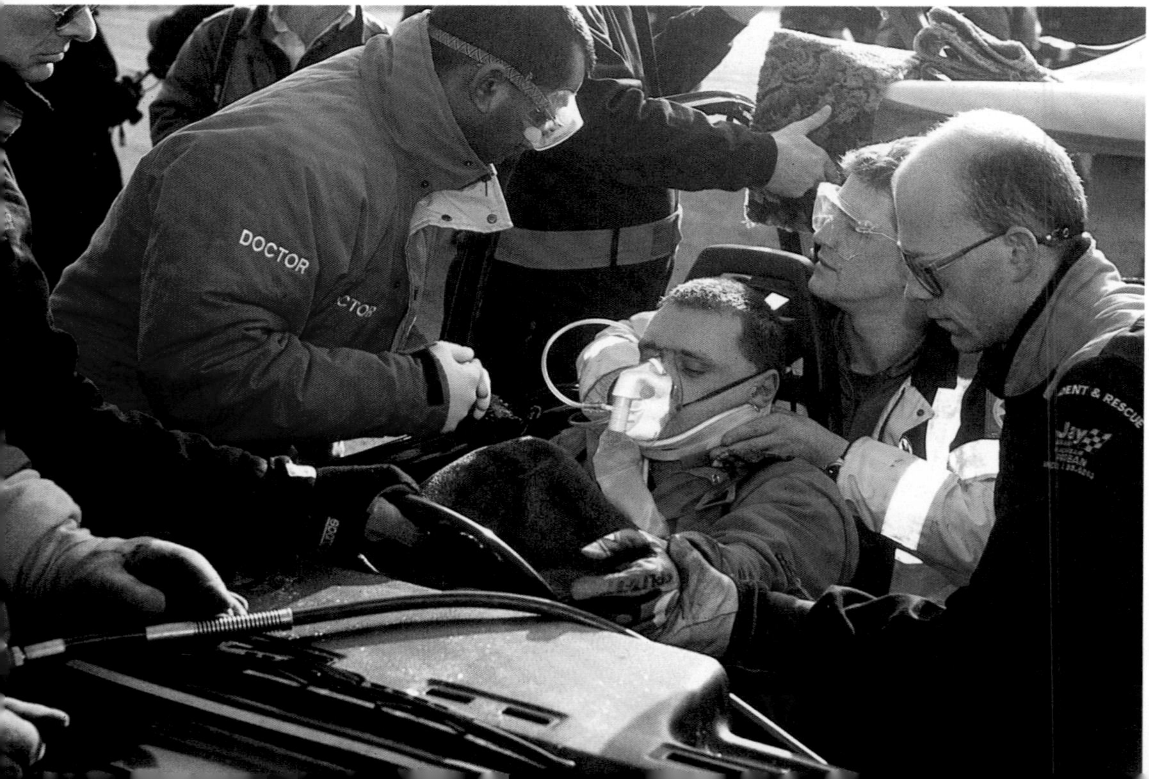

ChampCar trail in 2000 after their close friend Greg Moore was killed during the 1999 season finale at Fontana. But like Hunt they themselves became victims of the inherent politics of the sport.

Peter Browning, who was the general secretary of the British Racing and Sports Car Club in 1977, disagreed with Hunt's ideas. The BRSCC was generally adjudged to set the standard of the time for marshalling, so his views carried weight. While citing the rigorous training that British marshals routinely underwent before they were deemed ready for the international scene, he dismissed the possibility of a repeat of the Pryce accident on British soil. He also cited the problems that would inevitably arise with language difficulties at some races, and the sheer cost of the undertaking. But he did not dismiss Hunt's ideas without making proposals of his own. He suggested that the sport needed an elite group of experts in specific fields – in particular flagging, observing, and firefighting – who would be available to instruct marshals at overseas venues. At the time Monty Terrell of the BRSCC had already been sent to some Grands Prix in Europe as an advisor on overall standards.

Where Hunt and Browning were in agreement was the idea to have at least one professionally trained race-to-race marshal at each post around any given F1 circuit.

Today marshal training has built on the impetus provided by men such as Louis Stanley, and is given similar priority to other facets of racing. It is not difficult to see why marshalling attracts men and women and persuades them to give up their time to stand for hours on active duty at race meetings. It enables them to see the action close up, for a start, and that is undoubtedly what triggers many in the first place. But immediately one has to draw distinctions.

Those who do it purely for the chance to get in free are quickly weeded out in a

Proper training, allied to the right equipment, has ensured that the Williamson tragedy could not happen again. (Sutton)

country such as Britain, whose marshalling standards continue to be respected as the highest across the globe. At a typical British GP, for example, some 1,200 highly-trained volunteer marshals will be on duty. That includes 325 fire and course marshals, 108 flag marshals, 57 observers, 30 incident officers, 11 tender crews, and six rescue vehicles. Prior to that, more than 300 fire and course marshals will have taken part in a two-day intensive training session at the track.

There's the Snatch Squad, whose job is to retrieve vehicles stranded in gravel beds. Speed of response is vital here, in case other cars slide off the road at the same point. That's precisely what happened when Jenson Button spun in practice for the 2000 race, and was promptly joined in a separate accident by Eddie Irvine's Jaguar. The job is no sinecure, but then most marshalling falls under that umbrella despite external appearances.

The Snatch Squad must be at the scene in seconds, and is trained to react quickly and efficiently to remove a car as quickly as possible and to clear away any debris. The team knows it is really moving when it can clear away a car before the field reappears on the following lap. 'An F1 car sliding across the top of gravel at 120mph [193kph] with spray flying is exhilarating but also highly dangerous,' says Andy Hobman, a veteran of 16 years. 'Marshals must be fully alert to keep one step ahead at all times.'

Then there is the Incident Team, the rapid response unit which waits in the pit lane for a 'shout'. They will be called into action if there is a major accident. All members of the crew are trained in release manoeuvring, and can clear a damaged dashboard from a driver's legs in two minutes, and immobilise and extricate a driver from a wrecked chassis in little more than four.

British marshals have long been recognised as the best in the world, because of the standard of their training and their high levels of enthusiasm and dedication. They are often invited to help out at foreign circuits. It's worth remembering that none of them do it for remuneration, because there isn't any. It may be trite, but racing could not exist without the individuals who are prepared to give up their own time to perform a frequently overlooked task.

'F1 is the pinnacle of motor sport and F1 drivers are the elite,' says Gary Dearn, a former marshal who has progressed through the ranks over the past 15 years to become Silverstone's Chief Incident Officer. 'For the majority, marshalling at the RAC British GP is the ultimate achievement.

'In marshals, we look for enthusiasm, commitment and the determination to get it right. Our team strives for perfection. Although the Grand Prix is a gruelling four-day event for those behind the scenes, the team spirit and the sense of satisfaction when it all comes together is unbeatable.'

Marshalling is open to anyone from 18 upwards (16 with parental consent), and marshals come from many walks of life – engineers, builders, accountants, doctors, and students. On the track they are all equal, and all bound by the joint goal of making motor sport safer. Their training is literally an exercise in life saving. When critical minutes can separate life and death, and circumstance may prevent the circuit doctors from getting to an accident scene in time, marshals have to know what to do to prolong life until specialist help arrives. Via bodies such as the Motor Racing Safety Fund standards in Britain continue to be the envy of the world, though anyone who witnessed the incredible speed with which the marshals in Monte Carlo cleared away wrecks during the 2000 Monaco GP will appreciate that improvement has been universal. Serious progress has been made when it comes to rescue operations.

The FIA exercises strict control of all track personnel via Race Director Charlie Whiting. It is he who starts the race, and who makes the decision whether to deploy the safety car and the high-speed medical intervention car, or to red flag the race or practice session. In this he is helped immeasurably by the presence of television cameras all round the track. The Williamson tragedy, one likes to think, could never happen today.

Things have undoubtedly improved dramatically, though when you think that as recently as 1991 an insane marshal got away with running across the track just as the field was sweeping into Ste Devote at the start of the Monaco GP, you sometimes wonder just how much some people have learned.

Chapter 16

Medicine men

It all goes from the sublime to, shall I say, the highly imaginative. The alarming thing was to think of 22 Grand Prix drivers having a button that could fire rockets!

Professor Sid Watkins

At one stage in Formula One's frequently bloody history, drivers almost had to fend for themselves. That rambunctious sports car racer and Le Mans winner of the 'fifties, Duncan Hamilton, related a gory tale in his book *Touch Wood* of the doctor who operated on him while the ash from the cigarette drooping in the corner of his mouth dangled precariously over the open wound.

All of this was anathema to Louis Stanley of BRM. After a number of unacceptable incidents in the 'sixties, he decided that what was needed was the homogeneity of a mobile hospital. It would travel from Grand Prix to Grand Prix, dispensing the same standard of care regardless of location. Thus was born the International Grand Prix Medical Service, of which he appointed himself director general.

By any standard this was a fantastic undertaking, and it proved a landmark achievement when the mobile hospital unit was finally ready for action. Stanley, as was his wont, had really stirred things up in a hurry, and had started the project shortly after Jackie Stewart's accident at Spa in June 1966. By the time that the non-championship Oulton Park Spring Cup F1 race rolled round in April 1967, 'Lord Louis' was able to preside with justifiable pride as Lord Chesham handed over the keys and the Bishop of Chester dedicated the unit.

The raison d'être of the International Grand Prix Medical Service was to prolong life, to ensure that accident victims could be stabilised immediately prior to receiving intensive medical care within the most apposite hospital facilities in whatever region a race was being held. It would travel from circuit to circuit, just as the race teams themselves did, and there would be a roster of suitable surgeons who would proffer their skills as and when circumstance dictated. The hospital trailer was pulled by a Ford tractor unit and the whole thing cost more than £50,000 to equip, no small sum when John Surtees calculated that Honda's F1 budget in 1968 was around £25,000 ...

The hospital trailer featured a refrigerated blood bank, a revolutionary X-ray unit which could run off batteries and possessed automatic development facilities that obviated the need for a darkroom, the latest equipment for dealing with burns and fractures, a full staff of doctors, surgeons and nurses, and full anaesthetic facilities. The long-term plan was also to build up a card index of all members of the Grand Prix fraternity, in order to match blood types. There was also the capacity and facilities to undertake full operations if a specific crisis of sufficient magnitude arose.

'In those days one didn't do things for publicity,' Stanley says of his motivation. 'I was just so appalled at the safety standards, especially at the medical centres at tracks or at the hospitals. There was no one particular incident that got me started. It was an accumulation, really. And this country was no better. Brands Hatch was poor at the time, Silverstone too. The attitude was that drivers could take their chance in a shunt. At one time I inspected the medical centre and found the outline where bodies had lain on beds that were supposed to be in a sterilised area where somebody might be treated for burns. At Monza on another occasion the medical centre was full of beer cans and smoke.

'Standards were appalling. I remember the case of Richard Burton, the Formula Two driver. I had a call early one morning from Charles Lucas to say Burton had had a bad accident in France, there were burns, and they didn't know what to do. So I got through to Geneva, I got an air jet over and we got him to a proper hospital.'

On the face of it, the International Grand Prix Medical Service was a brilliant response to an obvious shortcoming, but more than once politics and nationalistic pride prevented it being used to full advantage. One such occasion was when Jochen Rindt crashed during practice for the Italian GP at Monza in 1970 (see Chapter 7). The Austrian sustained terrible injuries as the front bulkhead was torn off. Stanley is adamant that Rindt was still alive when he was taken from the shattered wreckage. The ambulance that was despatched to take him to hospital in Milan actually stopped by the medical trailer, but was waved on instead on its fateful hour-long drive into the city. Rindt was dead by the time it arrived.

Stanley had travelled in the ambulance with him, and though he was threatened with confiscation of his passport, steadfastly refused to sign a statement that was presented to him which said that a professor of medicine had been present during the ordeal. 'It was nonsense,' Stanley fumed. 'It was just me, a nurse and a medical attendant. I'm not saying that the International Grand Prix Medical Service could have saved him, because he was beyond that. But,' he added poignantly, 'he could have passed away there with his wife by his side, with some semblance of dignity ...'

It was one of Stanley's abiding frustrations that, impressive though his role as a prime mover in safety matters was in the 'sixties, the International Grand Prix Medical Services mobile hospital was never allowed to realise its true potential. 'It would be nice to think I had played a part,' he concedes. 'Over the years, if the Medical Unit had saved a life, I would have been satisfied. It would have done its job.' Alas, it was not allowed to do so.

If it did not appear in action at Grands Prix, the Medical Unit was also absent from test sessions. Had it been at Silverstone in August 1967 it might have helped Bob Anderson. The former motorcycle racer turned F1 privateer crashed while testing for a Canadian GP that he would not live to see, dying a horrible death as a result of poor medical facilities at the Northamptonshire circuit. His Brabham aquaplaned into a marshal's post on Club Straight, and was badly damaged.

'There was no proper ambulance,'

Stanley recalls. 'There was no doctor. After half an hour they got someone there to release him from the wreckage. The vehicle they put him in was full of mud, there was no bell, no suspension. Both of his lungs had been perforated and he was in agony. Halfway to Northampton he was met by a proper ambulance, but he was too ill to be transferred.' Anderson, like Rindt, did not make it to the hospital.

Gradually, despite such accidents and the obvious value of the International Grand Prix Medical Service, the impact of the unit was eroded. There was the need for different medical staffs at each circuit, which affected the smoothness and continuity with which it functioned. Race organisers did not react well, either. They were defensive and, it must be remembered, the unit arrived at a time when very few really took safety seriously. In those days the usual technique after an accident was to bundle the injured or deceased driver out of view of the spectators, and to continue a race as if nothing had happened. At Rouen in 1968, when Jo Schlesser perished during the French GP, it was a callous two hours before his widow Annie was informed that he had actually succumbed.

Stanley quietly ponders the past, and offers a rueful smile. 'Have you ever tried to tell a doctor that you'd be better off being treated by a vet? Because that is tantamount to what you had to tell some circuit doctors in those days. One, who shall remain nameless, came to the circuit hospital on one occasion so smelling of drink that I had to ask him to leave. Another man came smoking, and I asked him to get out. This was into a sterile atmosphere for operating. In Monza one time when Jackie Stewart had a burn, the doctor opened up his dispenser, and dropped his forceps and so on in the dust and never bothered to wipe them. I could go on ... One time in

The International Grand Prix Medical Service made a proud debut at Oulton Park's Spring Cup in April 1967. (LAT)

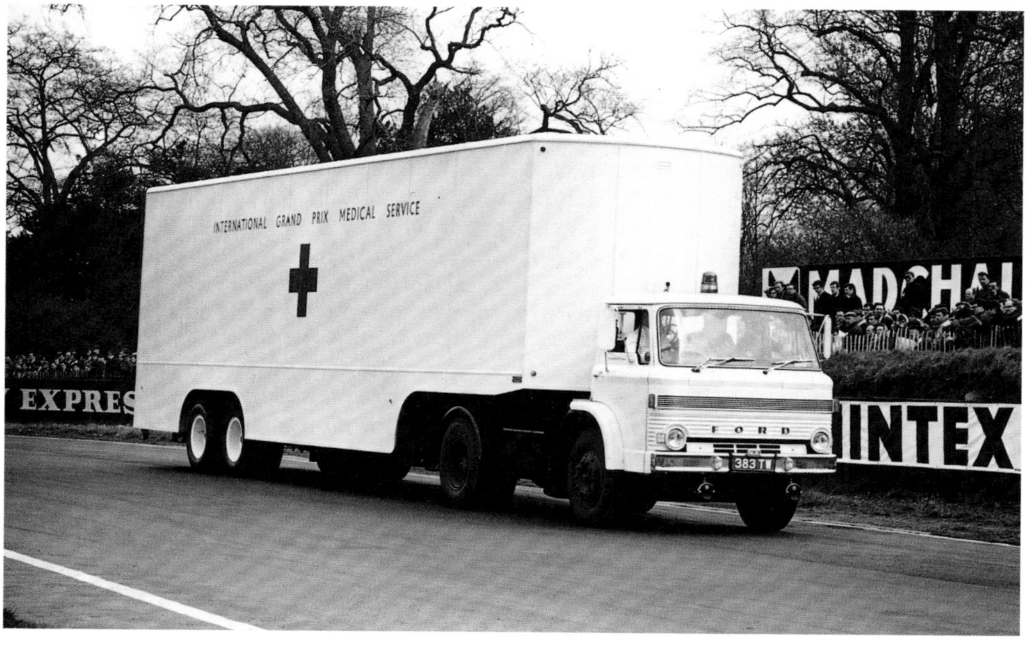

Sicily I asked the doctor about anaesthetising a driver and he said, "No, we'll wait for the pain to put him out". Well that's rather primitive.' That was the hapless Pedro Rodriguez, who went through agony having a broken ankle reset without anaesthetic after crashing his Formula Two Protos.

Co-operation was vital to the Medical Unit's success, and vested interests ensured that this was not always forthcoming. Also, it must be said, Stanley's resolute blend of ruthless determination, disdain for red tape, and sheer bombast often militated against acceptance of the unit.

The highly underrated F1 sleeper and sports car ace Brian Redman would also have benefited had the Medical Unit been at the legendary Targa Florio in 1971. Redman had retired at the end of 1970, concerned at the number of people being killed. He had convinced himself he was the next on the list. He emigrated to South Africa, but realised almost immediately that he had made a ghastly mistake. By the time he got back home he had lost his drive to Derek Bell, and was out of work until John Wyer called to offer him a ride in one of JW Automotive's Porsche 908/3s on the classic event that toured Sicily's tortuous terrain at very high speed. 'In May John rang and said, "Brian, Derek has never raced at the Targa, would you like to do it?" I thought, "Great!"'

But the chance to revive his career nearly had chilling consequences. 'The 908/3 was a better car than the 908/2,' Redman remembers, 'but we were nervous about sitting so far forward because of how they'd put the gearbox ahead of the engine. Six inches of your lower leg was ahead of the front wheels, and all you had there was some aluminium tubing and an oil filter! It was quite something, round places such as the 'Ring, but the actual driving of it was tremendous.

'Everything was fine, but at the end of practice Jo Siffert had had an accident and the car had quite a bit of damage. It was repaired but very unusually John Wyer said to me, "Brian, we want you to start the race because we don't want Siffert and Rodriguez hammering on each other."

'So I started the race, and straight away the handling was poor from the first corner. Just before the race Helmut Flegl, the Porsche engineer, had said to me, "Brian, if you must have ze accident, do not crash on ze right side", because that was where the fuel tank was!'

He was going downhill to one of the few corners with which he was familiar, because it was where his co-driver Dickie Attwood crashed two years earlier. Fortunately, he had slowed up for it more than usual. 'I turned in, and nothing happened. It went straight on into a concrete post, on the right-hand side, of course, and the fuel tank exploded. The steering had broken.

'I was extremely lucky to get out of that Porsche,' Brian admits. 'I held my breath automatically, shut my eyes, and hit the release buckle on the safety belt, and got out. But I was blinded because of the flames and I was burning from head to foot. I just rolled around and eventually the fire went out, but there was nobody there. I couldn't see, but I could hear somebody screaming in the distance. It was obviously me, but I didn't realise that. Then some peasants came and they were fanning me with magazines. It took the helicopter 45 minutes to get to me because it couldn't land in the mountains, and I had a really unpleasant time. I was taken to a hospital and nobody knew where I was. I was there 12 hours, unable to speak or to see, until Richard Attwood and Pedro Rodriguez found me and took me back to the hotel.'

Redman had burns to his hands, face and back, and swelling round the eyes had temporarily deprived him of his sight. 'It was an horrific experience.

Richard later told me the hospital was just a hovel. People were smoking and there weren't any nurses; the patients were being nursed by their families. There was a boy who had been hit in the race, who was dying in the same room, and his mother was screaming. It was like a scene from hell.'

* * *

Professor Sidney Watkins, of whom so much has already been heard in this book, appeared on the F1 scene in the late 'seventies. He did not need much time to make a lasting impact, and it is safe to say that his craggy face and ever-present cigar are the first two things any injured driver wants to see looming over him. He is the guardian angel of the sport. But he is no pushover, as everyone, Bernie Ecclestone included, discovered when Nelson Piquet crashed at Tamburello during practice for the 1987 San Marino GP at Imola.

Piquet was examined at the track's medical centre before being transferred to the Maggiore Hospital in Bologna for a routine brain scan. He then turned up for work on Saturday morning, having discharged himself. He and Watkins soon had angry words in a frank exchange of views. Besides being the FISA's chief medical delegate (a position he still holds) Watkins was then the leading neurological surgeon at the London Hospital. He stood firm by his view that Piquet was not fit to drive, and Nelson was not allowed out for free practice. But the Brazilian believed he should be allowed to defend his fastest time in that afternoon's qualifying session.

'Nelson first of all wanted to race, and certainly Prof said no,' recalls Williams technical director Patrick Head. 'I think Nelson had been talking gobbledegook – not that he necessarily didn't talk gobbledegook when he was otherwise – but he certainly had the most enormous impact. I would say that it subdued him for a bit. It was a physical thing rather than a mental thing. I think it literally subdued him. It was a very, very big thump.'

Had the Medical Service been available at Monza in 1970, Louis Stanley believes that Jochen Rindt's death would at least have been more dignified. (Phipps/Sutton)

Watkins now found himself at the epicentre of a growing storm that would become a crucial test case for Formula One. Despite mounting pressure from the politically active Piquet to be allowed to compete, he stood firm. Dr Raphael Grajales-Robles, Piquet's personal physician, agreed with Watkins, but Ecclestone and the organisers were extremely keen not to lose a key gate draw.

'Nelson was out of the car by the time I arrived, a bit stunned,' Watkins recollected. 'He didn't quite know where he was to begin with, but we took him to the medical centre and by then he knew who he was, where he was and what he was doing. He went off in the helicopter to the hospital in Bologna, where there's a neuro-surgical unit, and he had a brain scan and stayed overnight.

'The next morning he discharged himself, so I wasn't surprised to hear from Bernie when I arrived that he wanted to drive. Anyway, he came to see me and I said to him that he couldn't drive because he'd had a head injury and he might have some brain damage. And he said no, he hadn't got any brain damage. I said, "Well, why have you left your shoe off?" He only had one shoe on. So he said, "It's not because I forgot it, but because my foot is so painful and swollen I can't get a shoe on."

'I said, "Brain damage, foot damage, it doesn't make much difference. You're not fit to drive." So then there was a bit of pressure from the circuit people, about wanting him to drive, and I think Bernie probably wanted him to drive too. The chap who stayed right out of the argument was old Balestre, for which I gave him credit. Nelson didn't drive in the morning practice, and then there was some talk that he was going to be allowed to make some demonstration runs between the two practices, and if he went all right in that then he could participate in the Saturday afternoon qualifying practice. That upset all the Italian doctors, and me. The chief medical officer, who had got a statement from the neuro-surgeon who had looked after him overnight, said that there was no way the medical staff would see him either demonstrate or drive and maintain their responsibility for the circuit. So it became an impasse, really, and thereafter the pressure for him to drive sort of disappeared.'

Prof himself had been quite prepared to resign, head home, and watch the race on television had things really come to a head, and that would have been a long-term disaster for Formula One. Fortunately common sense prevailed. 'I think the Italian papers made a good deal of the fact that I'd prevented Nelson from driving so that Nigel, who was in the same team, could get an advantage ... Nelson later admitted – some months later – in some article I saw, that he wasn't himself for about three months after the shunt. He couldn't sleep, and he wasn't on form. So in retrospect he thought I'd been quite right, although at the time he was pretty upset. He cried a bit, and that sort of thing. But he didn't badmouth me.'

Two years later the Belgian driver Thierry Boutsen had a similar impact in a Williams while testing in Rio. Like Piquet he benefited from the immense strength of the Williams chassis and escaped virtually unharmed, but he too found that he was not fully himself for three months or more.

Imola 1987 became the test case for all other similar situations. And it confirmed that, unlikely as it might seem, the medical side of Formula One was the one thing that really could override the commercial considerations of the day. From that incident onwards, Professor Sid Watkins's word has been law.

'That was, I think, a sort of test of whether or not the medical advice could overcome the commercial value,' he reflects. 'And in the past perhaps the commercial value hadn't been serious enough, so I didn't have the contest, if you see what I mean. When Nigel banged his head in Ricard in 1985, he didn't want to race the next day so he went home instead. When other famous people, like Niki, hurt his wrist, he was sensible enough at Spa to say he didn't want to drive.

'It was one of those things, I suppose. Here was this crowd at Imola, with a big following for Piquet, and the removal of him from that particular competition reduced its hype value. He and Nigel were hard at it for the Championship, of course, but equity was restored later in the year when Nigel missed Suzuka because he hurt his back. And Adelaide, too. As it turned out it was almost one each effectively, and I felt all right about it.'

'Sid is fantastic,' enthuses Peter Wright. 'He just cuts through all the politics. He's the medical side of things, and if you like, the engineering side is myself, Charlie Whiting, and then the people we use, because the FIA is not a technical organisation but a political one. You need a strong man like him in the group.'

As the chief medical delegate, Watkins has certainly earned his right to his opinions, and to have his expertise respected. No more so than that day at Imola when he had to tend to his friend Ayrton Senna as he lay dying, a man for whom he had boundless respect which was reciprocated in full. Watkins has paid his dues.

He admitted freely that going back to Imola a year later was difficult, even for one so practised in keeping emotion at bay. 'Imola has been a catalyst for so much change on safety issues. That first time I came back, after Ayrton's accident, it was particularly difficult for me, as a friend. There was so much memorial to him still showing on the circuit. Once I had seen that, the first time I went round what had become almost a new circuit, I didn't look in that direction.'

Much of what has happened in the name of safety since Senna's death has borne Watkins's stamp, via the Expert Advisory Group that he was tasked with setting up in the wake of Karl Wendlinger's accident at Monaco in

Men of safety: Prof Watkins, Peter Wright, Charlie Whiting, Roland Bruynseraede, Derek Ongaro and Gerhard Berger at one of the FIA's frequent technical meetings. (Formula One Pictures)

1994. 'There's me, Charlie Whiting, Peter Wright, and Roland Bruynseraede,' he outlines, the last being the FIA's former race director. 'We lost Harvey Postlethwaite, so now we have John Barnard representing the designers. Michael [Schumacher] is probably going to replace Gerhard, because Berger is so busy now with BMW. And then we co-opt whomever we need. For example, we frequently co-opt Andrew Mellor from the Transport Research Lab, and right now he is doing fundamental research into a new helmet standard which we hope we will have by the end of the year. There is a lot of movement in different ways.

'What we have to do is develop our own criteria, which is what we do with TRL, and then we can get the manufacturers, whether of helmets or seats or whatever, to move in on it.' Watkins draws in the best brains from all over the globe in the relentless search for an overall answer that may not, he acknowledges, exist. 'Some people wonder how much there can be left to do on safety,' he admits. 'But a never-ending search is required. My job with the research group goes on. My responsibility is to look at possibilities to make further moves forward.'

Watkins believes that the head and neck protection system is the most significant safety development in the post-Senna era. 'That's been tested pretty well by people like Jos Verstappen and Mika Salo on a couple of occasions. Heinz-Harald Frentzen has also had a couple of big ones. Schumacher damaged his helmet by hitting the steering wheel at Stowe, but the column collapsed in the

Ready for its first crash tests, the special Confor foam safety headrest was but one of Prof Watkins' successes. (Formula One Pictures)

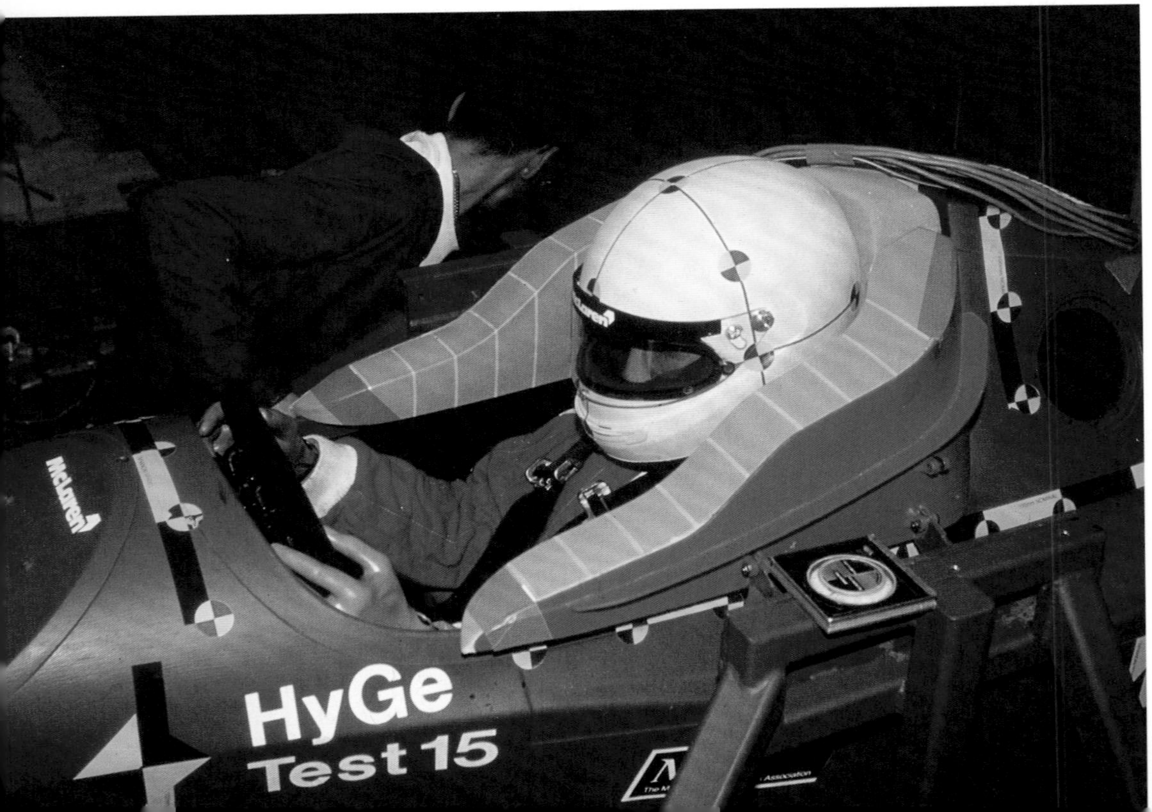

right circumstances. Cockpit safety has been a big advance.

'The whole thing about lateral head movement is quite precise, the amount you can allow. What we did was set up the dummies for a lateral impact test, and then progressively change the distance of the foam until we got one that gave us optimum in the foam and optimum in the head. If you take it too far out, the head improves but the neck gets worse. If you bring it too far in, the neck gets better but the head impact gets worse. So like most things, it's a compromise.'

He is also pleased with the big advance in barriers He is not sure why the Theobald Senna System was not adapted, but says, 'We do know that if you put the correct inserts into the tyres you get good performance. Of all the artificial barriers that we've tested, the rows of tyres properly linked together and protected with conveyor belt still offer the best solution in terms of practicability, cost, and lack of maintenance. And the reduction of the need to stop the race because somebody has gone off and damaged the barrier. That was exactly the problem with catchfencing.

'Tyres do degrade ultimately, but there isn't a formula that I am aware of for deciding when they need replacement. I don't know how much they degrade but I'm sure that they do, particularly when you have a lot of climatic change. Spa for example. They're frozen all winter, then have a couple of hot days!'

His Expert Advisory Group looked at the HANS system originally in 1995, 'when it was big and cumbersome, and we actually had Gerhard Berger wear it during tests in an F1 car. He never raced it, because it was too bulky and uncom-

Berger, Watkins and Whiting fine tune the initial concept. (Formula One Pictures)

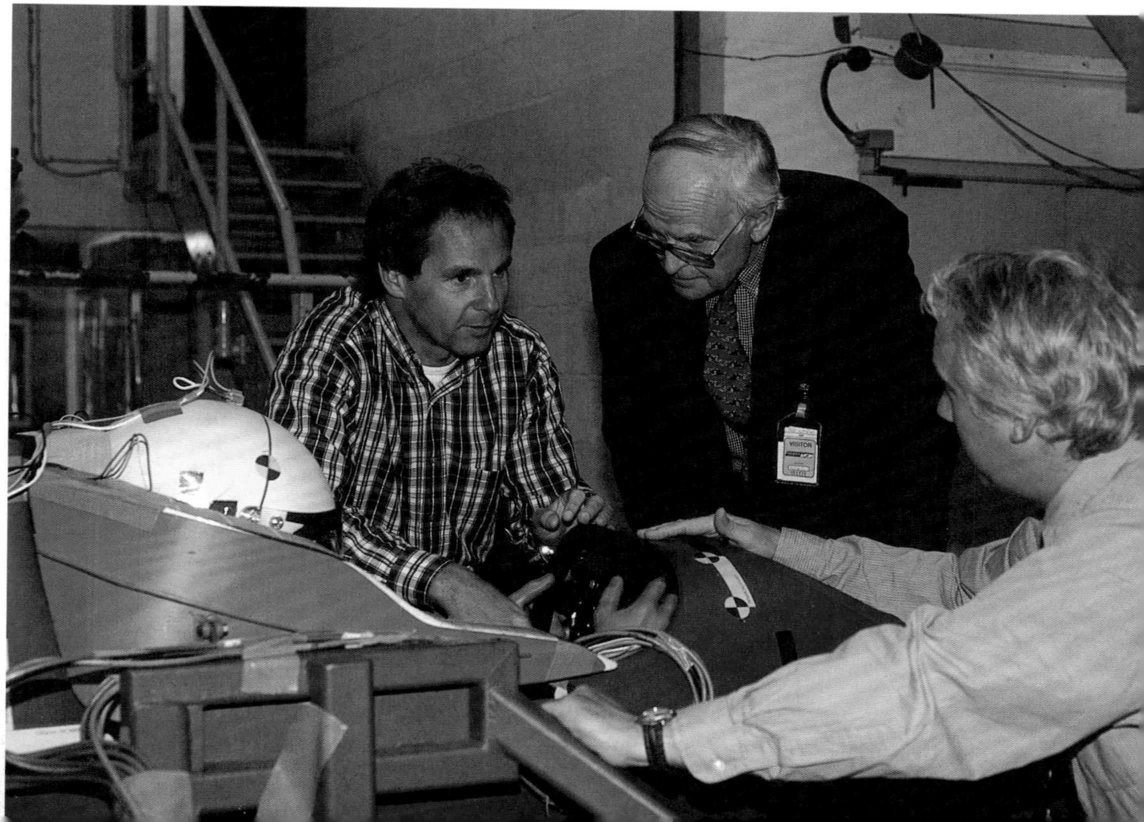

fortable. But it showed it was possible. The following year, with McLaren and Mercedes and after Hakkinen's accident in Adelaide, we started to redesign it with the help of its originator, Professor Hubbard from the United States. It got smaller and lighter and much more manageable. We started all that before the Hakkinen accident, and knew from the original clumsy one, which we tested with fully instrumented dummies and high-g sled tests, that it did work.

'Very early on, when we started to develop the cockpit safety system, after Senna's death, we came up with the head and neck foam protection which worked for lateral accidents, and worked for going in backwards. But it didn't work for head-ons. We were left with the problem of the frontal impact, which we partially hoped to solve with the collapsible steering column.

'We also tried an air bag with the automated dummies, and that worked. But there's a technical problem with air bags. I've always been in favour of them, and I still would be, if you could get the technology to work. If you had HANS and an air bag, then that would be another step forward. The speed of activation of an air bag is the problem, and the risk of accidental triggering.'

Better than most, he knows how easy, and dangerous, it is to become complacent about safety, and that great care is needed to avoid that. 'Somebody is going to get hurt, sometime,' he says very calmly. 'There is no question about that. You can't do these speeds, and nobody get hurt. But I had a patient who broke his neck falling off a barstool; you'd have thought that was a reasonably safe occupation …'

What pleases him most – and he suggests that perhaps this is Ayrton Senna's legacy to the sport that he loved – is that attitudes to safety have changed diametrically. There is no longer any inertia about safety matters. But he is not sure just where future research can go.

'I don't know whether we can go much more with the car. We've got the double tethers on the wheels now. There's the front and rear impact absorption. The Kevlar shield on the chassis. We are doing a bit more with the cockpit, increasing the amount of foam down to foot level to try to help the knees. That will come in next year and will mean increasing the size of the cockpit a little. That will help us when it comes to rescue. They are small things, but they may be significant.

'To do much more with the car, you'd have to transmit more energy to the driver, so again it's the compromise route. So long as some of the structures on the car can absorb energy, but leave the survival cell intact. But I believe that more focus will be on assessment of the geometry of the circuits, and close examination of run-off areas. We are searching, with little success, for a better way to decelerate the cars when they leave the track. The gravel, we know, is not as ideal as we'd like to have it. And a raised gravel bed would be a good launch pad …'

He laughs tolerantly at Eddie Irvine's views on the subject, and says, 'Good old Eddie! But really, you need to think these things through …'

The group examines all sorts of inventions. Watkins guffaws. 'We talked to some rocket scientists who said they could fire rockets upwards and give you big downforce and stop the cars. But the exhaust gas temperature from the rockets was a bit high … It all goes from the sublime to, shall I say, the highly imaginative! The alarming thing was to think of 22 Grand Prix drivers having a button that could fire rockets!

'Overall, I would say that safety standards are higher than they have ever been, but you can never get complacent. Whenever you make a change there is a consequence as a result, which you may not have predicted. Anything to do with safety soon makes you aware that you are aiming at a moving target.'

Chapter 17

Improving the breed

I think the biggest step forward in the last ten years has probably been changing attitudes. It's getting to the stage where all the F1 engineers are prepared to agree to something once it's shown it's necessary for safety. The only argument is, is this actually a safety measure?

Max Mosley

Max Mosley tells a wry tale of his Formula Two debut at Hockenheim, in April 1968.

'I had just moved up from Clubmans racing to Formula Two that year. My wife was a bit concerned, and asked if it was dangerous, and I said, "No. Provided that you are careful and go about it sensibly, no, it's not dangerous." And of course then I had to explain afterwards about Jim Clark, because he was obviously careful and was unquestionably a better driver than me, yet still managed to get killed. And that did rather start to put it into perspective.' Mosley counted 21 other drivers on that grid for the Lottery race at Hockenheim on 7 April. 'Two more were dead by July: Chris Lambert and Jo Schlesser …'

Like Jean-Marie Balestre, Mosley is no stranger to controversy. He was born in to it, for 11 weeks after he had made his appearance in the world in war-torn London in 1940 his mother Diana Guinness was incarcerated in Holloway Prison. His father was the notorious politician Sir Oswald Mosley, well-known at the time for stirring up pro-Nazi feelings in the East End of London as his Black Shirts marched against the Jews.

Educated almost on the hoof in a variety of establishments in England, France, and Germany, Mosley headed for Oxford in 1958 and emerged with an Honours degree in physics, a matter that would later be of some ironic amusement to frustrated designers as time and again he would oppose their ideas with the preamble: 'I'm no engineer, but any 15-year-old student of physics will tell you that …'

Interestingly, Sir Oswald wrote in his autobiography: 'We decided to give Alexander and Max another education because we hoped to make them good Europeans, and thought that a command of languages is a most desirable gift of parents to children.'

By 1964 Max had successfully read for

the Bar and begun practising as a barrister, but he had other interests, among them parachuting and activities in the Territorial Army. He also began to take up Clubmans racing on the British motorsport scene, and by 1968 had graduated to Formula Two.

It did not take him long to realise what the motorsport writers of the time already appreciated: his talents lay on the other side of the pit wall. In 1969 he combined with a group of friends to establish what would become one of the most remarkable British race car manufacturing companies, March Engineering. Robin Herd was fast emerging as a top racing car designer, having the previous year penned the M7A McLarens that were still winning races in Denny Hulme's hands as March was taking shape. Graham Coaker was financial guru. Alan Rees had driven an F1 Cooper-Maserati in the British GP, but was better known as a quick F2 driver who had been Jochen Rindt's team-mate in their days in Roy Winkelmann's Brabham operation. The March name was an amalgam of their initials – *M*osley, *A*lan *R*ees, *C*oaker, *H*erd – though cynics of the day lost no time in turning the acronym into Much Advertised Racing Car Hoax. But Mosley would have the last laugh.

Perhaps it says much of him that March's grandiose entry into F1 came at the same time as its much-publicised pledges to build customer cars for F2 and F3. At one of the numerous launches that March's multiple F1 sales demanded, it was bitterly cold at Silverstone. Mosley's fellow directors turned out wrapped sensibly against the cold, but he shunned an overcoat and appeared elegantly attired in a pin-stripe suit. As would so often prove to be the case in later years, however, external appearances did not tell the full tale. Beneath the natty threads Mosley sensibly wore his Nomex racing underwear for extra warmth …

March would succeed against the expectations of the cynics. Jackie Stewart and Chris Amon were the fastest drivers during practice for the maiden race in South Africa, and the Scot went on to win the Spanish GP, the next race on the calendar. But along the way Mosley left the company and was enlisted by his friend Bernie Ecclestone to look after the legal ramifications of his war with FIA president Jean-Marie Balestre. Together they went as far as to prepare regulations for a breakaway World Championship, the documents for which eventually became the Concorde Agreement by which F1 would in future be run when the FISA/FOCA war of 1980–1 was finally resolved.

Mosley's role led to another as a member of the FISA's F1 Commission, and deputy membership of the FISA Executive Committee and thereby involvement in the organisational promotion of various Grands Prix. At the same time he was heavily active in matters concerning safety and technical regulations. He quit in 1983 to pursue other business interests, before returning three years later as president of the FISA Manufacturers' Commission. He continued in that role until his successful election as president of the FISA and then president of the FIA.

Even before this upheaval, Mosley was keen to stress his major concern for the sport's future. In the light of events at Imola less than three years later, they were to be prophetic words.

'I think we are going to be under great attack from environmentalists and I think that it won't be long before people particularly active in those areas use motor sport as a platform because it would be a very quick and easy way to get publicity,' he said early in 1991. 'We've got to be ready for that, and I think that there's a great deal we can do to completely disarm those sorts of criticisms – both in Europe and the rest of the world. I think facile solutions are not the answer.

'We need to set up a strategic planning committee. We've got some very good people who would not be out of place in a government think tank. Under the present regime they would never sit and listen to long talk about operations but they would do something serious like this. That committee should sit down and look at the looming environmentalist, political, and financial problems and have a very clear idea of where they think international motor sport will be in five or ten years' time.'

That time has already arrived, and Mosley has faced and passed his major test. It came in the wake of the Imola weekend in 1994, when the very core of motor sport came under threat. 'I think the biggest step forward in the last ten years has probably been changing attitudes,' he says, looking back. 'It's getting to the stage where all the F1 engineers are prepared to agree to something once it's shown it's necessary for safety. The only argument is, is this actually a safety measure? And now there's no question any more about adopting these things. There's certainly a completely different attitude to, say, 30 years ago.

'Even before Senna and Ratzenberger, people were beginning to say things like: "It's too safe. That's why these drivers are always bumping into each other." But Imola stopped that. Now, really, there are only one or two people who say that, very much of the older generation. I don't think that many modern people say that now.'

For the past six years he has largely followed his own script. Today, he summarises his role thus: 'The thing is that team owners and engineers have their

Max Mosley (third from the right, standing), is warmly dressed back in his days as a director of the upstart March Engineering, as Ken Tyrrell unveils his new team for 1970. (Phipps/Sutton)

jobs. The job that I am supposed to do is a very genuine and very necessary job. You need somebody stood back, trying to make it all function sensibly. You might well say that it is the wrong person doing it. But you have got to have *somebody* doing it. I might not be the right person, but there must be somebody. And it really needs to be somebody capable of being fairly determined, should the need arise.'

He may not be universally popular, and there are those who believe that much of what he has achieved has been done with an eye to his own political aspirations. After all, he did once famously say that, 'the art of doing this job is to appear to be a gentleman while being totally self-serving.' But Mosley will be remembered as the man who meshed motor sport with road cars. His defusing of the post-Imola situation was an object lesson in politics, but the most personally satisfying aspect of his role as FIA president lies elsewhere, in what others perceive to be the arena of his future aspirations.

'It's a little bit out of racing,' he admits, 'but I think it has been transferring this attitude to road cars, and getting the ENCAP to work.' This is the European New Car Assessment Programme, where all the various different people were persuaded to compromise and join into one body. Within three years it became recognised as the body for crash testing cars. That in turn has had a huge impact on safety levels.

'There's always been crash testing; a magazine and a club in Germany used to do it. But never really on a big scale. One can see that from comparing the first batch of cars that were ever done,' Mosley says. 'That was what they called the super-minis back in 1997. Comparing those with results we published in February 2000, every single one except the worst in the last batch that we did, was better than the best of the previous batch. Two of them were up in the four-star categories, which three years ago people were saying was not possible for small cars.

'And that has really come straight from racing. What started that was after Senna and Ratzenberger, when we were setting up the Expert Advisory Group and were looking at all different sources of information. One of the first places to look was what had been done for road cars, and there we found that *nothing* had been done for 20 years. It was absolutely amazing. That discovery started a whole sequence of events. First of all with the European Parliament and the legislation, and then starting ENCAP.

'It was really our people, such as David Ward, who brought it all together. It existed in embryo. There was a Department of Trade and Industry (DTI) programme combined with the Swedes, but it was all piecemeal. I think what we achieved was to pull the whole thing together into one unit.'

Alan Donnelly was the president of the Automobile Users Inter-group in the European Parliament, so when the new crash test legislation was put forward by the Commission he had to go to the Parliament. And there he discovered that, in the Commission, initial proposals that had been put forward for crash testing had been watered down. 'So the scientists and technical people had agreed the standards for these crash tests, which was a new type of frontal impact test and a completely new type of side impact test. These had been agreed in 1985. By now it was 1995 and nothing had happened except that the Commission had downgraded the level of these tests. What we did, via Alan, was to ask the Parliament to put them back up to the level that the technical people originally set. The Commission said that we would never succeed in this, but in the end, through Alan's efforts and the lobbying we did with people such as Gerhard Berger, the Parliament voted unanimously to put the standards back up. In the face of this, the Commission gave in.

'So when these standards came in, in 1998 for the new models and 2003 for all new cars, they were back up to the standard that had been put forward in 1985.

'It's nevertheless disgraceful that there had been no change. Now we are seeing cars tested by ENCAP that are ten times safer in the side impact, which is the directly comparable test, than the legislative requirement; they are ten times safer than they are required to be. So instead of having a 50 per cent chance of injury, which will get you through the European side impact test, we are down to a five per cent risk with some of the best cars. Even small cars like Volkswagen's Lupo (if it has the side air bags, which are not standard) are ten times better. Bigger cars, such as Volvos, are double the requirement.'

Mosley says all this with evident pride. The inertia that had to be overcome here was extremely similar to the inertia that Jackie Stewart once faced in his crusade within the sport. Mosley warms to his theme.

'The parallels were incredible. Unbelievable. It was so similar to Formula One in the 'sixties and 'seventies. But once you get these things moving, you get much more media coverage. What happened was that the media picked it up, and it started affecting sales. Therefore the big car companies started using it in advertising. Now they all try to make cars up to this standard. So the speed at which this moves, compared to the speed at which legislation

Mosley is proud of the way in which the FIA's ENCAP tests have started to transfer the F1 safety revolution to road cars. (FIA)

can move, is enormous, an order of magnitude greater.'

And it will get better still, as competition to do better feeds off itself, and major manufacturers build into their overall umbrella small, F1-style engineering units that can react very quickly.

'One of the automobile chiefs said recently that what they like about F1 is the culture,' Mosley points out. 'If you've got a problem you don't have two or three years to sort it out. It's got to be sorted out by next week, otherwise there you are, live on television, looking really bad. I think that's a big element. The Japanese have known that for a long time. They've always sent their young engineers over to learn from F1.

Formula Zero, launched at the 2000 French GP, is Mosley's initiative to cut road deaths. (FIA)

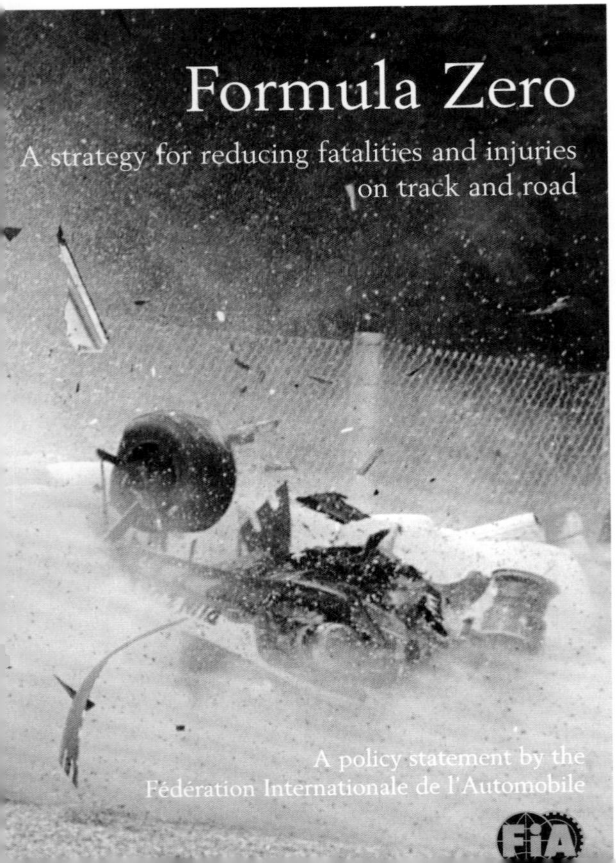

Formula Zero
A strategy for reducing fatalities and injuries on track and road
A policy statement by the Fédération Internationale de l'Automobile
FIA

'It's extraordinary how Formula One is beginning to become a catalyst, because it has those sort of benefits, and at the same time it opens all sorts of doors. It's amazing how many people are closet Formula One fans. If you invite some politician to discuss something, you've got much more chance of getting him to a Grand Prix and then being able to talk to him, than if you want him to come to a seminar on the environment.'

The wheel is turning full circle, and once again motor racing is improving the breed again. What it is bringing about may not be as visible as the disc brake or improved engine technology, but it is nonetheless equally important. Perhaps more important.

'It's beginning to drive the whole safety thing,' Mosley says, 'and that will grow in the next ten years. Instead of inventing a new brake, because we have gone way beyond that, motor racing is having this effect on safety. And the thing that is really going to transform safety is going to be electronics. And that's what we've had to stop with Formula One, otherwise the cars would be driving themselves. That was a deliberate decision that we took back in 1993, to stop what had been 100 years of working together in parallel with road cars, and recognising the direction in which road cars are going. And that, ultimately, is that they will drive themselves, like a personal train. With the racing car there is just no point, unless a human being drives it. Half the interest would be gone.'

Mosley becomes reticent when asked whether he is satisfied with what he has achieved in his frequently controversial role as president of the FIA. 'When you are inside an organisation, all you see is what's wrong,' he admits. 'You tend to see everything in a "cup's half empty" rather than a "cup's half full" way. But I think I have done as much as I could.

'The annoying thing is that we are distracted all the time, for example by all

The powerbrokers of F1: Max Mosley and Bernie Ecclestone face the media. (Sutton)

this business with the European Commission and competition. That sort of thing takes an enormous amount of time and energy that should be devoted to doing something useful and constructive. But life has always been like that. Whenever you try to achieve something, there are always a number of people putting obstacles in your way.'

It's not long before he glides away on another tangent, as the conversation turns to crash helmet research. 'Because of the Accident Data Recorders we know what happens in a car, and we now have a great deal of information,' he enthuses. 'If you get hold of the helmet of somebody who has been killed on a motorbike, for instance, you don't know what the forces were. So you try to replicate them in the laboratory, but you don't really know what you're replicating.

'For the first time there is research going on where you have a whole load of helmets, where we know exactly what the forces are. We can reconstruct the accident and then work backwards. This has all been done at TRL, and it's quite a big project. From it will certainly emerge a much, much better helmet than anything that is currently available.'

The TRL has data on accidents from fatalities right down to minor bumps, and a massive bank of information which is allowing it to plot the forces of accidents. Working back from that, designers are currently working on creating a new breed of helmet. Mosley believes that this is likely to be the next area of significant improvement. 'First you have to get the new specification right. But there are also some very interesting, completely novel ideas to do with helmets, which are being looked at. Some very, very clever ideas. I think it will be a whole new ongoing thing.

'It probably won't have the dramatic effect in Formula One,' he concedes, 'where, touch wood, heads are reasonably protected. But in other things it will.'

Some scoff when Max Mosley says that his aim is zero tolerance for safety risks, because he no longer regards it as acceptable that any driver should risk being killed in a racing car. But that won't stop him trying to realise that goal.

Appendix 1

In memoriam 1950–2000

Fatalities arising from accidents in international races, 1950–2000

1950
Raymond Sommer, Cadours
Joe Fry, Blandford

1952
Luigi Fagioli, Monaco
Bill Schindler, Pennsylvania

1953
Felice Bonetto, Silao, Mexico
Nine spectators killed by Farina's Ferrari in Argentina
Charles de Tornaco, Modena
Carl Scarborough, Indianapolis

1954
Onofre Marimon, Nürburgring
Guy Mairesse, Montlhéry
Eric Forrest-Green, Buenos Aires
Tom Cole, Le Mans

1955
Bill Vukovich, Indianapolis
Pierre Levegh, Le Mans, plus at least 81 spectators
Alberto Ascari, Monza
Mike Nazaruk, Langhorne
Don Beauman, Wicklow
Jim Mayers, Dundrod
Richard Mainwaring, Dundrod
Bill Smith, Dundrod
Jack McGrath, Phoenix
Manny Ayulo, Indianapolis

1956
Arthur Bryant, Oulton Park
Louis Rosier, Montlhéry
Benoit Musy, Montlhéry
Bob Sweikert, Salem
Annie Bousquet, Reims

1957
Eugenio Castellotti, Modena
Herbert Mackay-Fraser, Reims
Bill Whitehouse, Reims
Alfonso de Portago, Mille Miglia
Ed Nelson, Mille Miglia
37 spectators on Mille Miglia
Ken Wharton, New Zealand
Piero Carini, St Etienne
Bobby Myers, Darlington

1958
Peter Collins, Nürburgring
Luigi Musso, Reims
Stuart Lewis-Evans, Casablanca
Archie Scott-Brown, Spa-Francorchamps
Peter Whitehead, Tour de France
Erwin Bauer, Nürburgring
Pat O'Connor, Indianapolis
Jimmy Reece, Trenton

1959
Ivor Bueb, Clermont-Ferrand
Jean Behra, Avus
Jerry Unser, Indianapolis
Bob Cortner, Indianapolis
George Amick, Daytona

1960
Harry Blanchard, Buenos Aires
Jimmy Bryan, Langhorne
Chris Bristow, Spa-Francorhamps
Alan Stacey, Spa-Francorchamps
Harry Schell, Silverstone
A boy spectator killed by Dan Gurney's BRM at Zandvoort
Johnny Thomson, Allentown
Chris Threlfall, Aix Les Bains, plus three spectators

1961
Giulio Cabianca, Modena
Wolfgang Von Trips, Monza, plus 14 spectators
Tony Bettenhausen, Indianapolis
Shane Summers, Brands Hatch

1962
Ricardo Rodriguez, Mexico City
A marshal killed by Richie Ginther's BRM at Monaco
Pete Ryan, Reims
Gary Hocking, Durban
Johnnie Mansell, Ardmore
Dennis Taylor, Monaco

1963
Bino Heinz, Le Mans

1964
Eddie Sachs, Indianapolis
Dave MacDonald, Indianapolis
Carel Godin de Beaufort, Nürburgring
Timmy Mayer, Longford
Bruno Deserti, Monza
Glenn 'Fireball' Roberts, Atlanta

1965
Lloyd 'Lucky' Casner, Le Mans

Bobby Marshman, Phoenix
Tommy Spychiger, Monza
Stan Ryan, Dunboyne
Tony David, Dunboyne
Adam Wylie, Dunboyne

1966
Walt Hangsen, Le Mans
John Taylor, Nürburgring
Ken Miles, Riverside
Don Branson, Ascot
Dick Atkins, Ascot
Jud Larson, Reading
Lex Davison, Sandown Park

1967
Lorenzo Bandini, Monaco
Roby Weber, Le Mans
Bob Anderson, Silverstone
Gunther 'Bobby' Klass, Mugello
Boley Pittard, Monza
Tim Cash, Portugal
Doug Revson, Djurslandring, plus Ray O'Connor, whom he hit and killed, and circuit owner Jans Christian Legarth
Giacomo 'Geki' Russo, Caserta
Beat Fehr, Caserta
Guiseppe 'Tiga' Perdomi, Caserta
Ian Raby, Zandvoort
Georges Berger, Nürburgring
Eight spectators killed by Luki Botha, Lourenco Marques
Eric de Keyn, Spa
Wim Loos, Spa
Jean-Claud Bernasconi, Rouen

1968
Jim Clark, Hockenheim
Mike Spence, Indianapolis
Lodovico Scarfiotti, Rossfeld
Jo Schlesser, Rouen
Chris Lambert, Zandvoort
Dickie Stoop, Oulton Park

1969
Lucien Bianchi, Le Mans
Gerhard Mitter, Nürburgring
Chris Williams, Silverstone
Paul Hawkins, Oulton Park
Moises Solana, Valle de Bravo
John Woolf, Le Mans

1970
Bruce McLaren, Goodwood
Piers Courage, Zandvoort
Jochen Rindt, Monza
Hans Laine, Nürburgring
Giovanni Salvati, Taruma
Derrick Williams, Anderstorp
Chris Summers, Snetterton
Jean-Luc Salamon, Rouen
Denis Dayan, Rouen

1971
Ignazio Giunti, Buenos Aires
Pedro Rodriguez, Norisring
Jo Siffert, Brands Hatch
Peter Hawtin, Oulton Park
Klaus Reisch, Imola

1972
Jo Bonnier, Le Mans
Bert Hawthorne, Hockenheim

1973
Roger Williamson, Zandvoort
Art Pollard, Indianapolis
Swede Savage, Indianapolis, plus crew member Armanda Teran
François Cevert, Watkins Glen
Nasif Estefano, Argentina
Gerry Birrell, Rouen

1974
Peter Revson, Kyalami
Helmuth Koinigg, Watkins Glen
Silvio Moser, Monza

1975
Mark Donohue, Osterreichring
Four spectators including a photographer hit by Rolf Stommelen's Hill at Montjuich Park
B.J. Swanson, Mid-Ohio

1977
Tom Pryce, Kyalami, plus marshal Jansen van Vuuren
Two spectators killed by Villeneuve's Ferrari in Japan
Brian McGuire, Brands Hatch
Max Stewart, Calder

1978
Ronnie Peterson, Monza

1980
Patrick Depailler, Hockenheim
Hans-Georg Berger, Zandvoort
Markus Hottinger, Hockenheim

1981
Herbie Muller, Nürburgring
Martin Raymond, Brands Hatch

1982
Gilles Villeneuve, Zolder
Riccardo Paletti, Montreal
Jean-Louis Lafosse, Le Mans
Gordon Smiley, Indianapolis

1983
Rolf Stommelen, Riverside

1985
Stefan Bellof, Spa-Francorchamps
Manfred Winkelhock, Mosport
Peter Rogers, Donington

1986
Bertrand Fabi, Goodwood
Elio de Angelis, Le Castellet
Dick Parsons, Silverstone
Jo Gartner, Le Mans

1990
Rich Vogler, Salem

1991
Paul Warwick, Oulton Park

1992
Marcel Albers, Thruxton
Jovi Marcello, Indianapolis
Kesjar Csaba, Norisring
Akio Morimoto, Suzuka

1994
Roland Ratzenberger, Imola
Ayrton Senna, Imola

1995
Neil Bonnett, Daytona

1996
Jeff Krosnoff, Toronto, plus a marshal
Scott Brayton, Indianapolis

1997
Sebastien Enjolras, Le Mans

1999
Neil Shanahan, Oulton Park
Gonzales Rodriguez, Laguna Seca
Greg Moore, Fontana

2000
Adam Petty, New Hampshire
Kenny Irwin, New Hampshire
Paolo Ghislimberti, Marshal, Monza

Appendix 2

FIA crash tests

The mandatory chassis structure crash testing introduced by the FIA dates back to 1985, and is intended to provide the utmost means of safeguarding drivers in the event of foreseeable accidents. Most are conducted, under FIA supervision, at the Cranfield Impact Centre in Bedfordshire, though overseas teams may specify more local sites of similar standard.

TEST 1
An impact test against a solid barrier (introduced 1985)
This is the head-on collision, the most nerve-wracking for the designer since failure can compromise the entire structure. The purpose is to ensure that the car can adequately protect the driver's ankles and legs.

Test structure
Nose box attached to a complete survival cell.

Impact speed
12m/s.

Mass
780kg.

Deformation
Limited to the nose box and no damage to the fixings of the extinguishers or seat belts.
Driver's feet have to be at least 30cm from the front of the survival cell.

Max mean g
25.

Conditions
Full fire extinguishers fitted.
Fuel tank filled with water.
Dummy, weighing 75kg, must be fitted with seat belts fastened. During the impact deceleration in the chest of the dummy must not exceed 60g for more than 3ms.

TEST 2
A static load test on the top of the main roll structure (introduced 1991)
This is designed to assess the ability of the car to withstand inversion without its rollover hoop distorting or breaking under load.

Test structure
Main roll structure attached to a complete survival cell.

Test load
72.08kN, which corresponds to a combined load of 57.39kN vertically, 42.08kN longitudinally, and 11.48kN laterally.

Deformation
No greater than 50mm measured along the loading axis and no failure more than 100mm below the top of the structure measured vertically.

TEST 3

A static load test on the side of the nose (introduced in 1990)

This is also known as the 'push-off test', to make sure that the nose, with its energy-absorbing deformable structure, remains intact during a glancing type of blow, as if the car has struck a barrier at a relatively shallow angle.

Test structure
Nose box attached to a complete survival cell.

Test load
40kN at a point 55cm in front of the front wheel axis.

Time
Test load must be held for 30 seconds.

Deformation
No failure of the structure or of any attachment between the nose box and the survival cell.

TEST 4

A static load test on both sides of the survival cell (introduced in 1992)

This is the 'crush' or 'squeeze test', and is designed to ensure that the monocoque chassis will provide adequate protection against side impact. The tests are carried out at various points along the length of the chassis. Gary Anderson tells the story of Jordan mechanics driving to Silverstone one morning coming across a damaged racing car monocoque laying in a hedge. It was F1 sized, and it transpired that it was the Life (née First) chassis from 1990 which, having failed its crush test, had simply been discarded!

Test structure
Every complete survival cell.
All survival cells must be produced in an identical condition in order that their weights may be compared. The first is weighed and all subsequent units must be within five per cent of the initial weight.

Test load
25kN on the first survival cell, 20kN on all the subsequent ones.

Test method
A pad measuring 10cm x 30cm is placed against both sides of the survival cell and the load applied.

Position
A vertical plane passing through a point mid-way between the front wheel axis and the front roll structure.

Time
Test load must be held for 30 seconds.

Deformation
No permanent deformation greater than 1mm after the load has been removed. Furthermore, on all subsequent survival cells the total displacement across the inner surfaces must be no greater than 120 per cent of the displacement measured on the first survival cell at 20kN.

TEST 5

A static load test on both sides of the survival cell (introduced in 1988)

This is another part of the 'squeeze test', carried out at driver hip level.

Test structure
Every complete survival cell.
All survival cells must be produced in an identical condition in order that their weights may be compared. The first is weighed and all subsequent units must be within five per cent of the initial weight.

Test load
30kN.

Test method
A pad measuring 20cm diameter is placed against both sides of the survival cell and the load applied.

Position
A vertical plane passing through the anchorage point of the lap seat belts.

Time
Test load must be held for 30 seconds.

Deformation
Maximum displacement of 20mm and no permanent deformation greater than 1mm after the load has been removed.

TEST 6

A static load test on both sides of the survival cell (introduced in 1988)

This is another part of the 'squeeze test'.

Test structure

Every complete survival cell.

All survival cells must be produced in an identical condition in order that their weights may be compared. The first is weighed and all subsequent units must be within five per cent of the initial weight.

Test load

25kN on the first survival cell, 20kN on all subsequent ones.

Test method

A pad measuring 10cm x 30cm is placed against both sides of the survival cell and the load applied.

Position

A vertical plane passing through the centre of area of the fuel tank side.

Time

Test load must be held for 30 seconds.

Deformation

No permanent deformation greater than 1mm after the load has been removed. Furthermore, on all subsequent survival cells the total displacement across the inner surfaces must be no greater than 120 per cent of the displacement measured on the first survival cell at 20kN.

TEST 7

A static load on both sides of the survival cell (introduced in 1991)

This is another part of the 'squeeze test, which assesses the ability of the chassis to withstand an impact on the underside.

Test structure

Every complete survival cell.

All survival cells must be produced in an identical condition in order that their weights may be compared. The first is weighed and all subsequent units must be within five per cent of the initial weight.

Test load

12.5kN on the first survival cell, 10kN on all subsequent ones.

Test method

A pad measuring 20cm in diameter is placed against the underside of the fuel tank floor and the load applied.

Position

A vertical plane passing through the centre of the area of the fuel tank floor.

Time

Test load must be held for 30 seconds.

Deformation

No permanent deformation greater than 0.5mm after the load has been removed. Furthermore, on all subsequent survival cells the total displacement across the inner surfaces must be no greater than 120 per cent of the displacement measured on the first survival cell at 10kN.

TEST 8

A static load test on both sides of the survival cell (introduced in 1991)

This is another part of the 'squeeze test', carried out at the front bulkhead level.

Test structure

Every complete survival cell.

Test load

20kN.

Test method

A pad measuring 10cm x 30cm is placed against both sides of the survival cell and the load applied.

Position

A vertical plane passing through the front wheel axis.

Time

Test load must be held for 30 seconds.

Deformation

No structural failure of the inner skins of the survival cell.

TEST 9

A static load test on both sides of the survival cell (introduced in 1991)

This is another part of the 'squeeze test.'

Test structure

Every complete survival cell.

Test load
20kN.

Test method
A pad measuring 10cm x 30cm is placed against both sides of the survival cell and the load applied.

Position
A vertical plane passing through the front wheel axis and the seat belt lap strap fixings.

Time
Test load must be held for 30 seconds.

Deformation
No structural failure of the inner skins of the survival cell.

TEST 10
An impact test against a solid barrier (introduced in 1995 and upgraded for 1998)
This is designed to assess ability to withstand side impacts.

Test structure
Side impact absorbing structure attached to both sides of a complete survival cell.

Test load
7m/s.

Mass
780kg.

Position
525mm forward of the rear edge of the cockpit entry template.

Deformation
All deformation must be limited to the impact absorbing structure.
No damage to the survival cell is permissible.
Average deceleration must not exceed 10g.

TEST 11
A static load test on each side of the cockpit rim (introduced in 1996)
Another squeeze test to assess integrity of the cockpit opening.

Test structure
All survival cells must be produced in an identical condition in order that their weights may be compared. The first is weighed and all subsequent units must be within five per cent of the initial weight.

Test load
10kN on the first survival cell, 8kN on all subsequent ones.

Test method
A pad measuring 10cm in diameter is placed against each side of the cockpit rim.

Position
200mm forward of the rear edge of the cockpit entry template.

Time
Test load must be held for 30 seconds.

Deformation
No permanent deformation greater than 1mm after the load has been removed. Furthermore, on all subsequent survival cells the total displacement across the inner surfaces must be no greater than 120 per cent of the displacement measured on the first survival cell at 8kN.

TEST 12
An impact test against a solid barrier (introduced in 1997)
The rear-end equivalent of the head-on crash test.

Test structure
Rear impact absorbing structure attached to the gearbox.

Impact speed
12m/s.

Mass
780kg.

Deformation
All deformation must be limited to the area behind the rear wheel centre line.
Average deceleration must not exceed 35g and the peak must not exceed 60g for more than 3ms.

Index